Police are understood largely as 'crime-fighting professionals', yet some highly effective policing involves partnering with others to increase public safety, prevent crime, and respond to related social problems. In this engaging work Kerry Clamp and Craig Paterson explain how restorative policing can extend the earlier reforms of community- and problem-oriented policing. They offer striking examples of police working as 'street-level leaders', working with citizens, rather than simply doing things to and for them. The discussion extends well beyond theory and high level strategy, to the practicalities of program implementation, and an impressively accurate account of how conflict resolution processes actually work, and may help us 'to reconnect with one another'.

David B. Moore, *Restorative Justice Pioneer, Australia*

Kerry Clamp and Craig Paterson deal in this outstanding book with 'restorative policing', recognising the central role played by police in restorative justice practices and radicalising the importance of one of the most neglected aspects of community policing, more precisely the empowerment of the very same community. The new restorative police should act no longer as decision-makers, but as contributors to the construction of collective efficacy, or to the capacity of the community to solve its own problems. *Restorative Policing: Concepts, theory and practice* gives clever guidance in this endeavour. It is instructive, insightful and practical at the same time. A book that speaks clearly to a broad readership.

Paul Ponsaers, *Ghent University, Belgium*

Clamp and Paterson's inspired integration of restorative justice and policing scholarship provides both a compelling vision and a solid theoretical foundation to guide the evolution of restorative policing for generations to come. Particularly provocative is their discussion on 'lengthening' the restorative policing lens, as it offers a linchpin between restorative and transformative justice with theoretical implications well beyond the topic of restorative policing.

Paul McCold, *Independent Criminologist and member of the Global Steering Committee, Restorative Justice International*

Restorative policing is a new philosophy and practice of policing, which links to community policing and problem-oriented policing, but draws also upon restorative practices to provide a different way of working with local communities to solve conflicts whilst building the community. *Restorative Policing* draws together both theory and what has been found to be effective practice to take forward and develop what it means to police restoratively. It is a key text for both practitioners and scholars.

Joanna Shapland, *Edward Bramley Professor of Criminal Justice and Director* ~~~~~~~~~~~~~~~~~~~~~~~~~~~~~~ *arch, University of Sheffield, UK*

Restorative Policing

In the UK and elsewhere, restorative justice and policing are core components of a range of university programmes; however, currently no such text exists on the intersection of these two areas of study. This book draws together these diverse theoretical perspectives to provide an innovative, knowledge-rich text that is essential reading for all those engaged with the evolution and practice of restorative policing.

Restorative Policing surveys the 25-year history of restorative policing practice, during which its use and influence over criminal justice has slowly grown. It then situates this experience within a criminological discussion about neoliberal responses to crime control. There has been insufficient debate about how the concepts of 'restorative justice' and 'policing' sit alongside each other and how they may be connected or disconnected in theoretical and conceptual terms. The book seeks to fill this gap through an exploration of concepts, theory, policy and practice. In doing so, the authors make a case for a more transformative vision of restorative policing that can impact positively upon the shape and practice of policing and outline a framework for the implementation of such a strategy.

This pathbreaking book will be of interest to undergraduate and postgraduate students taking courses on restorative justice, policing and crime control, as well as professionals interested in the implementation of restorative practices in the police force.

Kerry Clamp is a Senior Lecturer in Criminology in the Department of Social Sciences and Psychology at the University of Western Sydney, Australia. She received her PhD from the University of Leeds in 2010 and also holds degrees from the University of Sheffield and the University of South Africa. Her research agenda focuses on the intersections of restorative justice and transitional justice, and of restorative justice and policing.

Craig Paterson is a Principal Lecturer in Criminology at Sheffield Hallam University, UK. His teaching and research interests include surveillance and commercial crime control, policing, crime prevention and criminological theory.

Routledge Frontiers of Criminal Justice

Restorative Policing
Concepts, theory and practice

Kerry Clamp and Craig Paterson

Routledge
Taylor & Francis Group

LONDON AND NEW YORK

First published 2017
by Routledge
2 Park Square, Milton Park, Abingdon, Oxon OX14 4RN

and by Routledge
711 Third Avenue, New York, NY 10017

First issued in paperback 2018

Routledge is an imprint of the Taylor & Francis Group, an informa business

British Library Cataloguing-in-Publication Data
A catalogue record for this book is available from the British Library

Library of Congress Cataloging in Publication Data
Names: Clamp, Kerry, author. | Paterson, Craig, author.
Title: Restorative policing : concepts, theory and practice / Kerry Clamp and Craig Paterson.
Description: Abingdon, Oxon ; New York, NY : Routledge, 2016. | Series: Routledge frontiers of criminal justice ; 39 | Includes bibliographical references and index.
Identifiers: LCCN 2016013998 | ISBN 9781138959071 (hardback) | ISBN 9781315660837 (ebook)
Subjects: LCSH: Community policing. | Restorative justice. | Crime prevention.
Classification: LCC HV7936.C83 C53 2016 | DDC 363.2/3–dc23
LC record available at https://lccn.loc.gov/2016013998

ISBN 13: 978-1-138-49953-9 (pbk)
ISBN 13: 978-1-138-95907-1 (hbk)

Typeset in Times New Roman
by Wearset Ltd, Boldon, Tyne and Wear

For Isabella Thandi Wood, who grew with this book and is now the perfect new addition to our family.

For Liz, Alexa and Jude.

Contents

x   *Contents*

Foreword

I predict this book will be recognised as the most significant and influential ever written on contemporary policing. As someone whose professional life has been heavily invested in restorative policing, I was taken by the eloquent way the authors challenge the reader to think about what restorative justice or practice/processes have to offer them as individuals and then, humanity. The title *Restorative Policing* suggests a whole new policing paradigm and to some extent this is argued as a serious consideration, not as a replacement for, but integral to existing policing practice. It also suggests that the 'bit' missing from policing is the 'R' word, relationships and that restorative dialogue, with its focus on harm, has the potential to change experiences and lives.

The authors present competing philosophies and theories and offer a whole new perspective on policing. In my view, this is a 'game changer'. It highlights the problematic nature of trying to drag restorative policing into existing policing paradigms because of its explicit and intentional focus on relationships. This takes the critics and commentators into uncharted waters. Throughout the book, many good and not so good examples of restorative policing were cited, and it was found that each had something positive to offer to someone. And on those occasions where restorative policing worked well, everyone was a winner! As I was reading the manuscript, I became frustrated because I was constantly responding to every critic. I needed to remind myself that we tend to see what we are looking for and that restorative policing when viewed through a different lens provides many different and exciting possibilities.

Never imagine for a minute that frontline police officers ascribe to the particular policing philosophy of their police service. Most probably they have no idea what it is because having never experienced a conversation about what they believe or what they think matters. The Wagga Wagga experience of restorative processes happened because police and the local community decided it was an ideal worth exploring. This initiative relied on two factors: The first involved the courageous leadership of Chief Inspector Kevin Wales, who was unfailing in his support for what was being attempted. The second related to the engagement of all stakeholders. This was done in a collaborative way through the use of restorative dialogue and resulted in police being given the mandate to look for better ways of dealing with young offenders. Clifford Shearing's idea of culture being like a storybook – change the stories and change the culture – was our experience.

Fundamentally, the restorative process is an invitation to a very different conversation. The restorative process works because it is innately human, involves an emotional investment and its strength is found through the dialogue that helps others to work out what matters. It creates the conditions that allow those experiencing dislocation to deal with their vulnerability in positive ways. Transformation [constantly referenced in this book] is what generally happens for someone as a result of a restorative experience.

Definitional issues can be contentious and the authors' argument that restorative policing is not a programme but a 'way of being' will confound the policing purists. While the suggestion that the organisational and institutional hegemony has a significant influence on policing practice would seem to be true, the dominant [policing] narrative excludes such discussion. The complexity of the issue was captured in a simple statement by a Thames Valley police officer: 'I love this restorative stuff. It has helped me personally and professionally, but I have realised that the only way this is sustainable is when we learn how to treat one another in a restorative manner.'

While the Wagga Wagga experience delivered some extraordinary outcomes and had the potential to provide a template for policing reform, it always had a limited 'shelf life'. For example, the implication of a 70 per cent reduction in the number of juvenile offenders placed before the courts over a two-year period was not seen as good news, but a fundamental threat to institutional policing arrangements, which went well beyond the police. The authors make a strong case that policing and police are two very different concepts. They also argue that restorative policing can position police as 'change agents', something that was very evident in Wagga Wagga where schools and various community agencies adopted the restorative policing model.

We live at a time in human history where some suggest the world is starting to implode. Police are increasingly operating in a climate of fear and, with the threat of global terrorism, are beginning to understand that traditional enforcement approaches are not working. Hilary Cottam [TED talk] suggests that our social welfare systems are broken because they are absorbed in system necessities and have lost sight of what matters, relationships. Sadly, far too many providers [police included] believe that those who struggle with life are incapable of working it out, even when given the right opportunity. Our collective restorative experiences prove otherwise. Imagine the possibilities if police were to develop a restorative narrative built around two simple questions: Will it cause harm? Will it improve relationships?

While this book argues the case for restorative policing, it invites the reader to contemplate what might be possible were the reader to take restorative processes seriously. I suggest that we have just begun to explore what restorative policing has to offer and, like the book, it will be better appreciated with ongoing experimentation and research. My hope is that this book becomes the catalyst for some new stories and different policing experiences, where making a difference in the lives of others can become a consistent and predictable experience.

I therefore recommend this book as essential reading to every police officer [and police department] and make one simple suggestion. Before trying to work out where 'restorative policing fits', start with a discussion on what you think policing is about – the answer about restorative policing will become self-evident. Finally, the authors leave you to ponder the question, 'what if restorative policing works?'

Terry O'Connell
Real Justice
May 2016

Acknowledgements

Writing this book has been more challenging than we expected. Perhaps the most significant challenge has been time zones. Craig is based in England and I am based in Australia, distance that doesn't encourage the sharing of ideas when while he was eating breakfast and just starting the day, I was eating dinner and just ending mine. Although Skype is useful, it is limited in that you cannot have the same types of discussions and debates that you normally would if your colleague was just down the hall. Another additional challenge was the sheer scale of the project, which we perhaps underestimated. Our investigations took us down routes that were unexpected and to literature that we had not considered before – all very stimulating endeavours.

Despite these challenges, we have found this process immensely valuable in terms of developing our own thinking and clarifying the particular nuances that we should have been taking into consideration in our previous publications on the topic. We have no doubt that our survey of the field will provide a springboard for much more collaboration on the topic – surprisingly we are still talking to one another at the end of this process – and hopefully initiate further debate and discussion on our findings. We see restorative policing as an immensely important area of study, not least because of the rapidly changing environment driven by changing financial, social and cultural climates.

In completing this journey, we were assisted and motivated by a number of people and thus we have a number of acknowledgements that we would like to make. At times, we needed clarification on particular aspects of restorative policing practice and people were kind enough to assist in suggesting literature, clarifying current practice and for general encouragement. These individuals included: Paul McCold (who has not only been kind enough to engage with me but whose work has been immensely valuable to our research in the area), Ted Wachtel, Laura Mirsky and Joshua Wachtel (International Institute of Restorative Practices), Jordan Diplock (RCMP British Columbia), Wendy Flanagan and Brad Hawkins (Detroit Police Department), Julie Keys (Hillsboro Police Department) and Bas van Stokkom. We would like to thank these individuals for answering our pleas for clarification, as well as our other colleagues whose work has driven our thinking and informed our analysis. That being said, all errors and omissions within the text naturally remain our own.

Our colleagues at both of our institutions have played an important part in allowing us to debrief when things got tough and to help us to clarify our thinking – these colleagues know who they are. We would also like to thank both Tom Sutton and Hannah Catterall at Routledge for their belief in the project and the help and support they provided, as well as the production team for getting the book ready for print. Last, but by no means least, we also need to acknowledge and thank, in particular, our spouses – Liz and Danny, who at times were single parents while we worked on the book. Their support and encouragement is not something that we could do without.

1 Restorative policing and policing reform

An introduction

Introduction

For most of the twentieth century, the dominant mode of thinking in Western democracies, or 'neoliberal states',[1] has been that the police could solve crime and disorder through a reactive approach. In the last two decades, however, this thinking has shifted to the belief that it is far more effective for proactive steps to be taken prior to crime occurring in the first place. This was not a new idea, but rather echoes the policing style proposed in 'The Instructions and Police Orders for 1829–30', largely attributed to Robert Peel, during the birth of the professional police in England and Wales:

> It should be understood at the outset, that the object to be attained is 'the prevention of crime'. To this end every effort of the police is to be directed. The security of persons and property, the preservation of the public tranquillity, and all the other objects of a police establishment, will thus be better effected than by the detection and punishment of the offender after he has succeeded in committing the crime.
>
> (*The Times* 1829: 3)

The introduction of community-based policing, problem-oriented policing and restorative policing during the 1980s and 1990s signalled a return to such thinking and offered the police an alternative to the reactive, incident-focused style that dominated previous eras (Paterson and Clamp 2012). These initiatives are characterised by an acknowledgement of the central role of the community in identifying, reporting and responding to crime, and it is thought that the police are more likely to successfully tackle crime where policing strategies are based within and informed by community members themselves. Such an approach has also created a need for the police to develop problem-oriented partnerships with other agencies (including probation, social work, education, housing and community-based organisations) to identify and deal with the underlying causes of, or potential triggers for, crime.

The multifunctional nature of policing means that it is subject to a range of tensions, including different priorities being set by upper and middle management to those of frontline officers and a perception amongst frontline officers that their peacekeeping role (i.e. mediation, negotiation and pacification) is not always valued as 'real' police work (Moor *et al.* 2009). So, despite this ideological shift, there has been a noticeable amount of resistance to these policy changes from frontline police officers who are used to drawing on their own expertise to determine what needs to be done at a local level. A critical body of literature has also emerged that questions whether or not shifts in power and responsibility are feasible, particularly given the extent to which 'community' has thought to have been lost in its traditional sense (Bauman 2001; Clamp and Paterson 2011; Hobsbawm 1995; McCold and Wachtel 1998b), and where it is feasible, the extent to which 'community control' merely 'emerges as a model of regulation' (Pavlich 2001: 56; see also, Cohen 1985; in relation to restorative policing in particular see White 1994).

This book is situated within the contours of this evolving police response to crime, and is focused on exploring the emergence, trajectory and complexities of restorative policing. A global body of literature on the subject of restorative policing has emerged over a 25-year period, key themes have waxed and waned across time and space, and, because of this, important insights have sometimes been lost (see also Hoyle and Rosenblatt 2016). So while this literature contains information about a number of distinct restorative policing initiatives from around the world, there has not as yet been an effort to consolidate it and to further interrogate and conceptualise what 'restorative policing' is in a single volume. In light of this, the book has two principal objectives.

The first is to survey restorative policing so that we may enhance our understanding of how the concept 'restorative policing' is used; the types of offences that fall within the general parameters of a restorative policing response; the similarities and differences between restorative policing programmes that exist or have existed worldwide; the research findings that have arisen from those projects; and the strengths and weaknesses of such an approach within an operational policing environment. By engaging in such a review, the book will dispel a number of myths that exist around what restorative policing is, how it is used and why police have embraced such an approach to respond to crime.

The second is to ground arguments within social and cultural changes that are taking place at the global level in the response to crime. Since the mid-1970s there have been a number of important departures from established Western social and legal norms, which suggest that the criminal justice system represents the most legitimate avenue for redress after harm or victimisation has taken place. Many developed nations have increasingly become aware that an exclusive adherence to a punitive strategy has not produced the desired result in terms of 'greater satisfaction with criminal justice or an increased sense of security or justice' (Roach 2005: 2). This challenge to the traditional mechanisms of state-oriented criminal justice that had prevailed throughout the twentieth century has subsequently resulted in concerted efforts to find new and innovative ways of managing crime, particularly in terms of developing partnerships with civil society and private sector organisations (Shearing 2001).

Thus, we suggest that policing in neo-liberal states is undergoing, in some cases, ebbs and flows and, in other cases, radical shifts that are influenced by the broader changes taking place across criminal justice landscapes. While traditional policing models utilised quasi-militaristic structures that historically led to forms of policing that are *done to* people, policing discourse has shifted, or is shifting, towards a more community-oriented and democratically responsive style that aligns with other modes of liberal democratic politics. These changes can be recognised at the global level, although the extent to which the language of a community-based approach translates into community-engaged practice remains open to question. Yet, it is clear that there has been a social, political and cultural shift towards a more democratic model of policing which, we argue, paves the way for the evolution of restorative thinking within the police service and other crime control agencies.

Indeed, as we will demonstrate below, we perceive restorative policing to be a particular reform movement that has naturally emerged from the traditions of community policing and problem-oriented policing, which means that much can be learnt from the experience of these reform endeavours. Restorative policing is situated within the general community policing experiment that sought to reduce the boundaries between the police and their local communities (Manning 2002; Ponsaers 2001) and the problem-oriented experiment which sought to provide police officers with the tools to address crime problems, as opposed to single crime incidents, in a more systematic manner (Bazemore 2000a). Yet, both community policing and problem-oriented policing remain partially complete endeavours that have largely retained traditional offender-victim dichotomies and which have met challenges in the shape of police organisational structures, culture and leadership (Mastrofski *et al.* 2002a; Skogan 2008).

We will develop the argument in support of the view that restorative policing erodes these boundaries, requiring officers to act as street-level leaders, to build legitimacy for their role from goals that have been set by both police organisations and local communities, and to seek resolutions to problems from within actively engaged communities. However, there are a number of challenges to this perspective. The first is the influence of existing social, economic and political structures and the symbolic meanings of crime and policing that they produce on the implementation of restorative policing within punitive communities. The second is the extent to which communities have the social capital and/or community capacity to actively engage in restorative policing. Restorative policing can only work if the myriad of cultures, values and practices that it exhibits secures the full appreciation of both the police and public.

This introductory chapter thus highlights a number of key themes that will be further interrogated throughout the book. It begins by providing an introductory analysis of the convergence of restorative justice with the new modes of policing that have emerged out of a landscape of persistent police reform. Next, given the breadth of literature that could be included in a book such as this, we identify a number of parameters around which our discussion and analysis will proceed. The final section provides an overview of the structure for the rest of the book.

Policing reform

Over the last four decades, policing has undergone a range of reform efforts that have departed from the dominant crime control model, aimed at making the police more effective in responding to and combating crime in local communities, and increasing their perceived legitimacy in the eyes of the public. The most prominent of these have been community policing[2] and problem-oriented policing which have called for increased partnerships between the police and the community in terms of drawing attention to and dealing with potential triggers for deviant and criminal behaviour that affect the quality of community life. The success of these reforms is subject to much debate, but they have led a number of commentators to suggest that change has a tendency to occur more in rhetoric than operational reality (see, for example, McCold 1998; McCold and Wachtel 1998a). A comparative analysis of community policing and problem-oriented policing supports this perspective, with the United States and Australia remaining wedded to a law enforcement ethos despite persistent community and problem-oriented policing reform attempts at the local level (Skogan 2008; Putt 2010).

On the one hand, some commentators have suggested that this is due to the fact that while significant theoretical work has often been undertaken, little thought has been given to how such work might be operationalised for the policing context (Moor *et al.* 2009; Pollard 2001). On the other hand, McCold (1998) has suggested that timing is the central issue. Quite simply, not all police departments have been or are ready for the changes that community policing and problem-oriented policing demand. Commenting on the Australian context, Fleming and O'Reilly (2007) confirm this position of community policing as a small-scale programmatic endeavour. At first glance, it would seem this is less the case in the United States and United Kingdom where a voluminous governmental literature exists on the subject of community policing. Nevertheless, this literature remains focused on the programmatic aspects, rather than on the philosophical and conceptual nature, of community policing, a particular limitation in current implementation strategies as we will argue later within the book.

In England and Wales, community policing philosophies and strategies are now embedded into all 43 police forces, yet a constant tension remains between the cost of high visibility, reassurance and preventative policing and the need to address evolving crime problems. Community policing is similarly embedded in other European states with regionalized policing structures (such as The Netherlands and Germany) although its evolution remains much more uneven in the European states that retain centralised control over the delivery of policing (see Brogden 1999 for a more in depth discussion). In all instances, the language of community policing is prominent even if the lived reality remains some distance away from community policing principles. Nevertheless, while the policy emphasis of central government and senior police leaders remains firmly within the gambit of community-oriented thinking there are tensions at different points of the police hierarchy in all countries with other priorities such as meeting performance targets, managing existing and emerging crime problems, and addressing issues of order maintenance remaining priority areas of focus. These challenges to community policing are cross-jurisdictional and indicative of a partially complete paradigm shift coupled with enduring tensions concerning the purposes of policing and who should own responses to crime and disorder (Manning 2010). Perpetual contests over the purpose of policing from within and around the organisation can mean that new innovations, such as restorative policing, can produce unexpected outcomes. This can include low levels of diversion where restorative approaches are perceived to be soft as well as inappropriate use where restorative policing is interpreted as a broadening of police discretion.

Across the globe, these tensions tend to be analysed by scholars through the lens of police culture, which results in often damning, or at least sceptical, accounts of the likelihood of success with community-oriented reforms. Yet, these structural narratives about police culture and reform tend to underplay the importance of police officer agency as well as the congruence between the restorative emphasis upon informal local resolutions and street-level police officer discretion (Paterson and Clamp 2012). An emphasis upon the dynamic nature of police culture and police officer agency permits a looser theoretical framework, which envisages change from the bottom-up and draws attention to the role of police officers as drivers of this process (Wood *et al.* 2008). Herewith, the role of police officers is understood as that of the street-level bureaucrat (Lipsky 1980), negotiating conflict via informal local resolutions that demonstrates an intuitive, culturally-informed appreciation of what restorative policing could look like. This perspective opens up potential links with the theoretical literature on 'collective efficacy' and its focus upon social disorganisation and the relationship between communities and crime (Sampson and Groves 1989). Important to this perspective is the potential for restorative policing to de-individualise responses to harm and, instead, address the collective problems and social justice issues that offenders, victims and communities face (Christie 1977).

In different ways, community, problem-oriented and restorative policing can be seen as components of a global police reform movement which is often imposed upon the police and thus exposes the tensions that exist between politicians, think tanks, academics, senior police leaders, managers and police officers. However, despite these similarities, there remain important distinctions in how each of the three proposed reform initiatives seeks to empower communities. Table 1.1 sets out an analytical framework in the form of a typology of these three participatory approaches to policy-making in policing. It is important to bear in mind that the framework is based on a simplification of a very complex set of initiatives and that, in reality; these are rarely as simple, straightforward or logical as they are portrayed here for the purposes of explanation and analysis.

Community policing and problem-oriented policing are often spoken of as if they are interchangeable,[3] so, the reason for adopting this typology is purely as an aid to conceptual clarification, and a means through which to draw attention to important differences between these three main sets of reform initiatives. These differences relate to their aspirations (*goals*), orientation (*approach*), the way they operate (*process*), the emphasis on and requirements of the officer during the

Table 1.1 A typology of police reforms: an analytical framework

Name of reform	Goals	Approach	Process	Police role	Public involvement
Community-oriented policing	To prevent crime, create a better quality of life and to change the reactive, control-oriented style of policing to a service-oriented style.	Building police-community partnerships by enhancing a sustained presence within the community.	Foot patrols, permanent geographic assignment of officers and the establishment of mini-stations serving a particular community.	Emphasis on interpersonal skills and an ability to develop a collaborative relationship with the community in terms of designing solutions to problems of crime and disorder.	Community participation limited to: (1) providing information to the police, (2) providing visible support for the police, (3) providing monetary assistance, and (4) statement-making (see further Buerger 1994: 270–271).
Problem-oriented policing	To prevent crime by looking for and examining the underlying causes of emerging crimes and disorders, and to find long-term solutions.	To develop fresh insights into problems of crime and disorder for the purpose of developing preventive approaches that engage partners from beyond the criminal justice system.	S.A.R.A. (scanning, analysis, response and assessment).	Emphasis on analytical skills in order to identify and solve the specific problems that police confront.	Not all problem-oriented police work is community-oriented, so the opportunity for community involvement is limited, although other commercial and public sector agents are engaged.
Restorative policing	To hold offenders to account. To repair the harm experienced by the victim/s. To prevent future harm.	To engage the victim, offender and the broader community (generally supporters of the victim and offender) in dialogue in order to respond to the incident and to develop a plan for future behaviour.	Restorative cautioning and conferencing.	Emphasis on interpersonal and communication skills and an ability to facilitate, rather than direct, decision-making.	Victims, offenders and others are actively involved in dealing with the causes and consequences of the offence and in making decisions about how best to deal with this.

process (*police role*) and the extent of community participation in the response to crime (*public involvement*). This framework suggests that restorative policing is distinct from community policing and problem-oriented policing in that it includes those most affected (i.e. victims – both direct and indirect – and offenders) in a process that is inclusive and where decision-making is primarily made by those other than professionals. This complexity will be further unpacked in each section dedicated to the three reform efforts, to which we now turn.

Community policing

Community policing is by no means a novel concept, it was rediscovered in the late twentieth century as a potential solution to the crisis of legitimacy being experienced by Anglophone police organisations. Since then, the Anglophone model of community policing has spread globally as the preferred choice for democratic countries.[4] Arguing that traditional authoritarian policing was proving to be inappropriate in a liberal society experiencing increasing levels of crime, John Alderson (1979: 199) developed this new style of policing in England and Wales, which aimed to, amongst other things, 'dispel criminogenic social conditions, create trust in communities, strengthen feelings of security and curb public disorder'. Thus, community policing sought to re-establish local accountability alongside localised, proactive policing strategies to reinvigorate the Peelian principle of policing by consent.

In practical terms, community policing philosophies incorporate a variety of strategies aimed at improving and maintaining engagement, co-operation, inter-action and trust between the police and the public in order to reduce crime and disorder and to improve the quality of life of local people. Friedman has defined community policing as follows:

> Community policing is a policy and a strategy aimed at achieving more effective and efficient crime control, reduced fear of crime, improved quality of life, improved police services and police legitimacy, through a proactive reliance on community resources that seeks to change crime causing conditions. This assumes a need for greater accountability of police, greater public share in decision making, and greater concern for civil rights and liberties.
>
> (1992: 4)

Community policing thus emphasises both proactive policing strategies as well as enhanced opportunities for police officers to use their discretion to respond to incivilities, underlying tensions between residents and low-level offending before they evolve into more serious conflicts. At the heart of this strategy, is the development of a collaborative relationship between the police officer and those who live on his/her beat. This requires the police to adopt a leadership position within the community by keeping the peace, mediating conflicts and coord-inating efforts to improve quality of life in the area more generally (Weitekamp *et al.* 2003). Such an approach is also said to have a number of positive effects on police officers, including: higher job satisfaction, a more positive response to the label of officers as problem-solvers and a feeling that what they do matters to the lives of those that they come into contact with (Wycoff and Skogan 1994: 379).

Despite these stated benefits, many question the extent to which community policing has transformed not only policing practice, but also police-community relations. Roche (2003) suggests that in reality, community policing has often been limited to: putting a few officers on bicycles, rebranding conventional policing practices, initiating Neighbourhood Watch Schemes and door knocking campaigns whereby police seek to elicit feedback about concerns from community residents. The problem with these strategies, he argues, is that they do not expose community police officers to the people with whom they would normally have the most contact: offenders and other marginalised populations. Alarid and Montemayor (2012) concur when they point out that even though the community becomes a more active partner in responding to crime and disorder, the role of victims and offenders remains minimal, or even non-existent.

Moore and McDonald (1995) have also highlighted a structural issue in relation to community policing: it offers a means through which police officers might go about their existing tasks more efficiently rather than offering a concrete break with past procedures or a means of addressing a different set of tasks. As such, the potential for dramatic change in policing practice, and/or the opportunity to secure long-lasting and meaningful outcomes, is limited, while Neighbourhood Watch Schemes; beat policing programmes and community consultative committees continue to operate in the current form and with their current rationale. At a strategic level, Moor *et al.* (2009: 7) argue that efforts to integrate community policing philosophies have too often been translated into 'organisational principles' rather than guidance about how this will alter 'practical professional choices, opportunities and solutions' on the ground. As such, the issue is not with the underlying philosophy of community policing, but rather with the manner in which the police hierarchy and, most notably, the front-line officer understands the implications of community policing for their role.

Mastrofski *et al.* (2002), Skogan (2008) and Willis *et al.* (2010) have provided compelling accounts related to why community policing approaches often fail. Their reasons include an incompatibility of community-oriented approaches with police department norms, conflicting priorities, cultural dispositions towards crime-fighting, and police officers and their supervisors not wanting to genuinely engage the public. A number of tensions therefore emerge in relation to community policing and the traditional command and control orientation of police hierarchies. First, enhanced discretion means less control over police officers, which leads to nervous leaders and managers. Second, questions about how police officers engage with communities arise, particularly those where there is a history of police-community tension. These issues point to the reasons why community policing has perhaps not taken as strong a hold as its proponents would have liked.

Problem-oriented policing

At the same time that Alderson was developing community policing in England and Wales, Herman Goldstein (1979), James Q. Wilson and George Kelling (1982) were making similar observations in the United States (although their conclusions about how to resolve crime more effectively were grounded within a cultural emphasis upon enhanced law enforcement). Frustrated with the general technocratic approach to dealing with crime that was dominant at the time (i.e. how fast calls were responded to), Goldstein (1977, 1979) and later Eck and Spelman (1987) developed the concept of problem-oriented policing. Problem-oriented policing works by identifying the root causes of recurrent problems in a community and solving them by using preventative evidence-based and long-term strategies. Such an approach requires the police to be proactive rather than reactive as they look for and seek out crime and disorder problems, a process which requires considerable research capacity (Reiss 1992). This involves officers undertaking an in-depth study of discrete police problems and developing preventative strategies that reduce dependence upon the criminal justice system through engagement with other public sector agencies, community groups and the private sector (Goldstein 2010).

Problem-oriented policing calls for close specification of problems through an analysis of the 'dynamics of offending' and deviates from the common misperception of the possibility of reducing 'crime' as a single entity. In other words, 'crime' must be analysed in the context of multiple variables, which are subjected to rigorous evaluation. This includes: who (the offender); does what (offence); to whom (victim); when (time); where (place); why (reason); how (method); and to what effect (possible impact of the offending). Once problems are found, problem-oriented policing embraces an evidence-based approach to solving issues through an analysis known as SARA: Scanning (clustering incidents together); Analysis (of the relevant offending dynamics); Response (action taken to address, reduce or prevent the crime or disorder problem); and Assessment (of the first three phases – particularly the response) that has emerged in different forms across the globe (Spelman and Eck 1987: 2–3; Leigh *et al.* 1996). The SARA model sought to communicate the purpose of problem-oriented policing to the front-line although it has been recognised that many attempts to implement problem-oriented policing, as initially imagined by Goldstein, have drifted towards beat officer problem-solving which, in practical terms, is more closely associated with community policing (Skogan and Hartnett 1997). As such, Goldstein (1997) has distinguished problem-oriented policing from community policing by arguing that the latter is focused on engaging the community in its existing tasks, whereas the former is broader in that it seeks to solve problems and devise solutions by engaging the community in problem-solving where the solution requires it.[5]

The purpose of policing, as interpreted by police organisations and many policing scholars, is largely focused upon issues of crime control, public protection and order maintenance carried out by uniformed officers which means, in practice, there is a tendency to marginalise work on the causes of crime. This underlying philosophy of crime control is evident in countless analyses of police culture as well as approaches to recruitment, training and development (Paterson 2011). Thus, change is imagined in pursuit of problem-oriented policing but rarely enacted in the shape of that imagined vision (Goldstein 2010). Organisational inertia holds court – largely because concepts of policing across the globe are infected with contradictory notions of crime control, violence and coercion which lead to the police being defined by their capacity to use force (Bittner 1970; Brodeur 2010) rather than their potential to secure justice and address complex social problems.

Even where deliberate attempts are made at problem-solving, a particular limitation of this policing strategy is that its emphasis upon resolving the underlying causes of crime extends beyond the police and into areas such as unemployment, education and other local community services such as garbage disposal and parking (Weitekamp *et al.* 2003). These are all areas over which the police have very little influence and control. Furthermore, Weitekamp *et al.* (2003) question whether a reduction in fear of crime, increased satisfaction with the police and more efficient responses to nuisance and incivility affecting neighbourhoods will result in a reduced crime rate. Rather, they stress the need to involve those stakeholders that are directly involved in offending in trying to understand its causes, consequences and solutions from the 'bottom-up'. The offender, they argue (and we would include the victim here as well), is a significant actor that is left out of both community and problem-oriented policing and without adequate attention and resources being devoted to this group; any crime reduction strategy will be limited in its effectiveness.

While the existing concepts of community policing and problem-oriented policing focus their attention upon improving the relationship between citizens and police officers, developing prevention strategies and addressing other problems faced by communities, they fail to provide a means through which such aims might be realised (Moor et al. 2009). This failure to engage with the science of implementation and organisational change has slowly been recognised by police organisations and we explore and interrogate this later in the book. In particular, we develop the calls by some commentators for a much more radical transformation of the policing role along restorative justice lines (Moore and Forsythe 1995; Bazemore 2000a). For our purposes, the growth in restorative policing can be understood to have been influenced by the shifts to both philosophies of community policing and problem-oriented policing strategies (Bazemore 2000a). Together, these processes encourage policing decisions to be made at as local a level as possible and oblige specific officers or teams to be responsible for, and familiar with, policing specific areas.

Restorative policing

According to McCold and Wachtel (1998a) restorative policing has been framed by three innovative developments in criminal justice. The first was the emergence of community and problem-oriented policing which sought to alter the dominant and often inefficient reactive policing style by increasing partnerships between the police and the community they serve. The second was the emergence of the theory of reintegrative shaming (Braithwaite 1989) which argued that informal social networks were more effective in bringing about remorse and actions to repair the harm caused than remote legal authorities. Finally, the restorative justice movement was seen as having offered a process through which the objectives of community/problem-oriented policing and reintegrative shaming could be realised.

The relationship between community policing and restorative justice has been investigated since the early 1990s (Bazemore 2001; Bazemore and Schiff 2001; Bazemore and Griffiths 2003; Pavlich 1996a, 1996b; Van Ness 1990) and it shares much in common with the ambitions of both community and problem-oriented policing. First, it focuses on preventing troublesome behaviour from evolving into more serious crimes. Second, it seeks to do this by prioritising problem-solving and conflict resolution approaches. Third, it seeks to embrace a future-oriented preventative model as a response to incidents and/or crime, which pose a threat to the safety and harmony of individuals and communities. Finally, it is premised on the fact that other networks, beyond the police, are needed in order to secure social control (see, for example, Hines and Bazemore 2003; McCold and Wachtel 1998a). However, it departs from community policing and problem-oriented policing because:

> ... it not only encourages police and the rest of the community to think carefully about how best to respond to juvenile crime, it also provides police and the general community with a new way of responding to that crime ... [and] a significant move to a fuller, more participatory form of democracy.
>
> (Moore and McDonald 1995: 146)

It does so by prioritising the participation of those who create harm and those who have been harmed or transgressed against in an inclusive dialogic process (for further detail see Chapter 2). The purpose of this meeting is to repair the harm that has been caused by devising a response to what has happened and to develop strategies so that future harm may be avoided. As an operational philosophy for police, McCold and Wachtel (1998a: 10) argue that restorative policing seeks to: encourage accountability, reparation, reintegration and healing; reduce recidivism; resolve conflict and eliminate ongoing problems; provide communities with a satisfying experience of justice; reduce reliance on the criminal justice system and formal processes; and, transform police attitudes, organisational culture and role perceptions.

Thus, the emergence of the restorative policing model (see further Chapter 3; Moore and O'Connell 1994; Moore and Forsythe 1995) has offered the police a framework through which to engage victims, offenders and communities in dealing with crime (McCold 1996; Vynckier 2009), an aspect that has largely been missing from the other reform strategies outlined previously. In doing so, restorative policing puts officers in direct contact with those communities most affected by their actions, leading Roche (2003: 146) to argue that 'restorative justice could help community policing [and we would argue problem-oriented policing] move beyond mere tokenism'. This is largely due to the fact that the police are facilitating the development of 'community' as well as its capacity to establish norms and social boundaries (see further Chapter 6) in relation to behaviour that is deemed acceptable and unacceptable (Hines and Bazemore 2003).

A particular limitation in relation to realising these grand aims, however, has been a rather unimaginative implementation of restorative justice within policing, largely due to a premature stifling of restorative policing pilots (see further Chapter 3). In some respects, this provides a challenge to previous assertions that what has undermined community policing and problem-oriented policing is a lack of translation of principles into practice. If restorative policing offers a framework and means through which the objectives of community policing and problem-oriented policing could be achieved, then perhaps we should have seen much more success of the model than we have up until this point. From our perspective, while restorative policing presents a radical shift in the expectations of how police officers should approach their job, and indeed the resistance felt in response to restorative policing confirms how radical a shift it is, it has not been implemented through a larger process of reform.

Instead, a short-term view of restorative justice has been adopted – one that offers a cost and time effective response to low-level offending – which has doomed it to the margins of police business. We see this as a mistake. Restorative justice holds a much broader potential for reform, but one that requires a much more significant reform project in order to be realised. We agree with Bazemore and Griffiths (2003) who suggest that restorative policing is the next logical step in police reform. Indeed, in the latter half of the book, we make the case for a much more transformative vision of restorative policing and outline what we believe would need to be done in order for this untapped potential to be realised. Before we provide an overview of how our arguments develop, we provide a number of acknowledgements about the necessary limits of its contents.

International focus and exclusions

Criminologists have undertaken most of the work conducted on restorative policing and so the lens through which this practice will be analysed will primarily be conducted from a criminological standpoint. That being said, we acknowledge the valuable contributions from other disciplines and where appropriate we have included both conceptual and theoretical frameworks from them to further deepen our analysis. A particular difficulty with documenting restorative justice practices generally, but restorative policing in particular, is the lack of systematic data. Information on the topic is routinely published in books, journal articles, and research reports and in more obscure outlets such as organisational newsletters and police operational reports. Furthermore, in some instances it was unclear from the available research whether or not practice was still ongoing, the nature of practice that was undertaken and issues relating to the particular nuances of the original schemes. Where possible, we sought contact with those who could provide further clarification and we are incredibly grateful for the time that these individuals took to provide this for us.

We are, however, under no illusions that we have managed to trace and include all information on the topic, not least because we are aware that both practice and research exists in countries where the first language is not English. This has meant that our analysis has been necessarily skewed towards the Anglo American model of democratic policing that evolved out of the United Kingdom from 1829 and diffused into Canada, New Zealand, Australia and the United States, which we are both more familiar with. This has not meant that we have ignored less well-documented practice; it just means that we were unable to produce a comprehensive account of all of the restorative policing models that exist around the world. For example, while the book predominantly focuses on the Wagga Wagga Model (i.e. police-led conferencing) in common law countries, we have also drawn attention to police mediation in civil law countries. We have also sought to bolster an 'international dimension' by drawing on the work of our European colleagues who have provided theoretical and conceptual insights that we felt was relevant to police-led conferencing, even though it has been developed in relation to police mediation.

The practice of restorative policing, if we adopt a maximalist perspective (see further Chapter 2), is diverse and offers a number of research opportunities to assess the strengths and weaknesses of the various models. This is particularly the case in England and Wales where currently restorative justice is known to most police forces around the country and much experimentation is underway. We have not explored practice in this region in significant detail because we wanted to look more broadly at the application of the Wagga Wagga Model in those locations that engaged in a sustained period of practice and where they were subject to evaluation. To provide a complete up-to-date overview of current practice would require full national surveys, something that falls far outside the scope of this book. We have, however, drawn attention to the nuances of different practices and the character of contemporary practices where they were useful for the analysis being undertaken.

What becomes clear is that there is scope and indeed a need for further research to be conducted on this topic. Indeed, there are times where we pose potential avenues for further research where we felt unsatisfied by the state of the field as it currently stands. We have also sought to integrate much more of the policing literature than is the norm on the topic. This has made discussions much more nuanced and, perhaps, provided a more integrated discussion of the realities of policing that in many ways mirror some of the developments in restorative justice. Such an approach has opened up the potential for new avenues of exploration, but we were unable (given space constraints) to explore all aspects in significant detail. In some respects, some of these issues that we raise cannot be authoritatively settled without empirical investigation and it is thought that this book might inform such empirical work. We thus see this book as a means of motivating discussion and further research activity and we look forward to engaging with our colleagues (i.e. you the reader) to further develop our understanding and arguments on the topic in the future.

Outline of the book

One way to think of this book is a tale of two halves. In the first half of the book, we focus on what restorative policing is (Chapter 2), what has happened in relation to the adoption and implementation of restorative practice within operational policing environments around the globe (Chapter 3) and the objections and counter arguments that have emerged in response to the practice as a result (Chapter 4). In this sense, it forms part of a review of the existing restorative policing literature. An essential starting point for any discussion on the topic of restorative policing, is an acknowledgement of the different agendas of restorative justice that exist in order to more fully appreciate the particular nuances that emerge when applying restorative justice to operational policing environments. Thus, Chapter 2 unpacks and explores some of the different interpretations of restorative justice; it provides definitional clarity on what restorative policing is (and therefore what it is not) and explores how this *concept* is being applied in operational policing environments around the globe.

Chapter 3 then traces the development of restorative policing practice since its inception during the early 1990s in Australia to the present day in England and Wales. Four countries are included in this discussion – Australia, the United States, Canada and the United Kingdom – primarily due to the fact that information on the schemes is readily available and they have all had empirical research conducted on them. Each section contains an overview of the inception of restorative policing practice, the character of the scheme, key research findings and where possible the reasons for its demise (or in the case of England and Wales its re-emergence). This provides a solid grounding for conducting a more thorough analysis of the relative strengths and weaknesses of the different applications of the Wagga Wagga Model over time, which we draw upon in the following chapter.

Chapter 4 highlights how police experimentation with restorative justice has perhaps stretched the application of restorative models the most as it relies on professionals – the police – rather than external and independent agencies in facilitating the process. There is a wide body of literature that is critical of an increase in restorative practice within the criminal justice sector generally and more specifically in terms of police facilitated restorative processes. Concerns about the involvement of police officers as facilitators of restorative processes, largely revolve around the perception that they are too heavily invested in particular outcomes. This ultimately led to a move away from police-led conferencing in Australia and significant scepticism from some scholars commenting on schemes from elsewhere. We highlight the potential risks associated with restorative policing and situate it within this broader critical literature.

However, we also felt it was important not to allow the critics to drown out some of the more positive contributions and claims that the supporters of the

Wagga Wagga Model have made. As such, we provide a challenge to those concerns on the basis of the available evidence and also devoted some space to dealing with the perceived benefits of the Model as well. In the same spirit, however, we have also drawn attention to research findings that challenge the tendency toward a utopic view of restorative policing.

In the latter half of the book, we have sought to further develop discourse on the topic. It will be evident to readers that we hold a transformative view of restorative justice (see Chapter 2) and thus our discussions are concerned with how transformation might be realised. As such, we have explicitly situated restorative policing within the policy changes that have taken place within criminal justice, and policing in particular (Chapter 5), devoted space to a reconceptualisation of restorative policing (Chapter 6) and then developed a potential framework for how our reconceptualised notions of restorative policing might be realised in practice (Chapter 7). Chapter 5 thus forms the basis from which we build our arguments in the remainder of the book. Most notably, we identify a global restructuring of the governance of security as a driver of restorative policing and explore the implications that this raises for the shape and sustainability of restorative policing. The chapter encourages scholars to explore not only the transformative potential of restorative practice for police organisations but also the impact of transformative changes in networks of policing and security at the global level upon the future shape of restorative policing.

We build on this narrative in Chapter 6 by altering our conceptions of restorative policing as a new mode of governing crime and a framework through which to further secure social capital. While social capital has been given some attention within the community policing and restorative justice literatures, there has been comparatively less attention given to the topic within the literature on restorative policing. As such we seek to plug this gap and in so doing make a case for broadening and lengthening the lens through which we view restorative policing. Finally, we explore the challenges that lie within the policy implementation process in Chapter 7 with a view to identifying some key principles that can underpin the development of a framework for change. We argue that under a restorative justice framework, police officers are no longer authoritative figures responding to disputes, conflict and crime but are rather required to become proactive community leaders who assist in addressing the harm caused by offending behaviour; use their discretion in a way that prioritises problem-solving over crime control; and view community residents as partners in responding to and managing crime (Clamp and Paterson 2013).

This is a dramatic change for police officers and other agents involved in this process as well as, most importantly, for communities. As such, we suggest that the transformation demanded by a move towards a more restorative approach needs to take place through a process that provides police officers with the necessary skills (such as communication, problem-solving, leadership and relationship-building), alongside strategies that will facilitate buy-in from front-line officers so that they may adequately adapt to this new way of engaging with the community (Clamp and Paterson 2013). Finally, Chapter 8 provides some concluding commentary on the central themes of the book and their implications for the future of restorative policing. In doing so, we conclude with a critical review on the futures of restorative policing and a more detailed reframing of a research agenda for the topic.

Notes

1 Cavadino and Dignan categorise these states as those based on free-market capitalism, epitomised by the USA but also including the UK, Australia and New Zealand (see discussion 2006: 14–17).
2 The literature reveals that scholars refer to either 'community policing' or 'community-oriented policing', although both terms refer to the same thing. We have decided to use the former throughout the book for the sake of consistency, largely due to the fact that, internationally, it appears to be more popular.
3 See, for example, Peak and Glensor (1996) who tried to integrate the two concepts that they termed 'Community Oriented Policing and Problem Solving'.
4 It is important to note that 'community policing' reflects a style of formal state policing rather than the informal, community-generated policing that exists in abundance outside of the wealthy West (Wisler and Onwudiwe 2007).
5 Weitekamp *et al.* (2003: 310) have elaborated on this by suggesting that, 'All community-oriented police work includes problem-solving strategies, but not all problem-oriented police work is necessarily community oriented.'

2 Restorative justice concepts and the operational policing environment

Introduction

Although restorative policing was not a deliberate experiment in applying restorative justice to policing practice, it has subsequently (and with good reason) become embedded within the broader discourse on restorative justice.[1] But what is restorative justice/restorative policing and how does it work in practice? These are misleadingly simple questions because they imply that a straightforward answer can and should be provided. The reality, however, is that restorative justice is a contested concept and so any answer that is given needs to acknowledge this problematic context. In seeking to develop a definition of restorative policing and a framework through which restorative policing might be understood, the nuances within the existing literature on restorative justice are therefore important. As such, we begin this chapter by reviewing two aspects of the restorative justice literature.

The first involves efforts to define restorative justice. Some would argue that such an exercise has been futile, as no consensus on the issue has been reached. However, understanding what restorative justice is and being able to assess the 'restorativeness' of an initiative is important for a number of reasons. On the one hand, Aertsen (2009: 68) argues that: 'Such conceptual clarity is needed, whether it is from the perspective of theory development, empirical research or reform of the police and/or criminal justice system.' On the other, as Declan Roche explains:

> To practitioners it may help critically inform the work they do. It may give practitioners ideas about how they can improve what they are doing. And even where practitioners' actions already conform to restorative justice principles, practitioners may benefit by becoming more self-conscious and deliberate about what they do.
>
> (2001: 342)

The second involves the trends and issues that arise when attempts are made to implement restorative justice. Such an exploration is essential in helping the reader to understand some of the nuances that arise in relation to the application of restorative justice, on the one hand, and the criticisms that arise in relation to that application on the other. This provides important contextualisation for the discussions of restorative policing that emerge in the chapters that follow.

Next, we consider the application of restorative justice to policing contexts in particular. Within this section, the features of restorative policing practice are discussed, the theoretical underpinnings of restorative policing put forward by its original architects are outlined and finally, definitional clarity on what restorative policing is (and therefore what it is not) is provided. In relation to policing practice, the diversity of what is included when people speak of 'restorative policing' is dramatic and to a large extent informed by the 'camp' to which proponents are aligned (i.e. 'purists', 'maximalists' or 'transformativists' – see the following section). The theoretical underpinnings of restorative policing are perhaps less diverse but have been an essential element in the emergence of this practice in particular. We end this section by calling for a reconceptualisation of restorative policing, something that we turn our attention to in greater detail later in the book.

Restorative justice: concepts and practice

Before beginning our conceptual and practical review, it is important that space be devoted to outlining the intellectual and philosophical roots that have facilitated the contemporary restorative justice movement. Dignan (2005) identifies three principal strands that have shaped both the way we think about and practice restorative justice: the 'civilisation' thesis, the 'communitarian' thesis, and the 'moral discourse' thesis. The civilisation thesis, expounded by the work of Cantor (1976) and Fry (1951) argued that efforts should be made to further 'civilise' both the procedures and sanctions that offenders were exposed to within the criminal justice process. These ideas have led proponents (see for example Cornwell *et al.* 2013) to suggest that the vast majority of crime could be dealt with through the civil, as opposed to the criminal, system and that the types of outcomes that should be pursued should be physical restitution and financial compensation.

The second strand, according to Dignan (2005), is situated between the two extremes of collectivism and individualism. While the communitarian thesis reflects some of the suggestions of the civilisation thesis, it argues that the moral and social implications of crime should be taken into account by including the views of both victims and the community. Such a view was epitomised by Nils Christie's (1977) *Conflicts as Property* whereby harm emanating from criminal acts was demonstrated to have a far broader effect than just on the state or on the immediate victim. Furthermore, in terms of the process for dealing with criminal acts, Christie's article argued for the fading of professionals into the background and the participation of stakeholders – victims, offenders and the community – to be the central focus. Such an approach, it is argued, would have the effect of not only dealing with crime more effectively, but also 'a means of reviving communities themselves and reinvigorating their capacity to exert informal social control over their members' (Dignan 2005: 98).

The third strand, rather than focusing on where justice should be done (civilisation thesis) and who should be involved (communitarian thesis), is largely about how justice might be made more effective. Exemplified by the work of Braithwaite (1989), the moral discourse thesis stems from an acknowledgement that a normative or moralising dialogue with the offender would provide a much more powerful response to crime control than the conventional criminal justice response. Braithwaite's theory will be discussed in further detail later in the chapter, suffice to say here that he distinguished between the destructive or disintegrative approaches of conventional responses to crime and a reintegrative approach which would seek to rally both victims and the people that the offender cares most about in demonstrating the harm caused. It is thought that denunciation by loved ones would be far more effective than that conducted by remote legal authorities. Such a discursive approach to crime has also been articulated by Duff (1986) and Tavuchis (1991), who explore the process and importance of apology in justice processes.

These intellectual and philosophical roots have had a number of policy implications, which Dignan (2005) refers to as 'abolitionism', 'separatism' and 'reformism'. *Abolitionists*, particularly influenced by proponents of the civilisation thesis see little in common between restorative justice and the conventional criminal justice system. As such, they have presented restorative justice as an alternative paradigm to criminal justice, which they believe should replace criminal justice completely. *Separatists*, on the other hand, while they agree with abolitionists that the values of restorative justice and criminal justice are incompatible, they acknowledge that the likelihood of the ambitions of abolitionists being realised is relatively unlikely (certainly in the near future). They therefore call for restorative justice to operate completely outside of the criminal justice system in a supplementary capacity. Finally, *reformists* view the potential for restorative justice values, principles and processes to transform criminal justice practice from the 'inside-out'. This can (and has) taken a number of guises, including: integrating restorative outcomes (such as reparation, compensation and community service) into sentencing and 'mainstreaming' whereby restorative principles and processes form a specific part of the criminal justice process (i.e. in diversion programmes or within system itself in relation to young offenders as in New Zealand, Northern Ireland and South Africa).

These historical influences and positions in relation to restorative justice as a 'movement' will be helpful for contextualising the different conceptions, applications and debates that feature throughout this chapter and later chapters in the book. In particular, they help to provide an appreciation for the diversity of practice in restorative justice that features in contemporary criminal justice systems around the globe. Before exploring such practice in more detail, the following section presents an overview of the different ways in which individuals interpret restorative justice.

Different conceptions of restorative justice

Every text on restorative justice will, at some point, mention that it is a contested concept. For the most part, this is due to the fact that there are a number of broad approaches that distinguish how people define what restorative justice is. Purists are concerned with *process*. For them, both the victim and the offender (and others, depending on the type of process) must meet to discuss the incident and collectively decide on a way to repair the harm that was caused. The most popular purist definition is:

> A process whereby *all* the parties with a stake in a particular offence come together to resolve *collectively* how to deal with the aftermath of the offence and its implications for the future.
>
> (Marshall 1999: 5, *emphasis added*)

In order to achieve these broad procedural aims, restorative scholars have singled out a number of values that should guide any process that claims to be 'restorative'. These are quite diverse and are concerned with how participants should be treated, how the process should be run, the types of behaviour the process should elicit and the outcomes that it should generate when the process has been successful (Clamp 2014a). Braithwaite (2002a, 2003) has helpfully grouped these values into constraining values, maximising values and emergent values. Constraining values are those that should be actively enforced because they keep the process focused on the interests of *all* stakeholders. These include non-domination, empowerment, honouring legally specific upper limits on sanctions; respectful listening; equal concern for all stakeholders; accountability and appealability; and respect for individual rights as outlined in international human rights documents (Braithwaite 2002a: 569). The key here is that stakeholders should be given an *equal* voice in the discussion and resolution of the incident, thus creating an environment in which the needs of each individual will be met. Maximising values are those that should be actively encouraged, and represent a means through which the process may be evaluated (Braithwaite 2003). These relate mostly to the extent to which self-worth, relationships, physical items and harmony have been restored; services have been accessed (social justice); and further injustice or bad behaviour has been prevented (Braithwaite 2002a).[2] Finally, emergent values are those that may or may not result from the process and include remorse, apology, censure of the act, forgiveness and mercy. Braithwaite (2003) asserts that facilitators should not explicitly require such outcomes, but that they should rather be viewed as outcomes that emerge naturally when a restorative process has been successful.

Maximalists, on the other hand, are concerned with *outcomes*. While restorative justice proponents in this camp would prefer an encounter to arrive at ways in which harm can be addressed, they are also supportive of any action that seeks to repair. This increases the boundaries of what might be considered restorative to include approaches that do not necessarily involve all stakeholders and to a more inclusive transformative project of justice processes more generally. Both Braithwaite (1999) and Dignan (2002, 2003), for example, have put forward models of how the conventional criminal justice system can be made more 'restorative' by increasing both reparative opportunities for victims as well as sanctions that will hold some meaningful value for the offender. For them, the priority is that steps are taken to repair the harm that is caused, which they argue is not guaranteed by the involvement of all interested parties in a single process. For this reason, they view any action that addresses the causes and consequences of offending behaviour to be worthy of the label 'restorative justice'. The most popular maximalist definition is:

> Restorative justice is every action that is primarily oriented towards doing justice by restoring the harm that has been caused by a crime.
>
> (Bazemore and Walgrave 1999: 48)

One attempt to bridge the purist and maximalist approaches has been to distinguish schemes on the basis of which stakeholders are able to participate in them (see McCold 2000; McCold and Wachtel 2003; van Ness and Strong 2002). It has been suggested that where all stakeholders are able to participate this should be considered *fully* restorative (such as conferencing initiatives and peace-making circles), where only two out of the three stakeholders participate this should be considered *mostly* restorative (such as victim-offender mediation and victimless conferences), and where only one out of the three stakeholders are the focus of the scheme, it should at best be considered *partially* restorative (such as reparative boards, victim services and offender family services). It should be stressed that the aim of these schemes must be underpinned by restorative values and the desire to repair harm rather than being based on stakeholder participation alone in order to be considered 'restorative'.

Added to this complex terrain is a smaller camp of proponents who view restorative justice as a way to transform the manner in which we view crime, our responses to it and as a means through which to reduce social distance (see, for example, Braithwaite 2003; Christie 2004; Johnstone and Van Ness 2007). Criticisms have been levelled against restorative justice for its tendency to reinforce stereotypical notions of victimhood (see Walklate 2005; Young 2002) largely due to the fact that it relies on established legal definitions of victims and victimhood that exist within criminal justice (Pavlich 2005). This conception of restorative justice is distinct in that it seeks to resolve these issues by transcending the criminal justice lens that frames the other conceptions outlined above. Clamp (2016a) for example, argues that rather than using the legal definition of crime we should instead embrace a social harm definition similar to that put forward by Henry and Milovanovic (1994, 1996) who distinguish between 'harms of reduction' (where individuals experience some form of material loss) and 'harms of repression' (where individuals experience future loss i.e. aspirations and development). She suggests that:

Refocusing crimes as harms means that the consequences of any behaviour, policy or action is propelled to a higher status than determining *who was responsible* for the harm and what needs to *happen to them* in order to restore the moral balance.

(2016a: 30–31, *emphasis added*)

Such an approach articulates two transformative consequences for the role of practitioners: (1) a rethinking or reconsideration of the role of the state and the broader community in responding to crime; and (2) a need to see crime problems in their social context with 'a forward-looking (or preventative) problem-solving orientation' (Marshall 1999: 5). While this conception has received compara- tively less attention than the purist and maximalist conceptions outlined above, it has received strong support from those who first designed the restorative polic- ing model (see, for example, McDonald and Moore 2001). We will therefore give further consideration to this in the section on defining restorative policing later in this chapter and subsequently in more detail in Chapter 6 where we develop a 'transformative vision' for restorative policing.

Despite these points of contention in defining what restorative justice is, a number of key features may be discerned that distinguish restorative justice from other types of conflict resolution (see generally Dignan 2005; Galaway and Hudson 2007; Weitekamp *et al.* 2003; Zehr 2002). First, there is a general focus on putting right the harm caused by responding to needs rather than sentencing on the basis of culpability. This may be in the form of either material gestures (such as money or the replacement of damaged items) or symbolic gestures (such as apologies or undertaking some type of specified work) by the individual responsible for any emotional or physical loss or damage. Second, the com- munity, victim and offender should receive balanced attention and tangible bene- fits from engaging in the process. While the victim and/or the community has a right to some form of reparative redress and this will form a significant part of the discussion and subsequent agreement that emerges, there also needs to be a focus on the offenders' accountability, well-being and the underlying motiva- tions for offending. Finally, it is thought that meeting these features should occur within an inclusive, non-coercive decision-making process in which those most directly involved and affected by the offence should have the opportunity to participate fully in the response should they wish to do so.

In the following section, we consider how restorative justice has been opera- tionalised within a criminal justice setting. While the debate surrounding what restorative justice is within the academic literature is quite complex, this is somewhat less convoluted in practice. What has emerged is a distinction between the use of the terms 'restorative justice' and 'restorative practice', the preference for which often depends on the programme and its organisational and policy setting. According to Aertsen (2009), criminal justice agencies in particular tend to favour the use of the concept 'restorative practices' to describe the schemes that they initiate. Part of the reason for this, he speculates, is that the use of the word 'justice' may be somewhat overwhelming for practitioners who may feel that it would require too dramatic a shift in practice. Perhaps most telling is that discussions related to justice are largely missing when police organisations and scholars discuss the role and purpose of policing (Manning 2010).

Restorative justice in action

The application of restorative justice processes within criminal justice is just as diverse as the concepts underpinning it. This is largely due to the fact that the conditions for referring a case to a restorative process, the types of offences that are eligible and the stage of the criminal justice process at which restorative processes are used vary considerably between criminal justice agencies (police, prosecutors and courts) and countries around the world (see Chapter 3, *this volume* in relation to restorative policing in particular). Furthermore, programmes differ in terms of their location, resources and sustainability as well as the extent to which stakeholders are allowed to participate in them (O'Mahony and Doak 2009). Where schemes are based, for example, can have a considerable impact on their functioning – some are incorporated into the criminal justice process and others are run independently by community or non-governmental organisations.

While many restorative justice proponents would prefer restorative justice initiatives to be independent from the criminal justice system, this does not necessarily guarantee success. Criminal justice agencies often have more funding and resources at their disposal, while independent schemes often struggle with resources and logistics (O'Mahony and Doak 2009). Furthermore, attracting referrals can be problematic for independent schemes because they rely on gatekeepers (such as the police, prosecutors or courts) being aware of and supportive of those schemes. Where gatekeepers feel that the scheme offers a 'soft' approach for dealing with a particular type of offence or where they are not familiar with the scheme, they will be unlikely to refer cases on thus leading to a lack of sustainability (see, for example, Clairmont and Kim 2013; Crocker 2013; Marinos and Innocente 2008). As Shapland (2003: 203) notes, 'state agents tend to be very loath to let many cases escape their grasp'. There is thus an argument for restorative justice initiatives to be housed within criminal justice agencies to overcome this tendency to protect their 'fiefdoms'. This will not only increase the likelihood of sustainability in terms of case referrals, but also the potential for transforming the approach to dealing with crime within that agency (not all restorative proponents agree with this assertion however, see further Chapter 4, *this volume*). Despite this potential, restorative justice has traditionally been kept at the margins of the criminal justice process, offering no real challenge to the *status quo*.

Nevertheless, restorative justice is perceived to hold a number of benefits for the criminal justice system. This includes reducing repeat offending, diverting less serious offences away from the costly criminal justice process,[3] providing victims with an increased role in the resolution of their cases (which is related to increasing the perceived legitimacy of the process) and improving the capacity of communities to deal with problems at the local level (Moore 2004). As such, much like within the policing literature, practitioners within criminal justice have embraced early intervention as the key to preventing ongoing and increasingly serious offending (Bradley 2009; Krammedine *et al.* 2013). Crawford therefore notes that:

> This early interventionist logic within the institutionalisation of restorative justice, results in a focus on low-level crimes and anti-social activities which themselves may fall outside or on the cusp of the frame of 'crime' narrowly defined and the processes of criminalisation. Restorative cautioning and police-facilitated conferencing often operate in this liminal space.
>
> (2015: 477)

As such, restorative justice processes have most often been implemented as a diversionary measure or an early intervention mechanism whereby the particular act in question would not normally result in a charge being pursued or where the offending is relatively minor in nature. The primary purpose of restorative justice applications within this approach has been to try to bring home to young offenders that their actions do have an impact on others, that their behaviour has been unacceptable, but that they can take steps to repair the harm that has been caused. Given the range of due process concerns that arise from such interaction, most restorative justice schemes that are used within the criminal justice setting (and elsewhere) require the offender to first admit responsibility for the offence and for participants to consent to their participation in the process.[4]

However, it is important to note that not all programmes that are run by criminal justice agencies include *all* stakeholders. This is particularly true in terms of the presence of victims and/or their supporters with many restorative justice schemes being characterised by low victim participation. In many respects, this is due to the fact that criminal justice is predisposed to focusing on offenders rather than victims and so established timings and procedures do not naturally lend themselves to victim engagement (see, for example, Crawford and Newburn 2003 in relation to youth offender panels in England and Wales, or Bazemore and Umbreit 2001 in relation to Vermont's reparative boards).[5] Given the time constraints associated with criminal justice processes, there has been a tendency to use surrogate victims and/or community representatives in place of direct victims (see, for example, O'Mahony *et al.* 2002). However, a number of restorative proponents have raised issues with this approach given that these individuals do not hold an emotional connection to the incident and so their contributions may be interpreted as having an air of moral superiority that is perceived to disrupt the restorative potential of the process (McCold and Wachtel 1998b).

Likewise, an expectation within conceptualisations of restorative justice that the community be involved has also raised questions about which 'community' is being referred to. Although many tend to think of community as referring to those that reside within a geographic setting, within the restorative justice literature, community is often conceptualised in much narrower terms. McCold and Wachtel (1998b), for example, refer to a 'micro-community' that emerges following an incident whereby those who were previously strangers have been brought together to collectively try to resolve the causes and consequences of the crime. A further way to think about the community is in relational terms, such as the supporters or 'communities of care' that victims and offenders bring to conferences (Boyes-Watson 2005). In practice, Hoyle and Rosenblatt (2016) draw attention to the tendency for criminal justice practitioners, such as the police, to interpret these 'communities of care' in a restrictive way by placing too much importance on immediate family members (i.e. parents).[6] They suggest that such an approach does not take into account the contemporary shifts in 'the political, social and cultural landscape' whereby support structures are more widely interpreted to include friends and social networks (see also Moore 1992). In order to deal effectively with what has happened and to prevent any future harm from occurring, they therefore argue that it is important that practice evolves to asking participants who they consider their supporters to be.

Regardless of whether the case is kept 'in-house' or referred on to another (often independent) service provider, the process remains broadly the same. A key actor known as a 'facilitator' (or in some initiatives a 'coordinator') is responsible for arranging the meeting (i.e. setting and communicating a mutually convenient time, date and location), ensuring that all parties are able to contribute fully to both the discussion (i.e. respecting each other's human rights) and overseeing the contents of the agreement reached (i.e. that the contents do not contain illegal or overly coercive elements). In keeping with the philosophy of restorative justice, facilitators should not dominate proceedings or allow a meeting to take place where the offence has not been acknowledged by the offender or where there are significant disagreements about the particular aspects of the offence in question (Shapland 2003).

Where a process is held, it often follows a similar pattern with offenders and then victims (where the process includes additional stakeholders, then the victim's supporters and finally the offender's supporters) being able to share their views on what happened (Roberts and Masters 1999). It should be noted that unlike in legal processes, the actual discussion that takes place during the process is something that is not linear. Often, contributions from participants will tend to involve referring to particular aspects of the incident and then talking about issues that, at face value, appear to be unconnected to it (providing a significant departure from the type of information shared within a trial). This, according to Shapland, is largely due to the fact that:

> [...] restorative justice, by its nature, does not limit itself to discussion of the instant offence, bounded as strictly as the evidential rules of formal criminal justice would ensure. Simply because ordinary people do not see the offence as a time-limited slice of action carved from ongoing social interaction, participants at restorative justice sessions will not discuss the offence alone. They will raise the circumstances around the offence, previous incidents, previous interaction between offender and victim and matters which have occurred since the offence. Nor, given the purpose of

restorative justice, will they be wrong to do so. It is not possible to have a problem-solving, forward-looking orientation to the session and omit all these other circumstances.

(2003: 205)

At the end of the session, it is expected that all participants will draft and agree to the contents of an action plan. While many assume that victims will want some form of material reparation (i.e. financial recompense or a replacement of damaged goods), research tends to show that many victims are far more concerned with symbolic reparation (i.e. apologies and some form of convincing indication that the offender will refrain from similar types of behaviour in future) (see Coates and Gehm 1989; Maxwell and Morris 1993a; Moore 1993a; Moore and Forsythe 1995; Strang 2002; Umbreit 1994; Wright 1991). Where there are particular items that are agreed to, the contents of plans can be affected by the relationship of the referral scheme to the formal criminal justice process. In the Northern Ireland Youth Conferencing System, for example, the co-ordinator needs to balance the wishes of the participants against what is likely to be approved by the courts in relation to the agreements that have been reached (see Campbell *et al.* 2005).

It should also be noted that the point at which the scheme is an option for referral in relation to the criminal justice process has an impact on the types of consequences that there are in terms of not fulfilling what has been agreed. For example, in terms of offenders not complying with agreements that emerge from community justice panels in England and Wales there may be no consequences or merely the requirement to attend another panel session to explore why the conditions have not been met and another action plan put in place (see Clamp 2014a). In other schemes, such as the Northern Ireland Youth Conferencing System, every opportunity is afforded to the young person to fulfil the original requirements of the agreement. In the relatively small amount of cases where this does not happen (around 6 per cent), the court can impose an 'attendance center order in addition to the youth conference order' or it can impose 'a new order whilst revoking, amending or extending the youth conference order' (Campbell *et al.* 2005: 116).

While many view restorative justice as a positive challenge to the monopoly traditionally held by the state in response to crime (Christie 1977), others suggest that restorative practices offer potential benefits that extend beyond securing outcomes for participants of the process alone. Wachtel and McCold (2001), for example, suggest that restorative practices might motivate people to become more interested in each other (thus breaking down the isolation that traditionally exists in urban areas), thereby increasing mutual accountability and social capacity to resolve conflict without having to rely on the state (see further Chapter 6, this volume). Perhaps given the fact that police officers act as gatekeepers for the rest of the criminal justice process, the potential for realising these grand aims is often thought to be located within this particular agency. Further support for this assertion will be outlined in the discussions that follow.

Restorative policing: a review of its application, theory and definitions

In this section, we move beyond the broad conceptualisation and application of restorative justice within criminal justice to focus on restorative policing in particular. We begin by looking at how restorative policing is being applied to operational policing environments. In purist terms, restorative policing is based solely on one restorative process: conferencing. Conferencing differs from other restorative processes in that it relies on public officials rather than trained volunteers as facilitators, it allows for a much more directed style of facilitation than had previously been viewed as appropriate and the number of participants is much broader (Umbreit and Zehr 1996a). However, there is also a body of literature which is more expansionist/maximalist in its approach which includes a variety of day-to-day activities undertaken by police officers which may broadly be considered 'restorative' and which also includes referrals to conferencing/ mediation schemes that are not run by police officers themselves. This literature will be explored (albeit briefly) in this section as well. However, given that the next chapter deals with the emergence of conferencing and programme specific restorative policing case studies in some detail, particular examples of a purist or police-facilitated approach will not form part of this discussion.

Next, in general, theories of restorative justice guide our understandings of *how* and *why* restorative processes work and have focused on particular emotions – shame, legitimacy, trust – that elicit positive responses from victims and offenders and reduce further offending (Rossner 2008). The original architects of restorative policing have spent considerable amounts of time exploring the theoretical explanation for the outcomes that they have observed during conferencing processes and these will be discussed in more detail here. It should be noted that the focus of the discussion in this section will therefore be in relation to conferencing alone. Nevertheless, we seek to expand preceding discussions by drawing on the often overlooked theoretical literature that underpins policing – the value of which helps to contextualise some of the specific trajectories that practice in this area has followed as outlined in later chapters.

Finally, we consider various attempts to define the parameters of restorative policing and how this has evolved over time. While we draw attention to the particular limitations of these attempts in this section, we will not develop our own conceptualisation for restorative policing until later in the book (see Chapter 6, this volume). The rationale for this is in part informed by space constraints but also for the benefit of narrative. Our argument is that conceptions of restorative policing to-date have been quite limited and so we argue for a more transformative agenda in this area.

Restorative policing practice

According to Vynckier (2009) restorative policing practices differ in the way cases are selected, who is involved, the processes used and the role that the police play within them. Shapland (2009) suggests that police officers can facilitate restorative processes themselves, refer suitable cases on to specialist policing teams that are trained in restorative practice, or some other specialist agencies outside of the police service or statutory criminal justice system altogether. Aertsen (2009) and Dandurand and Griffiths (2006) add to this by suggesting that police officers can also apply restorative justice principles within their daily interaction with members of the public, by mediating conflicts and resolving problems as part of their routine activities, informing the public about restorative justice processes, monitoring outcomes of agreements that emerge from restorative processes and informing the prosecutor and/or courts of the outcome of mediated agreements. Restorative justice has also been used internally in cases of alleged police misconduct (see Davey 2007; Hoyle and Young 2003; McLaughlin and Johansen 2002; Walker *et al.* 2002). As such, the scope for restorative justice within policing organisations is significant, 'limited only by the imagination and skill sets' of police officers themselves (Dandurand and Griffiths 2006: 63) and the operational constraints within which they work.

There is a distinction in the literature, however, between those who define restorative policing as meetings facilitated by trained officers themselves known as the 'Wagga Wagga Model' (see McCold 1998; Moore 1994) and those who expand the boundaries of restorative policing to include activities of referral, monitoring and the integration of restorative principles into routine police practice and referrals to external diversion schemes known as the 'New Zealand Model' (see broadly the chapters included in Moor *et al.* (2009) for case examples of both models). Some of these procedural differences emerged out of two of the earliest models of conferencing that developed in New Zealand and Wagga Wagga in New South Wales (see further Chapter 3, this volume). Although both share a commitment to restorative principles, the New Zealand Model reflects a 'community justice orientation' whereas the Wagga Wagga Model reflects restorative processes within a 'community policing orientation' (Hipple and McGarrell 2008: 556).

The institutional arrangements that exist within countries have a significant impact upon the extent to which restorative policing is able to feature and thus the type of model adopted. For example, in civil law jurisdictions, such as Europe, police officers do not hold the same level of discretion as their neoliberal counterparts (Daly 2001). Decision-making about the offences that are channelled into and away from the criminal justice process is often determined by prosecutors rather than police officers (Clairmont and Kim 2013). As such, the opportunity for restorative practice to be used by police officers is restricted because they are unable to decide on how a case should be dealt with on their own or in consultation with the affected parties (Daly 2001; Vanfraechem 2009; Vynckier 2009). Instead, officers, with the approval of the prosecutor, are able to refer non-criminal and formally agreed to minor categories of offences to neighbourhood mediators or to mediation services that may be located within a local police station or elsewhere (see Aertsen 2009; Vanfraechem 2009; van Stokkom and Moor 2009; Vynckier 2009). In these countries, therefore, it is the New Zealand Model that is the most prevalent.

Practice in civil law jurisdictions have largely been eclipsed by practice in common law jurisdictions due to a lack of accessible information and data in English. Nevertheless, two notable examples may be briefly mentioned here. The only jurisdiction to experiment with police-led conferencing in Europe (as far as we could ascertain) has been the Netherlands. However, this practice ceased in 2000 due to a refocusing of the police on 'crime fighting' and 'detection' thus forfeiting some of their traditional local peace/order functions (van Stokkom, personal communication). Van Stokkom and Moor (2009) suggest that mediation and comparative alternative approaches are viewed as 'soft options' that take more time than they are worth and interfere with 'core' police business. In nearly all municipalities in the Netherlands, the police now refer cases to diversion programmes such as Halt and other local neighbourhood mediation centres (sponsored by local authorities and housing organisations). These practices have blossomed in the last few years (for example in Amsterdam, 250 mediators participate in more than 2,000 cases on a yearly basis) but a lack of documentation in English has meant that little is known about them beyond those who speak Dutch (van Stokkom, personal communication). Despite the move away from police-facilitated conferencing, both van Stokkom and Moor (2009) and Vanfraechem (2009) draw attention to a range of informal 'restorative' and 'peace-making' activities undertaken by police officers in the Netherlands within the course of their daily business whereby individuals are encouraged to resolve issues themselves before they resort to any formal processing. However, van Stokkom and Moor (2009: 113) stress that these activities 'remain within the logic of "incident-driven" work' and that the dominant crime control ethos means that officers (including beat police) are involved less and less with the public in any proactive way. As such, the authors argue (as we do later in the book) that the police should play a significant role in conflict resolution and proactive policing activities to increase local community capacity.

In Belgium, both federal and local police exist and it is at the local police level that restorative practices, or more specifically, mediation programmes exist (Aertsen 2009). Vynckier (2009) draws attention to the fact that the discretion of the police is not formally recognised in Belgium and that it is the public prosecutor who ultimately serves as the gatekeeper to the system. Despite these constraints, two particular programmes have emerged in response to minor offences at the discretion of the prosecutor, one in the Flanders called 'damage mediation' and another in Brussels called 'local mediation' (Aertsen 2009; D'haese and Grunderbeeck 2009; Vanfraechem 2009). In both locations, while police identify suitable cases (i.e. the victim must be known; the offender must admit responsibility and the consequences of the offence must require an element of restitution) they then refer them on to be facilitated by a civilian mediator at a local police station (Aertsen 2009; Vanfraechem 2009). Nevertheless, drawing on a range of Dutch literature, Vanfraechem (2009) makes the argument that police officers do engage in mediation within their day-to-day tasks, as in the Netherlands, in the form of peacekeeping. This is not an infrequent statement within the literature on routine policing practice (even beyond these specific cases) and as a result of little documentation on these practices; it perhaps presents an opportunity for further research and reflection on these 'hidden' restorative moments within police work.

In common law countries, however, there has been a tradition of 'decentralization and compartmentalization in criminal justice system decision-making, allowing for local moral entrepreneurs (i.e. rule creators crusading for the passage of certain rules, laws, and policies), police discretion, and space for restorative approaches to develop' (Clairmont and Kim 2013: 364). As such, it is within these jurisdictions that most conferencing projects, and especially the Wagga Wagga Model, have been implemented (Vanfraechem 2009). It should be noted that all police work takes place prior to the formal prosecution of offences in neo-liberal or common law states. Thus, the use of restorative processes within this context predominantly takes place as a diversionary option, or in other words, as an informal resolution of the case without formal prosecution through the courts once an offender has admitted responsibility (Clamp and Paterson 2013). While some conferencing processes tend to be facilitated by trained neutral third parties as in civil law jurisdictions outlined above, it is the police rather than an external and/or independent agency that oversee the process in what is traditionally thought to be 'restorative policing'. In many respects, this has stretched the application of restorative models as the process relies on professionals who have a vested interest in the resolution of the offence facilitating the process and, as a result, this has drawn much scepticism about the practice (see further Chapter 4, this volume).

The most extensive use of police facilitated restorative practice in neoliberal jurisdictions has been located within the common law systems of police warnings and cautions for those who are first-time offenders or who have committed relatively minor (and in some schemes, moderate) offences. Police officers are able to use their discretion in such instances to warn offenders and/or apply certain conditions on those who admit responsibility for the act. The manner in which such disposals have traditionally been approached has often been labelled 'degrading ceremonies' (Lee 1995) whereby the offender will receive a 'telling off' by the police officer and then sent on their way (also see O'Connell 1992). In an attempt to move away from this stigmatising approach, restorative justice principles have primarily been incorporated into what has become known as 'restorative cautioning', whereby the police seek to get the offender to understand the consequences of his/her actions and to highlight ways in which they might repair any harm that has been caused (this would conform to the 'partially restorative' model outlined above) or 'restorative conferencing' whereby officers expand the participants to include the victim and their supporters (this would conform to the 'fully' or 'mostly' restorative model outlined above). It is thought that through such a process stakeholders will subsequently have a deeper understanding of the circumstances and consequences of the offence; that all participants will have agreed and contributed to the drafting of a behavioural or task-oriented contract to which the offender has to adhere; and that all participants will experience a sense of procedural justice – that they will be satisfied that they have been dealt with in a fair and equitable manner. Where the process breaks down or where the offender does not meet his or her obligations as agreed to during the conference, the officer retains the right to pursue the charge through the normal adversarial channels.

Some have suggested that such an approach would be more appropriate in rural or semi-rural areas largely due to the fact that people living in urban areas are much more able to practice avoidance as a means of dealing with conflict resolution.[7] However, Meyer *et al.* (2009: 338) suggest that peace-making efforts (such as restorative policing) are a far more effective means of dealing with conflict because it deals with the underlying causes of the problem and 'it can address situations that fall outside the rubric of the formal adversarial process due to failure to meet legal requirements of proof, evidence, and magnitude of harm'. This further extension of the public voice in policing will, at times, require police officers to act as facilitators and silent stakeholders rather than as decision-makers, a process that requires police officers to interpret and undertake their role in innovative ways (Paterson and Clamp 2012). Thus, rather than police officers identifying perpetrators, considering the severity of the incident and deciding on an appropriate response, a restorative framework requires them to seek to include all those involved in decision-making processes (Clamp and Paterson 2013). This allows participants to feel some level of ownership over both the processes that their cases proceed through and the outcomes that are generated from those processes, thus leading to increased acceptance of and satisfaction with the outcome. Solutions are thus achieved between parties through consensus, rather than through externally imposed mandates (Meyer *et al.* 2009). Many of these assumptions are underpinned by theories that have emerged during the last three decades about the importance of the process of justice. In the section that follows, we draw attention to the key theories that have been important to the emergence of conferencing, in particular.

The theoretical perspectives underpinning restorative policing

Moore (1993a) distinguishes the theoretical starting point for restorative policing from the conventional criminal justice process. He does so by linking the traditional police caution and other community-based sanctioning mechanisms with theories that locate the causes for an individual's offending as an issue of low self-control (see Gottfredson and Hirschi 1990 for a more detailed explanation of this theory). The manner in which attempts are made to rectify any offending under this approach is through a 'combination of threat and suasion' (Moore 1993b: 206). Although not developed within the theoretical literature on restorative justice, the work of Sykes and Matza (1957) is relevant here by way of explanation for why crime control responses are, for the most part, ineffective. The authors are located within a camp of theorists who locate the causes of offending within processes of social interaction and they argue that it is easy for offenders to deny responsibility where their victims are 'physically absent, unknown or a vague abstraction' (1957: 668). In the absence of being confronted with the consequences of one's actions, the offender is able to rationalise and justify his/her behaviour so that it is deemed acceptable.[8] The implications of such thinking is that the only way to address offending by a particular individual is to place them in a social context in which they are unable to deny the personal and social ramifications of their actions. Restorative justice processes more broadly, but conferencing in particular, seek to create the conditions in which this can occur.

The theoretical framework of the Wagga Wagga Model complements Sykes and Matza's theory in that it is underpinned by the belief that people offend because of 'an unwillingness or inability to empathise with other people' which has both individual and social causes (Moore 1993a: 207).[9] As such, this model creates a social context wherein the consequences of the offenders' actions – in terms of the impact on their victim/s, the victim/s family and their own family – are communicated to the offender and the circumstances of the offender in terms of providing an impetus for offending are reviewed and integrated into an action plan to prevent further offending.[10] The starting point for theoretical debates regarding conferencing in general and restorative policing in particular, has been Braithwaite's (1989) reintegrative shaming theory (McDonald and Moore 2001; Moore 1994, 2004). Contrary to other crime control theories, which emphasise doing things to offenders (i.e. incapacitating them in some way), Braithwaite argued that those who had the most to lose from offending were the most likely to abstain from such behaviour. In terms of crime control then, he deduced that creating meaningful conditions through which offenders can view their behaviour as hurtful (not only to victims but to their loved ones as well) was the key to reducing further crime. This reasoning emphasises psycho-social factors such as a sense of personal control and the presence of social support: 'If individuals feel they have some sense of dignity, a sense of hope for the future, and significant positive relationships, then they have a great deal to lose from behavior that damages those relationships' (Moore 2004: 76).

As such, Braithwaite (1989) argued that the moral educational function of punishment is far more important than the deterrent function (also see Moore and Forsythe 2005; O'Connell 1992). This perspective draws on Durkheim's 'moral education' (1925) and Foucault's conception of 'biopolitics', which describe how attempts are made to foster the well-being and orderliness of populations on behalf of the nation state and sovereign law (Foucault 1991). In seeking to demonstrate the veracity of his theoretical position, Braithwaite (1998) explained why some countries have higher crime rates than others by drawing on two types of shaming: reintegrative shaming and disintegrative shaming (or stigmatisation). The former, it is argued, can produce constructive behaviours on the basis that the aim is the social reintegration of a person who has committed a shameful act, whereas the latter traditionally produces destructive behaviours on the basis that the primary aim is to distinguish that person from those who are law abiding (Moore 1993a).[11]

However, two general objections have been raised in respect of the conscious use of shame as a crime control technique within the literature (Moore 1993a). First, is the perception that a renewed focus on civic duties and collective responsibilities may serve to undermine the individual rights that underpin liberal political and legal systems. Second, shame has traditionally been thought of as a negative emotion, which has led some to suggest that guilt might be a better topic of focus. However, as Roberts and Masters (1999) convincingly argue, while some might feel it is desirable to move away from using the concept of 'shame', to do so would undermine our understanding of why these processes work as well as they do. Chatterjee and Elliot (2013: 356) suggest that confusion about the term can be further illustrated by the use of the concept 'shame' as a noun or a verb.

In respect of the former, shame is a 'self-derived emotion' wherein the offender is expected to recognise his or her responsibility for the harm to his or her relationships. Where the facilitator is competent in working with the participants to manage shame in a collective way, the authors argue that this presents no compromise to the integrity of the conferencing process. In addition, if the emotion of shame is felt by the collective as proposed by McDonald and Moore (2001), the transition to a constructive process resulting in healing becomes the responsibility of the collective, i.e. the conference participants, who might be expected to ensure harm reduction by the offender. Where shame is used as a verb, however, the authors suggest that it is easy to become bogged down in the (mistaken) perception that conferencing is inherently about deliberately humiliating individuals. Chatterjee and Elliot (2013: 356) point out the potential exists for *any* sanctioning process to be used in this way rather than just conferences led by police officers (also see Roberts and Masters 1999) and that where this happens, it 'creates a contradiction between process and values'. Rather, what proper conferencing expects is for facilitators to become more deliberate in their attempts to reintegrate, not to shame, particularly given that the conferencing process already has shaming inherent within it.

In engaging with Braithwaite's work, Moore (2004) suggests that questions increasingly arose about the psychology of what happens during the conferencing process. He reflects that as facilitators followed the script, participants appeared to move through a series of stages, dominated by a small number of emotions resulting in a profound emotional turning point in the latter half of the (most well-convened) conferences. This similar pattern of emotional dynamics, it is reported, appeared to arise regardless of distinctions in the 'nature of the offence, the number of participants present or their cultural backgrounds' (Moore 2004: 77). Following a significant period of evaluation, reintegrative shaming was believed to be limited in its capacity to describe what was happening because it focused on one individual experiencing shame. Rather, what was happening was a collective experience of 'vulnerability' and subsequent transformation of perspectives and feelings of all participants,[12] as Moore notes:

> What seemed to be happening physiologically was a shift in affects, or 'basic emotions'. The shift begins from the moment the convenor, quite transparently, shifts the focus from judgments about *individuals* to analysis of *actions* and/or *events*. This shift in subject matter begins the first affective shift, from emotions most associated with conflict – anger, fear and contempt – to the emotions of distress, disgust and surprise. These emotions are

consistently expressed about harmful actions (in cases where the conference is dealing with undisputed harm), and/or about the general set of circumstances (in cases where the conference is addressing many disputes). When a picture has been painted, collectively, of what has happened and how people have been affected, the convenor creates a space for reflection, asking some or all participants whether they have anything to add. This is a logical break, the divide between looking at the past and the present, and looking to the future. Again, in parallel with the structural logic of the process, this is also a profound affective turning point. Various metaphors describe the physiology of participants at this point. They will, for instance, look at though they have 'had the wind knocked out of their sails'.

(2004: 87, *emphasis original*)

Although they are under no obligation to do so, Moore (1993a) reports that during the process the majority of offenders offered genuine apologies for their actions and more often than not victims almost invariably forgave offenders. In explaining why this occurs, he draws on the 'microsociology' of destructive and constructive conflict of Susanne Retzinge and Thomas Scheff, the affect theory of Silvan Tomkins and Donald Nathanson, and the moral philosophy of Jean Hampton and Jeffrie Murphy (see Moore 1994). What emerges is the belief that the process provides a forum for the resentment of victims to be dealt with by offering a mechanism through which they might secure symbolic and/or material reparation and for the general indignation of indirect victims (both offender and victim supporters) at a breach in social norms to be vocalised which ultimately leads to the moral education of offenders in empathy and the subsequent feelings of shame (also see O'Connell 1992; Wachtel and McCold 2001). Thus, Moore (2004: 22) suggests that the conference is designed 'to strengthen the internal control of conscience and the external control of social bonds'. This line of theoretical inquiry has also been adopted by Bazemore (2000a) and Sampson and Laub (2003) in their work on collective efficacy and community capital, although Manning (2010) bemoans the lack of impact that these theoretical explorations have had upon policing scholarship. Given that 'good theory assists good practice', it is important that theoretical insights are shared within and between different fields of professional practice, about the principles and practices with which we work (Moore 2015: 73).

Conferencing may therefore be thought of as a process of cooperation between participants leading to a subsequent transformation of perspectives, feelings and circumstances (Moore 1993a). In some cases attitudes to others may not change significantly, in others there may be less transformation as a result of the process and more due to the outcome that follows from the action plan that parties put together, for others still the process of coming together and talking through what happened may be the outcome (Moore 2004). This provides a challenge to the perception held by White (1994: 188) who views conferencing as a form of control and extension of police power, 'a state-run, top-down model, one which is constructed to involve members of the community, but not in a manner which actually places real decision-making power into the hands of that community'. It would be negligent to say that here are no poorly run conferences (indeed Chapter 3 will show that there are), but in theoretical terms, good conferences that adhere to the theoretical and philosophical underpinnings of conferencing do empower stakeholders. Daly (2003) suggests that the extent to which conferences are successful or not lies in the varying degrees of 'readiness' that participants have to make the process work. She explains that:

> Offenders and victims are not equally disposed to be restorative towards each other, to listen to each other, or to be willing to repair harms. Some come to conferences with negative orientations and closed minds that cannot be changed, and others come with positive orientation is an open mind. The conference process may engage restorative orientations already present in victims and offenders, or it may create openings for those orientations to emerge. However, for those victims fixed negative attitudes (e.g. those who think the offender is a bad person), the conference process is unlikely to move them in a more positive or restorative direction.... We should expect variations in restorative processes and outcomes; without it, we would be unable to test the theory restorative justice. Variation occurs because there is both potential for and limits on transforming relations between victims and offenders in the aftermath of crime.
>
> (2003: 49)

Other theories, which have proved to be influential in respect of police-led conferencing are Tyler's (1990) theory of procedural justice (which can also be viewed as a process-based model of regulation see Tyler 2003, 2006a) and Sherman's (1993) defiance theory. Both theories complement Braithwaite's theory of reintegrative shaming in that they are concerned with respect and legitimacy in the *process* of dealing with individuals and the activation of internal motivations to become law abiding. Tyler (2006b) suggested that in an increasingly punitive society, criminal justice institutions have attempted to enforce compliance through the application of sanctions. The outcome, he argues, is an increasingly hostile reaction from the population, particularly in relation to the police. As such, he argues for the treatment of individuals with procedural justice and respect because where individuals believe that they have been treated fairly, they are more likely to view legal authorities with legitimacy. The importance of legitimacy for governments and criminal justice institutions is described by Wrong simply as: 'Legitimate authority is more efficient than coercive or induced authority' (1979: 52). In other words, 'If authorities are judged to be legitimate, they need not justify each decision they make, nor enforce it through the use of rewards, threats of punishment, or both' (Tyler 1997: 335). It is widely asserted that the more legitimate citizens view the state and criminal justice institutions to be, the more likely they are to voluntarily obey the law (Tyler 1997; Sunshine and Tyler 2003). The effect is that people then become self-regulating, taking on the personal responsibility for following social rules (Tyler 2006b). As such, Tyler (1990) argues that the ways in which people are involved in justice processes might be more important than the outcomes that they generate.

Similarly, Sherman's (1993) theory of defiance emerged in light of the insights provided by Braithwaite and Tyler outlined above (amongst others). He proposed a general theory of sanctioning effects which posited that where individuals were disrespected and disempowered during the sanctioning process it would lead to defiance.[13] According to Sherman (1993: 461) defiance will arise in the presence of four conditions. First, the offender must interpret the criminal sanction as unfair which can be related to the treatment by the sanctioning agent or because the sanction is perceived as 'arbitrary, discriminatory, excessive, undeserved, or otherwise objectively unjust'. Second, the offender must be 'poorly bonded' to the sanctioning agent or the community that the agent represents. Third, the offender must interpret the sanction as stigmatising and therefore rejects the sanctioner (this point, in particular, has overlap with Sykes and Matza's techniques of neutralisation outlined above). Finally, the offender must fail to acknowledge the shame that the sanction has caused him or her to suffer.

Legitimacy is a central concept in defiance theory and the social bonds that an offender has are viewed as an important factor in the type of responses that emerge in relation to 'unjust' sanctions. On this basis, Sherman (1993) predicted that three responses would emerge in relation to punishment defined as unfair. The first is that a poorly bonded offender will accept the shame, but the perceived unfairness of the sanction would weaken the deterrent effect on similar behaviour in the future. The second is that a poorly bonded offender will deny the shame and the sanction will increase future offending with victims becoming vicarious substitutes for the sanctioning agent. The third is that a well-bonded offender may deny the shame, but the strength of social bonds means that while the perceived unfairness may weaken the effect of the sanction, they would be somewhat shielded from defiance (i.e. further offending). On the basis of this theory, given that conferencing seeks to deliberately increase social bonds through a respectful process, participation in such a process is thought to be more likely to reduce recidivism than conventional justice approaches.

Defining restorative policing

Drawing on the 'balanced and restorative justice model' of Bazemore and Umbreit (1994)[14] and the 'restorative/enhancement approach to community crime prevention model' by Brown and Polk (1996),[15] Weitekamp *et al.* (2003) sought to conceptualise restorative policing. The authors argue that what is missing from these traditional models are the police themselves, the central actors in any attempt to increase feelings of community safety, reduce fear of crime and develop crime prevention strategies. In their model, they therefore include the offender, the victim (depending on the type of offence, this could be an individual or the community more generally), the community and the police as the key stakeholders that should be involved in any response to crime and disorder. Moore *et al.* (2009: 23) hold a similar position when they suggest that police work is an essential part of restorative practices, given that in order for restorative justice processes to take place there needs to be an identifiable suspect, that suspect needs to acknowledge responsibility for the act that has occurred and that those who have been affected by the offence (including the offender) need to participate in the process. Police officers are integral to all three of these conditions of restorative practices being realised and they therefore argue that they be given due consideration as a central actor in restorative justice practice.

It is interesting to note that while many would view restorative policing as an example of deliberative democracy because of its emphasis on participation, equity, deliberation and non-tyranny, Moore (2004: 86) has rejected such an approach because it risks 'prioritising process over outcome'. As such, he calls for a reframing of conferencing as a model of restorative justice to a model of transformative justice (not too dissimilar to the transformative conception of restorative justice outlined previously). McCold and Wachtel (2001) appear to hold a similar view when they suggest that restorative justice has been interpreted relatively narrowly within the criminal justice system which has meant that the results of the policing experiment has not been as progressive as it could be. If criminal justice practitioners were able to expand their conceptions of restorative practice to include transformative conceptions of restorative justice, this could have much more dramatic consequences for the criminal justice system. In fact, we dedicate space to further unpacking this orientation later in the book, suffice to say here that given the theoretical underpinnings of restorative justice and some of the more progressive experimentation that has occurred within policing (particularly in relation to some community policing models), the promise of restorative policing holds much more value for developing community capacity for informal social control and community-police relations than has previously been discussed before.

Even though the primary discourse around criminal justice in contemporary society is on 'law and order' or 'crime control', in reality policing is essentially about 'peace-keeping' or 'peace-making' (Meyer *et al.* 2009; O'Connell 2008). As such, the more progressive perspective of restorative policing is not necessarily limited to a process, but rather a means through which officers can transform themselves from officials primarily concerned with managing conflict to those concerned with making peace (see, for example, Clamp and Paterson 2013). A number of attempts to define restorative policing can be drawn on which focus on different aspects of restorative policing. For example, Superintendent Mel Lofty from Thames Valley Police sought to define restorative policing in terms of its operational features:

> Restorative policing is not 'yet another' new policing model or initiative, competing with all the other things we do. Rather it supports and builds on the ideas of problem solving policing whilst acknowledging the need to detect and reduce crime in the short and long term. Restorative policing can be a range of tactics and strategies, whose end result, when done right, is that offending behaviour is prevented or curtailed, conflict between

communities is reduced and victims are given back their own confidence and sense of well-being.

(2002: no page)

Others have sought to situate restorative policing within the established discourse on community policing:

> [...] restorative policing ... is ... consistent with the values and goals of community policing, and the general historical purpose of policing itself: to stop crime from occurring, and to keep people safe within their own communities.
>
> (Hines and Bazemore 2003: 412)

There has also been an attempt to define restorative policing in terms of the manner in which it alters the policing role. For example:

> Restorative forms of policing require officers to act as community leaders in addressing the harm caused by offending behaviour; to use their discretion in such a way that prioritises problem-solving over crime control; and to see the community as partners in responding to and managing conflict within the community.
>
> (Clamp and Paterson 2013: 294)

Terry O'Connell (1993: 226) conversely seeks to define restorative policing in terms of the transformative effect that it has on responsibility for offending and the harm caused by offending, largely due to the fact that:

> It challenges police to consider juvenile offending in a more appropriate light. It requires police to become facilitators and mediators, by ensuring that the best possible outcome is achieved for all involved in a cautioning conference. Juvenile offenders are no longer automatically charged unless they have committed a serious indictable offence, have been refused bail or have had onerous bail conditions placed upon them.... The model is fundamentally good policing practice: it provides all those connected with a crime with an opportunity to ensure that justice is both seen to be achieved and is actually achieved.... No longer can communities expect governments, legislators or police to solve the problem of harm caused by offending, nor can various community agencies afford to operate in isolation. Our ability to develop the type of communities and the quality of life for which we all strive, will be largely determined by the level of community resources and involvement committed to resolving those problems that threaten community cohesion.
>
> (O'Connell 1993: 226)

There have been faltering attempts at developing restorative policing in this regard, largely due to the fact that such notions have been limited to individuals working within policing organisations that have held transformative visions of what restorative justice actually offers in terms of conflict resolution. However, attempts to drive this change have often been undertaken within a top-down approach, which has not resulted in a significant transformation of policing or police relations with the communities that they serve more generally. Restorative policing, according to us, therefore holds the potential to drive a shift within policing from a force ethos to a service ethos (see further Lofty 2002[16]) and from an institution which seeks to enforce compliance to one which seeks to generate voluntary compliance (see Ritchie and O'Connell 2001). The work of Clifford Shearing has contributed much to this discussion within the context of policing and security through detailed exploration of the emergence of non-police (i.e. state) agencies that police through an emphasis upon soft power and voluntary compliance. We argue for the continuation of such a transformative project in the remainder of this book.

From concepts to practice

This chapter has provided a conceptual and theoretical overview of restorative justice and restorative policing, an essential task given the breadth and contested nature of this area of research. What we have tried to achieve by engaging in this review is to provide the reader with a sense that restorative justice offers much more than a process that brings victims, offenders and their supporters together to talk about the offence and to develop an agreement for action. Restorative justice holds a much more transformative potential in terms of altering the way that we perceive and do justice. We have also sought to instil in the reader an appreciation that conferencing has strong theoretical roots which has helped to not only guide how practice has evolved, but also to advance our understanding of why it produces the outcomes that it does.

It has also been acknowledged that restorative policing takes many forms (much like restorative justice) that can be traced along the practice continuum of 'fully', 'mostly' and 'partially' restorative schemes. Two principal models that are discussed within the literature have also been presented (albeit briefly) here: the New Zealand Model and the Wagga Wagga Model. The key difference between the two relates to the role of the police officer within the delivery of the scheme. In the former, the officer may only refer a case on for facilitation or attend the meeting between the stakeholders, while in the latter the officer will play a much more significant role by arranging and facilitating meetings themselves. The Wagga Wagga Model has stimulated the most activity at the levels of policy, practice and research and so the focus for the remainder of the book will remain solely on restorative policing in the form of this model. Research has shown that not all restorative justice is good restorative justice (Rossner 2008), and the next chapter will confirm this in relation to restorative policing in particular.

Notes

1 Although, see Moore (2015), it has been suggested that the alignment of conferencing with restorative justice may have inadvertently constrained both the conceptual discussions and practice of conferencing.

2 However, Braithwaite (2003) does raise a caveat here. He argues that constraining values should always take precedence over maximising values because it is the stakeholders who should have control over decision-making rather than any professional or facilitator. Unfortunately, this does not always occur in practice. In criminal justice settings, the restorative process is considered successful if participants are satisfied with the process, agreements or behaviour contracts have been completed and/or repeat offending has been prevented – objectives that have often not necessarily been prioritised by stakeholders, but rather by the state and professionals, who are motivated by the wish to increase perceptions of their legitimacy.

3 For example, as Daly (2001: 61) notes, conferencing in particular 'may be viewed as a less costly method of disposing of cases; it can rely on the labour and good will of citizens, especially with its rhetoric of decentring professional authority',

4 However, see Crawford and Newburn (2003), Campbell *et al.* (2005) Moore (1992) and Polk (1994) who question how voluntary a process can be when the alternative is having one's case proceed through the normal adversarial process.

5 However, see Mason (1992) and Gardner (1990) whose research in Australia provides a challenge to the perception that victims want to be involved in a process that sanctions offenders.

6 See further Moore (1993a) who responded to some of these concerns over 20 years ago and stressed that nowhere does it state that supporters should be interpreted as family, particularly as he acknowledges that offenders can interpret themselves as 'victims' of their family circumstance.

7 Merry's (1979) research further illustrates this in terms of those, particularly from lower incomes, using the criminal justice process as a means of dealing with conflict rather than resolving disputes themselves.

8 Sykes and Matza (1957) distinguish between five neutralisation techniques that allow offenders to perceive their behaviour as justifiable: (1) the denial of responsibility (i.e. it was an accident or someone else's fault), (2) denial of injury (i.e. no-one has really been hurt), (3) denial of the victim (i.e. he/she deserved it), (4) condemnation of the condemners (i.e. those seeking to chastise the offender are hypocrits or prejudiced), and finally (5) appeal to higher loyalties (i.e. the attachments to siblings, gangs or others are stronger than those of society).

9 See O'Connell (2008) for his reflection on a prison inmate in the United States who had not realised that his offending had had any impact on his family.

10 Although, see Harris (2006) whose research demonstrated no difference between perceptions of stigmatisation in conferences and court processes.

11 This provides a challenge to White (1994) who argues that conferencing continues to emphasise behaviour rather than their social conditions. We certainly agree that more progressive models can and should be adopted in this regard and we outline what that might look like in Chapter 6.

12 See Rossner (2008: 1744) who holds a similar position when she argues that 'collective feelings of solidarity drive success [in restorative processes], not specific instances of reintegrative shame or procedural justice'.

13 Also, see research conducted by Harris (2006), which supports the position that the way in which offenders manage feelings of shame will have an important impact on how they react to an event.

14 The idea behind this model was to develop a programme for community supervision of the juveniles, which protected the community and meant that the offender was held accountable in a meaningful way (Weitekamp *et al.* 2003). The model includes four

key elements: accountability (achieved by the offender providing reparation to repair harm caused), community protection (achieved by minimising the risks to victims and the community), competency development (achieved by giving offenders skills to lead productive, crime free lives) and balance (achieved through equal attention being given to victims, offenders and the community) (Weitekamp *et al.* 2003: 316).

15 Essentially, the model shifts the attention from state-level criminal justice agencies to local community initiatives and links ongoing restorative justice approaches to a broader community enhancement perspective (Weitekamp *et al.* 2003).

16 The former can be described as: reactive, focusing narrowly on law enforcement, militaristic, hierarchical, having a blame culture, being backward-looking (i.e. solely concerned with what laws have been broken), reliant on tradition and rule tightening. The latter is said to focus on: problem solving, community safety, individual responsibility and accessibility, reflective, forward-looking and innovative. While many police agencies are thought to be keen to move away from a 'force' approach, not many have achieved the status of a 'service' (Lofty 2002).

3 Tracing restorative policing
The Wagga Wagga Model in action

Introduction

Up until the late 1980s, restorative processes were primarily thought of in terms of mediation programmes that brought victims and offenders together, either in a face-to-face meeting or via messages delivered by a trained volunteer known as a mediator (Umbreit and Zehr 1996a). Following the emergence of family group conferencing in New Zealand, the nature and practice of restorative justice changed dramatically. Facilitators became trained officials[1] rather than volunteers and the number of participants increased to include friends, families and other interested parties (Umbreit and Zehr 1996a). This initiative subsequently elicited a flurry of international academic study and police experimentation with this new and innovative approach to dealing with crime, as Umbreit and Zehr note:

> Rarely has a new criminal justice idea received such quick exposure and interest from audiences as widespread as activists, professionals and the general public. No other restorative justice approach has so quickly brought such numbers of law enforcement officials 'to the table' as active stakeholders in the restorative justice movement.
>
> (1996a: 4)

As outlined in the previous chapter, restorative policing can generally be discussed in relation to two models of conferencing: the New Zealand Model and the Wagga Wagga Model. The New Zealand Model operates on a statutory basis, conferences are generally facilitated by welfare practitioners, and no script is used to guide the meeting between victims, offenders and their supporters. The Wagga Wagga Model, on the other hand, is purely a diversionary approach for dealing with less serious offending, the police facilitate the process and they use a script to guide the discussion that takes place between stakeholders. While the Wagga Wagga Model was developed in Australia, and contrary to popular belief, it is the New Zealand Model that now prevails within this jurisdiction. Nevertheless, there have been and, in some instances, continue to be a number of notable examples of the Wagga Wagga Model in the United States, Canada and the United Kingdom.

In this chapter, only case studies that fall under the Wagga Wagga Model will be discussed. The only exception will be a brief overview of the emergence of conferencing in New Zealand, which provides a context for the other case studies. The reason for choosing to focus on these initiatives is two-fold. First, whilst there is a great diversity of police-led conferencing schemes in operation across the world, it is the Wagga Wagga Model that has received the most academic and policy attention. Second, these case studies have all been 'subjected to large-scale independent evaluations, thus providing more reliable data than are available from other police-led schemes' (Young 2003: 196).

The chapter begins by situating the emergence of restorative policing within this evolution of the restorative justice landscape by looking at the practice of conferencing in New Zealand and subsequently in Australia. The subsequent spread of the conferencing model, particularly within policing organisations, beyond Australia occurred as a result of a Churchill Fellowship that Terry O'Connell secured to embark on a study tour around the United States, Canada and the United Kingdom in 1994 (McCold 1998).[2] During this trip, O'Connell engaged in training workshops in the United States, Canada and the United Kingdom where the police went on to use conferencing as part of their response to offending just as had been practised in Australia. Further detail about the schemes that emerged in these jurisdictions will subsequently be presented in this order.

Australasia: the birthplace of conferencing

This book is concerned with a particular form of restorative practice: conferencing (see further Alder and Wundersitz 1994). Its emergence was situated within the approach to dealing with young offenders, which represented a shift in the manner in which young offenders were dealt with in two important respects (Moore 1994). First, rather than being viewed as rational individuals to be held accountable for their actions; young offenders were dealt with in a forum that included their families, friends and/or supporters thus acknowledging that offending occurs within a social context (Moore 1993a). Second, the process introduced a much greater concern with the role of *emotions* in dealing with the effects of offending behaviour (as demonstrated in the theoretical discussion in Chapter 2). Prior to this, and in most adversarial systems of contemporary justice, only facts relevant to establishing culpability were generally allowed (except for the relatively recent introduction of victim impact statements, see Erez and Rogers 2001). Conferencing has subsequently become a feature of juvenile justice in both New Zealand and Australia, although in all legislation, the offender remains the primary concern rather than victims (Daly 2001).

New Zealand

Conferencing first emerged in New Zealand and the practice became world renowned with the passing of the Young Persons and Their Families Act 1989.

Under this Act, young people were no longer to be dealt with through an adversarial process, but rather a process which sought to keep young offenders out of the criminal justice system by making far greater use of diversion, by including offenders, victims and their families in decision-making and increasing the flexibility of the approach for more culturally appropriate outcomes (see further Maxwell and Morris 1994a).[3] It is important to note that restorative justice was never at the heart of the legislative changes that happened in New Zealand, but rather the label was subsequently applied to conferencing and the approach to youth justice contained within the Act (see Bradley *et al.* 2006). As Morris and Maxwell note, the system:

> [...] aims to heal the damage that has been caused by juvenile offending, to involve those most affected by the offending in determining appropriate responses to it and to make things better both for young people who have committed offences and for their victims ... a new system that clearly shares the ideas underlying restorative justice.
>
> (1998: no page)

Figure 3.1 below provides an illustration of the youth justice system in New Zealand and the highlighted sections illustrate the main points at which offenders may be formally dealt with in a restorative way. Like most other criminal justice processes, the police are the first point of contact for those who have committed criminal acts and those who have been offended against. The police have three options at their disposal: they can issue an informal warning, they can arrest the young person (two requirements need to be satisfied: first, there must be sufficient grounds for arrest – the act needs to be serious enough – and second, there must be sufficient evidence to charge the young person) or they can refer the case to Youth Aid. Each police station has at least one Youth Aid Officer who works with the community to prevent offending by juveniles and who works with juveniles after they have offended. Once a referral is received, Youth Aid Officers can issue a formal warning to the young person in front of their parent/s and, in some cases, negotiate informal sanctions with the child's parents that may involve: an apology to the victim, reparation, community work, counselling, changes in residence and recreational activities (Maxwell and Morris 1993b).

Where sanctions have previously been unsuccessful or if the offending is more serious, the Youth Aid Officer will normally refer the case on for a family group conference, which they will also attend (Maxwell and Morris 1993b). These conferences are facilitated by welfare workers employed by the Department of Social Welfare and they are responsible for preparing all participants (victim/s, offender/s and their families/supporters) for the conference. Conferences are most often held on the Department of Social Welfare premises,[4] which it is argued, is less intimidating for the victim (see Morris and Maxwell 1998). During the conference, all involved seek to determine the best way to put things right (Pratt 1996) in the form of a conference plan. The role of police officers

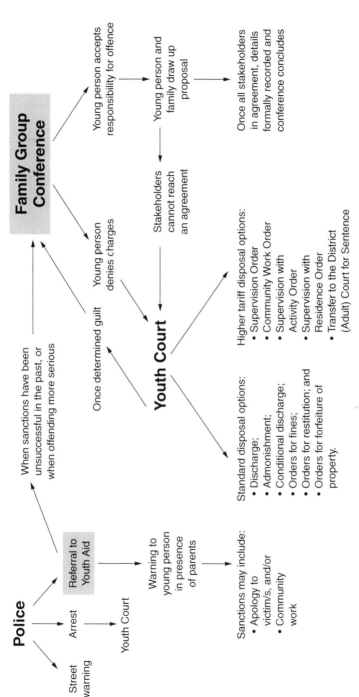

Police

Street warning

Arrest → Youth Court

Referral to Youth Aid → Warning to young person in presence of parents → Sanctions may include:
- Apology to victim/s, and/or
- Community work

When sanctions have been unsuccessful in the past, or when offending more serious →

Family Group Conference

Young person accepts responsibility for offence → Young person and family draw up proposal → Once all stakeholders in agreement, details formally recorded and conference concludes

Young person denies charges → Stakeholders cannot reach an agreement

Once determined guilt →

Youth Court

Standard disposal options:
- Discharge;
- Admonishment;
- Conditional discharge;
- Orders for fines;
- Orders for restitution; and
- Orders for forfeiture of property.

Higher tariff disposal options:
- Supervision Order
- Community Work Order
- Supervision with Activity Order
- Supervision with Residence Order
- Transfer to the District (Adult) Court for Sentence

Figure 3.1 An overview of the New Zealand Family Group Conferencing System.

during the process is limited to describing the offence, and possibly the impact on the victim, although they retain the right to comment on the outcome of the agreement by the family in terms of it being too lenient or excessive. Young offenders are also entitled to have a youth advocate present, however, their role is limited to providing advice on legal issues relating to the young person's rights and they may also provide comment where they feel that proposed penalties may be excessive.

Probably the most important achievement of the new system was the success in diverting the vast majority of young offenders from criminal courts and a reduced reliance on the use of institutions (Maxwell and Morris 1996;[5] Morris 1999).[5] Around 82 per cent of all cases were dealt with informally by the police, 8 per cent via family group conferences at which the police played a prominent role, and only 10 per cent were dealt with by the Youth Court (Maxwell and Morris 2000; O'Connell 1992). Indeed, it was this particular aspect (i.e. court processing) that drew interest amongst criminal justice reformers in other jurisdictions, resulting in a flurry of international delegations to learn more about how the process worked. The conferencing model thus spread around the globe in a variety of forms. Although many examples of the New Zealand Model are present in Australia, only the Wagga Wagga Model will be discussed in the following sections.

Australia

The emergence of the Wagga Wagga Model can be traced to a trip taken by John McDonald (Principal Adviser, Youth and Juvenile Justice, New South Wales Police Service) and Steve Ireland (Policy and Planning Branch of the New South Wales Police Service) in 1990 to New Zealand (Daly 2001). During that visit, they found a striking contrast between the youth justice context in New Zealand and New South Wales. In New Zealand under the new conferencing model, 90 per cent of youths were diverted out of the criminal justice process, but in New South Wales over 80 per cent of youths were being charged and brought before the courts (Moore and O'Connell 1994). When they returned, they therefore had a strong basis from which to argue that conferencing could be used to reduce the proportion of individuals appearing from court by adapting and integrating conferencing into the response to juvenile offending in New South Wales, with two key areas of departure.

First, it was suggested that rather than involving more government departments in dealing with cases that could be diverted out of the criminal justice process, that this should be dealt with by the department with the first point of contact, i.e. the police (Moore and O'Connell 1994). Second, John McDonald made a connection between John Braithwaite's (1989) theory of reintegrative shaming and conferencing (see Chapter 2) and in mid-1991 David Moore suggested that Braithwaite's terminology be used when discussing the Wagga Wagga pilot (Moore 1994). This not only enhanced the status of the proposed programme, but it also gave the architects a particular reference point with clearly articulated and defensible values (Moore and O'Connell 1994). While the

proposals received significant support from a range of state government departments and agencies, police patrol commanders were less enthusiastic. When the
proposals were sent to Terry O'Connell, the Police Association Deputy President, he therefore argued that if there was a commitment to the idea of involving the community in responding to offending that they should be canvassed as
well as those officers who would be facilitating the process where the trial was
due to take place (Moore and O'Connell 1994; Moore and Forsythe 1995). This
idea was supported and O'Connell began canvassing both the community and
police officers in Wagga Wagga early in 1991. In order to understand why
Wagga Wagga became the pilot site, one needs to look at the broader changes
that were taking place in this force.

By the end of the 1980s, attempts were being made to increase the engagement of the community in policing matters which resulted in the establishment
of the Wagga Wagga Community Consultative Committee in 1987 and a number
of Neighbourhood Watch and Safety House programmes.[6] However, these initiatives lacked the support of the police and it was not until November 1990 that a
tangible commitment had been made to adopt a more proactive style of policing.
A 'Beat Policing' initiative was developed at the request of the Community Consultative Committee, underpinned by the ideas of community and problem-
oriented policing as outlined in Chapter 1 (Moore and Forsythe 1995; O'Connell
1993). While little empirical research had been conducted on this initiative, it
was believed that improved police-community relations and a proactive approach
to dealing with problems arising at a local level was leading to a reduction in the
amount of crimes being reported[7] (O'Connell 1993).

In the following year, Chief Inspector Wales surveyed a number of police
officers to explore attitudes to juvenile justice that revealed officers were frustrated with the lack of offender accountability, the lack of justice victims
received and the costs of juvenile crime borne by communities (O'Connell 1992,
1993, 1998). On the basis of positive outcomes of the Beat Policing programme
and these associated concerns; Wagga Wagga was thought to be a prime location
to further evolve policing approaches within the community (see Moore and Forsythe 1995: 7–8, Chapter 1 for a detailed overview of the broader policy
context). However, early reports from the canvassing exercise being undertaken
revealed that the proposals were met with some scepticism by officers who
viewed conferencing as a 'soft option' (not an unfamiliar first reaction as other
case studies will reveal). So the next task was to get police officers to support a
trial of the proposed scheme. The strategy for this was to create a panel of sergeants who would meet once a week to review all juvenile matters and decide
which cases would be eligible for caution and to invite officers to observe the
process (Moore and Forsythe 1995; O'Connell 1998). This slow and considered
approach to developing the new cautioning process in this way was broadly
acknowledged for helping the police to subsequently accept the merits of the
programme (see O'Connell 1993, 1998).[8]

The programme was designed to take place within existing (and rather broad)
initiative guidelines for police cautioning, so no policy issues arose in respect of

piloting this new approach (McDonald and Moore 2001; Moore 2015; Moore and Forsythe 1995). The 'effective cautioning scheme' (as it became known) officially began in 1991, although it should be noted that the samples remained small while officers developed the process and an understanding of what worked and what did not work (see further Moore and Forsythe 1995).[9] The scheme was distinct from traditional cautioning in that the arresting sergeant was no longer giving the young person a verbal warning, but rather bringing together those affected by the incident within a conferencing process (Moore 1994; O'Connell 1992). Furthermore, while the traditional caution focused on the character of the offender with the ultimate aim of the individual consciously altering their behaviour, the new restorative cautioning arrangements focused on the incident and drew in a collective community of affected participants to respond to the causes and consequences of the incident (Moore and Forsythe 1995). Under the conditions set within legislation for police cautioning, the pilot included young people aged 7–10 who admitted responsibility and had committed non-indictable offences (Moore 1994). Other eligibility factors included: the nature, type and seriousness of the offence/s, the number and age of offenders involved, prior offending history, the number of victims, any compensation/reparation sought and the recommendation of the investigating officer (Moore and Forsythe 1995). According to O'Connell (1992), the only offenders who were automatically charged included those who committed serious indictable offences.

The programme was administered by the local 'Beat Police' unit who were 'expressly dedicated to the philosophy and practice of community policing' (Moore 1994: 74). The basic design of the scheme was simple: the victim and offender were brought together, along with their family members or friends, to a meeting that a police officer facilitated at a police station (Moore 1992, 1993a; Moore and Forsythe 1995). The conference itself was carefully scripted, to ensure both the restorative quality and the consistency of process (McDonald *et al.* 1995; O'Connell 1998), with open-ended questions to encourage a less formal setting and a safe structure for participation. A clear distinction was made at the beginning of every meeting between the offender and the act that that young person had committed, given that the causes of crime were seen to be located not within the individual but within a context of failed control by families and other intimate communities (Moore 1993a). The role of the police officer was to facilitate these discussions, to intervene when difficulties arose, to witness any arrangements for material restitution and to refer significant social problems that emerged from the process onto other relevant professionals (O'Connell 1992).

The script began with a statement of the restorative purpose of the conference, followed by a series of open-ended questions, asked first of the offender, then the victim, then the victim's supporters and then the offender's supporters. Emotions – shame, anger and aggression – were not prohibited but rather viewed as a positive expression that needed to be expressed before the restoration of both individual self-respect and collective social bonds could occur.[10] Sharing the personal experience of the incident between stakeholders was perceived to encourage empathy within offenders and by encouraging the offenders' supporters to discuss the positive aspects of the offenders' character was perceived to reinforce a positive identity (Roberts and Masters 1999). But the process was not merely concerned with developing empathy; it was also concerned with dealing with the triggers for the offender's behaviour as well as harm caused by that behaviour, thus leading to the reintegration of the offender (O'Connell 1993). The victim was then asked what they want to get from the conference, when consensus was reached with the rest of the parties it was formalised in a contract, which everyone signed. At the end of the conference refreshments were always provided to facilitate an opportunity for informal interaction between participants. Following the cessation of the conference, offenders and their families were required to participate in 'Stage 2', which involves the completion of an activity booklet dealing with crime and its consequences. They were then involved in a one-off two-hour session run by local community members which 'places a strong emphasis on offering remedial skills' to them (O'Connell 1992: 18; also see Howard and Purches 1992).

The Wagga Wagga Model has been evaluated on two occasions within New South Wales. The first was a process evaluation conducted by Moore and Forsythe (1995) which analysed the conference process, gathered the views of conference participants (including police officers and other government officials) and grounded the findings within a theoretical model. The research report produced some interesting insight into what stakeholders thought about the conferencing process sometime after it had taken place and about what they thought could be improved about the process. On the basis of these insights, recommendations were drafted and implemented to further improve the manner in which conferences were run. Of note, the research revealed that the numbers of cases being processed by the courts reduced by 50 per cent without any net-widening (the amount of cases reported to the police began to decrease) and without increasing the recidivism rate (in fact it is reported that there was a 40 per cent reduction); 93 per cent of offenders fulfilled the agreements reached within the conference and high levels of victim and officer satisfaction (Moore 1994; O'Connell 1992).

The second was a randomised trial run by the Australian Federal Police in 1995 which evaluated a pilot of the Wagga Wagga Model in the Australian Capital Territory.[11] The Canberra Reintegrative Shaming Experiments (RISE) trained over 100 police officers in conferencing (O'Connell 1998) and set out to measure both procedural justice and recidivism in relation to restorative policing (Daly 2001). The project included four kinds of cases: drunk driving, juvenile property offending with personal victims, juvenile shoplifting detected by security officers and violent youth offences (Sherman *et al.* 1998; Strang *et al.* 1999). Despite continuing negotiation, serious political kudos and agreed parameters, less than 20 per cent of eligible cases were referred by the police to RISE for allocation to the random distribution between restorative justice and court processing (Strang 2000). Furthermore, while it was expected that all officers would learn how to facilitate conferences as a standard method of police work, experience showed that some were far more enthusiastic than others and the tendency towards specialism (i.e. a smaller cohort regularly fascilitating) increased over time (see Sherman *et al.* 2003).

RISE researchers in Canberra found that victims of crime whose case went to conference rather than court were presented with greater opportunities for material reparation, yet they were less likely to ask for money as part of the case outcome; they were significantly less distressed and angry; they were four times as likely to receive an apology; they rated higher in sympathy and trust (particularly if they were victims of violent crime); they were more satisfied with the process and its outcomes and the 'fair and respectful treatment' they received (Strang 2002). Furthermore, compared with those who went to court, conferenced offenders reported greater fair treatment and respect, greater opportunities to repair the harm they had caused and increased respect for police and the law (Strang *et al.* 1999). Offenders also reported higher levels of being treated fairly and with respect (i.e. procedural justice), more opportunities to repair harm caused and an increase in respect for both the police and the law than those that went to court (see Sherman *et al.* 1988; Strang 1999).

While Moore (1992) notes that it was difficult for a conservative government to be publicly opposed to community-based initiatives such as the cautioning programme,[12] as early as 1992, pressure was already being exerted on the patrols involved to refocus their attention on securing arrests and arranging Neighbourhood Watch Meetings. There were also a number of minor setbacks in 1994 including an introduction of a new state-wide computerised operational policing system (COPS) which diverted attention and resources away from the pilot, a change in the Head of the Beat police (Terry O'Connell had changed his role the year before) and by 1995 the New South Wales Attorney General was seeking to limit the role of police officers in the programme (Moore and Forsythe 1995). Moore and Forsythe (1995) further point to the political support for the development of 'community aid panels' around the same time as a particular obstacle to the developments in Wagga Wagga but which, they argue, focused only on the needs of the offender rather than additionally those of victims and the community (also see Daly 2001). Despite the positive evaluations and international popularity of the model, responsibility for facilitating conferences was ultimately transferred to juvenile justice agencies in 1998 and trained community members now facilitate police diverted conferences. As such, the Wagga Wagga Model is no longer in operation in any state within Australia (Kurki 1999; Richards 2010).[13]

North America

The United States

The first jurisdiction outside of Australia to experiment with the Wagga Wagga Model was the United States. In 1995, O'Connell and his colleagues provided training in both Minnesota and Pennsylvania (O'Connell 1998). Much of the training, following O'Connell's visit, was undertaken by REAL JUSTICE (a private not-for-profit organisation) which reportedly trained more than 2,000 conference facilitators in more than 30 states, including 368 police officers from 141 different police departments (McCold 1998). Although nine police departments were identified as having officers who were actively involved in restorative practice (see Nicholl 1999), due in part to space constraints, but also the availability of sufficient literature they will not all be discussed here. There are three programmes that will be given further attention due to their prevalence within the literature: the Bethlehem Police Family Group Conferencing Project, the Woodbury Police Department's Restorative Community Conferencing Programme and The Indianapolis Restorative Justice Project.[14]

The Bethlehem Pennsylvania Police Family Group Conferencing Project

The Bethlehem Police Department had an active crime prevention and community policing project and they were keen to further develop the community policing philosophy across the force (McCold 1998, 2003). Sponsored by the National Institute of Justice and in conjunction with the Community Service Foundation, the Bethlehem Police Department embarked on a two-year pilot study of police-based family group conferencing. The study sought to evaluate the effectiveness of the Wagga Wagga Model and to test the concerns that had been raised about police-led conferencing within the literature (see McCold 2003; McCold and Stahr 1996). The project, much like the RISE project undertaken in Canberra, involved the selection of eligible cases and the random assignment of those cases either to court or to a diversionary police run conference. Developing the parameters of the project proved to be quite difficult given that Bethlehem straddles two counties and thus the support of gatekeepers had to be secured in both jurisdictions (McCold and Wachtel 2012). It was subsequently agreed that eligibility for referral to the programme was to be limited to: first incidences of offending by juvenile offenders where they had admitted responsibility; offences committed within the jurisdiction of Bethlehem; and summary offences (no drug or alcohol crimes, no sex offences) that included minor assaults (no serious bodily harm, no weapons), thefts and property crimes (McCold and Stahr 1996).

The study began with the training of 18 police officers who had volunteered to be a part of the programme and who were already supportive of the community policing philosophy (McCold and Stahr 1996). The process for case selection at Bethlehem followed a similar approach to that in Wagga Wagga, although on a smaller scale. A Police Liaison Officer (PLO) reviewed arrest records and selected cases that met the eligibility criteria. All cases were then randomly assigned into a control group (i.e. proceeded without diversion to court) or a treatment group (i.e. became part of the sample eligible for conferencing). In all treatment cases, the PLO contacted the offender and their parents/ guardians to explain the conferencing process and to see if they would be interested in participating. Only once the offender's participation was secured was the victim contacted. Where both the victim and offender agreed to participate, the case was assigned to one of the trained facilitating officers and they became responsible for contacting the participants and coordinating a mutually convenient time for the conference to take place. Victims and offenders could withdraw their consent at any stage of the process and where this happened, the case was processed through the normal adversarial system (McCold and Stahr 1996). In instances where the conference proceeded and the contract/agreement that emerged from the conference was fulfilled, the charge against the offender was withdrawn (McCold and Wachtel 1998a).

McCold and Wachtel (1998a) report that 189 cases were assigned for conferencing out of the eligible sample, 80 participants agreed to participate, while 109 declined and opted to have their case heard before the courts. Where a conference was arranged and facilitated, three researchers also attended to observe and evaluate the process according to a number of set criteria. The outcomes revealed that despite all officers receiving an intensive three-day training course prior to cases being referred for them to facilitate, some officers were unprepared for the conference – only meeting some of the participants for the first time on the day and with low levels of supporters in attendance. Some strayed from or paraphrased the script, while others decided what the outcome should be rather than allowing the participants to have control over this, and there were others still who reverted back to a traditional stigmatising cautioning approach. As such, the author's report that the initial three-day training provided to these officers was insufficient and in-service training became essential for reinforcing the reintegrative aspects of the conferencing process. Following performance evaluations, six officers did not facilitate any further cases as a result of them withdrawing from the scheme but for those who continued, they were perceived to comply with conference protocol in nearly 90 per cent of the conferences that were facilitated subsequently.

The effect of the programme was measured through surveys of victims, offenders, offenders' parents and police officers and by examining and comparing outcomes of conferences and formal adjudications (McCold 1998: 3). Some key insights into police facilitation of conferencing emerged from this study. First, unlike with the study undertaken in Wagga Wagga, the researchers reported that they did not find that involvement in conferencing resulted in a cultural shift across the force (see McCold and Wachtel 1998a). Nevertheless, a moderate change was detected amongst those actually delivering conferencing towards a more community-oriented problem-solving approach (McCold 2003). In part, McCold (2003) suggests that the lack of cultural change could have been due to the fact that conferencing was a marginalised activity kept separate from the broader policing activities taking place on a day-to-day level and that both officers and supervisors saw conferencing as an additional task to be undertaken which interfered with patrol and responding to calls for service. Real change, he argues, cannot take place without sufficient organisational and managerial support.

Second, officers were able to facilitate conferences in a manner consistent with due process and restorative justice principles where ongoing support and training was offered. Third, victims (96 per cent) and offenders (97 per cent) were satisfied with the process, just as much as with those VOM programmes facilitated by non-police officers and nearly all respondents confirmed that they would opt to participate in a similar process again and recommend it to others (McCold 2003). Fourth, much like in the Wagga Wagga findings, 94 per cent of offenders fulfilled the contents of the agreements reached during the conference (McCold 2003; Moore 1995). All outcomes were agreed to by the victim and were perceived to be reasonable[15] in relation to the nature of the offence committed.

The Woodbury Police Department Restorative Justice Programme

In 1995, the Woodbury Police Department developed the *Restorative Community Conferencing Programme.* According to Hines and Bazemore (2003), the Woodbury Conferencing Programme represents an important case study in the transfer of discretion to a police department from the prosecution service (Hines and Bazemore 2003). The project began with the initial training of a few interested police officers which was then subsequently rolled out across the force through training days which involved a minimum initial training of 24 hours in theory, process and practical involvement, role play and debriefing meetings between facilitators (Roberts and Masters 1999). Where officers presented resistance to the idea of conferencing and the facilitation of cases, they were offered the opportunity to view a conference for themselves and the positive impact that the process yielded. Where officers remained uncomfortable with the process, they were not pressured to be a part of the programme (Hines 2000).

Eligible cases were selected by the Programme Coordinator on the basis of the seriousness of the offence (only homicide, sex crimes and very serious assaults were automatically excluded), previous contact with the juvenile justice system[16] and the offenders' attitude (Umbreit and Farcello 1997). For very minor offences with first time offenders, officers were encouraged to engage in street-based conferences to save resources for more serious and complex cases (Hines and Bazemore 2003). In fact, Hines (2000) notes that a number of cases were conferenced with repeat offenders as well as felony level cases. Where the Coordinator was satisfied that the case would be a good fit for the programme, where the offender admitted responsibility and, along with the victim, agreed to participate it was referred to one of six officers trained to facilitate conferences (Hines and Bazemore 2003; Umbreit and Farcello 1997). The facilitators had the final say over whether or not the conference would proceed on the basis of their assessment of the participants and where a conference did not go ahead, the case was processed through the courts (Roberts and Masters 1999).

For eligible cases, the Coordinator was responsible for contacting all stakeholders (usually by telephone) to inform them of the process and to arrange a convenient time for the meeting to take place. The vast majority of conferences were held at the Woodbury police station or at a local school and lasted typically between 1–2 hours. The conference was scripted (see Umbreit and Farcello 1997 for a copy of this) which meant that all conferences began with a description of the process (i.e. purpose, order for participants to speak and the consequences of the meeting breaking down and/or the agreement not being met) and the laying of ground rules. Unlike in other police-led conferences up until this point, after an agreement had been noted, the coordinator made a strategic exit on the basis of completing administration associated with the conference and invited participants to share refreshments together. The amount of time generally provided was around 15–20 minutes so that the participants could interact in a less pressured environment. When the coordinator returned, the terms of the agreement and the consequences of not fulfilling the agreement (i.e. cases being processed through normal adversarial channels) were explained and then all participants are asked to sign the document. Agreements were expected to be completed within 90 days.

An internal evaluation of the Programme was undertaken through the use of self-administered questionnaires provided to all participants at the end of the conference, which they were invited to return. The questionnaire asked participants to rate their answers on a sliding scale from 1 (lowest) to 10 (highest). Umbreit and Farcello (1997) report that the return rate was around 90 per cent, that all participants rated their satisfaction with the conference process at 8 or above, their satisfaction with the outcome of the conference at 8 or above and their treatment during the conference at 9 or above. Furthermore, 82 per cent of victims, 96 per cent of offenders and 95 per cent of parents said they would choose the Programme over court should they come into contact with the criminal justice system again. The qualitative aspect of the study confirmed the overall positive perceptions held by participants, although a few victims felt that the offender's attitudes had not been changed because they did not perceive that they were remorseful. Furthermore, although officers participating in the Programme were initially sceptical of the potential of conferencing, all subsequently became vocal advocates of the practice. However, the authors provided some caution regarding the results given the relatively small sample of cases that were evaluated and they called for a much more extensive evaluation to be undertaken using control groups.

Hines (2000) further reports that 50 per cent of all cases dealt with by the Woodbury Police were dealt with by way of a restorative process. An internal evaluation demonstrated that in 2000, 72 per cent of youths whose case was processed by the courts reoffended, but that those cases that were conferenced, recidivism dropped to 33 per cent (Hines 2000). This outcome was largely attributed to involving those with a stake in the outcome and the strong links developed with the community to support stakeholders during the conference and in meeting the contents of the agreements. As Hines and Bazemore (2003) explain it is the community who provide the impetus for policing activities as cases emerge from the community. This means that the relationship between police and communities is essential and it is largely in the best interests of the police to undertake activities to both develop and maintain this relationship. As such, the authors further argue that the community is key to both the success and long-term sustainability of restorative policing, success that relies on the maintenance of a strong partnership.

A particular strength of the community, according to Hines (see Roberts and Masters 1999), is that the location of the Programme within the police service meant that there were plenty of potential cases to choose from. As such, he argues that the police are an essential partner for the success of any diversionary restorative justice initiative and that perhaps the greatest potential for restorative justice lies within community policing initiatives that already exist within police departments. The community was seen as essential to the success of the Programme and they were given educational material on a regular basis, which both described and promoted the project. However, Hines (see Roberts and Masters 1999) noted that the biggest threat to the project, despite the wide support it received from both police officers and the community was a lack of input and ownership of the project by the community. He suggests that system changes are needed where true partnerships between the police and the community mean that the sustainability of such initiatives could be secured. For example, he suggested that co-facilitation could occur between police officers and a community member in order to create more balanced power and stronger police-community bonds (see Roberts and Masters 1999).

The Indianapolis Restorative Justice Project

In 1995, a number of key senior criminal justice officials, the mayor and the Hudson Institute in Indianapolis learned about restorative justice and conferencing at a briefing delivered by Professor Lawrence Sherman. Sufficient interest was garnered for the police department to send two police officers to be trained by REAL JUSTICE with a view to trialling the Wagga Wagga Model locally (McGarrell *et al.* 2000). These officers were strategically selected because of their reputations as good street cops and their popularity amongst their fellow officers, a key factor in the subsequent success of the model within the department. During 1996 and 1997, the two officers with the agreement of the juvenile court began conducting conferences as an alternative to arrest for relatively minor offences that they encountered during their patrol. In 1997, the officers became involved in training their colleagues – a crucial means of overcoming the scepticism that was present. Where participants in the training were uncomfortable with the idea of facilitating conferences themselves, like in Woodbury, they were offered the opportunity to observe a conference. McGarrell *et al.* (2000) report the vast majority of officers that accepted this offer were impressed with both the process and outcomes.

The Indianapolis Restorative Justice Project formally began in September 1997 as a court diversion option. The initial eligibility criteria included: offenders 14 years old and younger who were being charged for the first time and who had admitted responsibility for an offence limited to 'battery (assault), trespass, mischief, conversion, and felony D theft' (McGarrell *et al.* 2000: 25). Eligible cases were randomly assigned to conferencing or other diversionary programmes and between September 1997 and September 1999, 458 cases were eligible, 232 were assigned for conferencing and 182 conferences were conducted. The identified and agreed upon process for arranging a conference mirrored previous programmes: once eligibility was satisfied, a coordinator would contact the young offender and their parents to explain the process, to assess willingness to participate and to acknowledge responsibility and where these elements are satisfied, to contact the victim. Where both parties agreed and a conference was successfully scheduled, both victims and offenders were encouraged to identify a group of supporters to attend. The actual process during the conference was guided by the script devised by Terry O'Connell, and given that has been described earlier; it will not be repeated here.

In stage one of the evaluation, all conferences were observed by researchers who found that conference coordinators generally followed the principles of restorative justice in distinguishing between the offender and the offence, by not lecturing youths, by keeping the discussion focused on the incident and being effective in involving all attendees. In just over one-third of conferences, coordinators were observed to make suggestions regarding the contents of the agreement, although this was largely due to a lack of forthcoming discussion by participants and where suggestions were made, participants were able to modify them as they wished (see McGarrell *et al.* 2000). More than 90 per cent of victims reported satisfaction with the process, 97 per cent felt they had been involved, 95 per cent felt that they had an opportunity to express their views and 98 per cent said they would recommend the process to others. Additionally, 97 per cent of offending youths felt that they had been treated with respect, 84 per cent felt that they were involved in the process and 86 per cent felt they had an opportunity to express themselves (McGarrell 2001; McGarrell and Hipple 2008). Perceptions of parents/supporters were also positive, with 80 per cent reporting that they had been involved and 90 per cent saying that had an opportunity to express their views (McGarrell 2001). Eighty per cent of youths who participated in the scheme apologised to the victim, completed the reparation agreement and did not reoffend (McGarrell 2001).

Despite these positive outcomes, recent contact with these police departments has revealed that this practice has all but withered away in favour of referring cases out to community-based organisations (i.e. the New Zealand Model). A lack of comprehensive legislative framework across the United States for police-led conferencing has been cited as a potential reason for the demise of this practice (see Katz and Bonham 2006). However, McCold suggests that a more likely reason is that:

> [...] there are largely no centralized police organizations beyond municipal semi-autonomous agencies and restorative justice has not received much (any?) police academic or professional attention. That is bad for diffusion of new approaches, but also makes the introduction to restorative justice potentially available to any single agency with progressive leadership. Nevertheless, the institutional pressures on policing continue toward a paramilitary model.
>
> (Personal communication)

Over the last ten years, attention by REAL JUSTICE has been focused on the implementation of restorative practices in schools; however the intention is to once again undertake training with police officers and other criminal justice practitioners (Ted Wachtel, personal communication). Furthermore, some police-based mediation/conferencing training continues to occur primarily in relation to school-based and community conflicts within the Detroit Police Department and the Hillsboro Police Department (personal communication with members from these departments). As such, we may see further practice emerging in this juris-diction once again in the near future.

Canada

Attempts to implement community policing throughout the 1990s in Canada were plagued by organisational apathy, resistance and scepticism. For many police officers, community policing was not perceived as real police work and many mid-managers, supervisors and patrol officers were reluctant to move away from practising professional law enforcement through the use of long-standing and quantifiable performance measures (Duekmedjian 2008). Duekmed-jian (2008) highlights that in the early 1990s, policy advisers to the National Royal Canadian Mounted Police (RCMP) saw the overlap between restorative justice and community policing and in 1992 a national policy report was issued, which argued for direct RCMP involvement in developing and promoting com-munity mediation programmes (also see Chatterjee 2000). A significant limita-tion of the report, however, was that it 'did not specify how mediation aligned with RCMP's community policing mandate' and so this attempt to stimulate change was not successful at that time (Duekmedjian 2008: 122).

It was not until 1995 that experimentation with this practice by the RCMP first began (Chatterjee and Elliott 2003; Duekmedjian 2008). Sergeant Bouwman, along with local defence lawyer Glen Purdy, founded the Sparwood Youth Assistance Program, which was based on the Wagga Wagga Model but differed in that used community volunteers to facilitate conferences and, unlike other initiatives up until this point, without the initial training by the Australian pioneers (Chatterjee and Elliot 2003; Duekmedjian 2008; O'Connell 1998; Standing Committee on Justice and Legal Affairs 1997). The purpose of the Program was to allow young persons involved with the law to be dealt with outside of the traditional court system, through a means of dealing with the young person, the victim, the young person's family and the community as a whole, in an effort to reduce repeat offences by young persons, increasing the role of the police in proactive policing, and also, bring a greater sense of parti-cipation to all concerned (Aertsen *et al.* 2010). Under the scheme, Bouwman and Purdy (1997, cited in Richards 2010) explain that where young people commit-ted relatively minor offences, they were first taken home to be dealt with by their parents, but where offending was more serious and/or parents are unable or unwilling to deal with the offending behaviour, a conference was convened. While participation was voluntary, once an offender and their parents agreed, attendance was mandatory. The programme dealt with 65 young offenders in the initial two years of its operations (Standing Committee on Justice and Legal Affairs 1997). According to Braithwaite (2002a: 57), no young offenders went to court during this time and reoffending rates for youths that participated in a conference was reportedly 8 per cent in 1995, 3 per cent in 1996, 10 per cent in 1997 and 0 per cent for the first nine months of 1998. Victims were satisfied with the process in 95 per cent of cases and where victims were uncomfortable with offenders undertaking work directly for them as reparation, the scheme had a number of partnerships with community organisations and businesses (Committee on Justice and Legal Affairs 1997). The programme gained further notoriety because of its reported 50 per cent annual reduction in youth offending (Duekmedjian 2008), the success of which was (in view of its founders) based on the level of community support the scheme enjoyed (Standing Committee on Justice and Legal Affairs 1997).

This resulted in a visit by RCMP executives to both Australia and New Zealand in 1996 to view for themselves the conferencing model in action (Chatterjee and Elliot 2003). Upon their return, convinced that the model offered significant benefits and aligned with its community policing philosophy, match funding between the RCMP and the Department of Justice was agreed to roll out a restorative process known as 'community justice forums' (CJFs) across the country in 1997 (Chatterjee and Elliot 2003; Katz and Bonham 2006). This spurred two priorities. First, a communications strategy was developed to sensitise police officers to restorative justice and second, John McDonald and Transformative Justice Australia were contracted to train 2,000 rank-and-file officers across the country in CJF facilitation over the following three years (Duekmedjian 2008).

The context and scale in which such change was being introduced was a cause of concern to executives as they were keen to ensure that what ultimately transpired was not the mere development of yet another diversionary programme (Duekmedjian 2008). Rather, CJFs were to become the preferred pre-charge discretionary mechanism for addressing a wide array of offence categories, from mischief, vandalism and most property offences to assaults. As such, Transformative Justice Australia were expected to change the long-standing mind-sets of officers who were inculcated into policing as professional law enforcement officers and who viewed the courtroom as the principal and valued means to address offending. Transformative Justice Australia attempted to do so by identifying and training an initial 50 members who would be most receptive to CJFs (Chatterjee and Elliot 2003; Duekmedjian 2008). According to Duekmedjian (2008: 126), such a model 'provided a highly structured framework in which RCMP and community members could frequently practice problem resolution through local constant consultation' within a conferencing forum.

Widespread publicity campaigns followed in 1998 and 1999 by senior government officials (including the Prime Minister at that time) and the distribution of success stories and best practices within RCMP that were generated from facilitators reported experiences (Duekmedjian 2008). This was further enhanced by the publication of an evaluation of the programme in March 1999 which revealed that 1,700 police officers had been trained to facilitate conferences and that 98 per cent of participants had expressed at least moderate overall satisfaction

(87 per cent of whom were quiet or very satisfied) with the process and 94 per cent of participants (but 100 per cent of the victims) perceived the CJF process to be very or quite fair (Chatterjee 1999). The majority of participants indicated their participation to be voluntary, 90 per cent of all participants reported that the outcome was quite or very fair and in almost all cases offenders fulfilled the agreement (Chatterjee 1999). Furthermore, 90 per cent of offenders said that their participation assisted them to understand the harmful consequences of their offences on others and to take responsibility for their actions. The majority of participants – 88 per cent of the offenders, 94 per cent of the victims, 95 per cent of offenders' supporters and 88 per cent of victims' supporters, stated that they would choose CJFs over the court if they had to do it all over again (Chatterjee 2000). These findings reflect those of the RISE evaluation (Chatterjee and Elliot 2003).

However, the RCMP never achieved stability and implementation in restorative policing based on the Wagga Wagga Model. Indeed, the highly sought after critical mass of organisational and public support was simply lacking, and executives subsequently and effectively cut the programme. In 2001, with a less supportive environment, the initial evaluation report was undermined with accusations that the study had been subject to the fallacy of self-selection and that definitive conclusions could not be drawn about the effectiveness of CJFs in reducing reoffending rates. In 2002, RCMP executives together with the Department of Justice eliminated their multimillion-dollar national funding commitment and it was officially stated that restorative justice was no longer a strategic priority (Duekmedjian 2008). As it turned out, the RCMP's inability to anchor community policing in the mindset of their members, and their inability to integrate the community in decision-making complemented shifting central (and indeed global) tides in thinking about tackling crime (Duekmedjian 2008; also see Chapter 5, this volume).

It was not until the implementation of the Youth Criminal Justice Act (YCJA) in April 2003, which increased the discretion of police officers to use restorative processes in certain offences (Marinos and Innocente 2008), that a return to the original role of the police as peacekeepers in Canada began (Chatterjee and Elliot 2003: 352; Dandurand and Griffiths 2006: 62).[17] Under the Act, police officers have the following options at their disposal: taking no further action, warnings, police cautions, Crown cautions, referrals (with consent of young person) to community programmes agencies that address the root causes of the offence, and extrajudicial sanctions. Extrajudicial sanctions are considered the most onerous and, as such, the young offender needs to have admitted responsibility, the Attorney General has to ensure that there is sufficient evidence to pursue prosecution and have authorised the programme in order for a referral to be made (Chatterjee and Elliot 2003).

Under extrajudicial measures, community justice forums continue to be used, although facilitation is now primarily undertaken by trained community volunteers (Bazemore and Schiff 2015; Chatterjee and Elliot 2003; Crocker 2013; Munro 2006). Munro (2006), for example, draws attention to the fact that of the

40 facilitators for the Nanaimo Restorative Justice Program, 12 are police officers so the potential for police-led conferencing remains, although it is not
standard practice. Furthermore, Bazemore and Schiff (2015) highlight that in the
Edmonton Restorative Justice Programme in Alberta, officers had initially facilitated most conferences themselves 'on the street', but the more serious offences
are now referred on to neighbourhood restorative justice groups. Jordan Diplock,
a Criminal Intelligence Research Analyst at RCMP in British Columbia, has
speculated that the general move away from police-facilitated conferencing may
be due to operational factors:

> I believe that most programs have focused on training volunteers, and that
> occasionally local police officers who were particularly interested were
> trained as facilitators. When programs start, sometimes a particularly inter-
> ested RCMP member will get it running and do facilitation, but given how
> regularly our members get posted to new communities and how relatively
> few have been trained as CJF facilitators, my thought is that a program
> would not last very long if it was only facilitated by police members.
>
> (Personal communication)

Europe

England and Wales

The proliferation of police experimentation with restorative justice in England
and Wales is nothing short of remarkable. Thames Valley Police are world
renowned for their attempts to embed a restorative approach across a force that
services roughly two million people. However, in what began with some fervour
in 1994, came to somewhat of an abrupt end in the early 2000s due to a shift in
political support and the introduction of a new target culture in the form of the
National Crime Recording Standards in 2003 (Barton 2011; House of Commons
Home Affairs Committee 2011; Shewan 2011). In the decade that followed, a
broader performance management culture that took hold over the criminal justice
landscape in England and Wales (Shewan 2010) and targets became the
dominant external factor that informed the sociocultural context of policing. This
had the ultimate impact of severely curtailing restorative policing practice and
police officer discretion.

The next significant initiative in this area did not happen until 2008 when
Youth Restorative Disposals were piloted across eight police forces. These disposals were used for low-level offences that brought victims and offenders
together to collectively decide how to deal with the offence. More systematic
change did not happen until 2010, when a new Liberal-Conservative Government announced that they intended to reduce governmental control over the
police and redistribute power back to individual forces to help deliver budget
cuts and re-emphasise the importance of individual police officer's professional
discretion (Shewan 2011). Restorative justice has since become the potential

vehicle through which this could be realised (see Home Office 2010, 2011; Herbert 2011). Restorative policing is now supported by the Association of Chief Police Officers and this has led to sustained interest in its development as a 'low-bureaucratic disposal for low-level offending and as a critical tool within Neighbourhood Policing to assist in problem-solving and meeting community expectations' (Shewan 2010: 2). In the sections that follow, we look at some key case studies that have emerged within England and Wales.[18]

Thames Valley

The impetus for the use of police-led conferencing emerged in Thames Valley in 1994 through a number of pilots that experimented with the use of 'restorative cautions', notably the Milton Keynes Retail Theft Initiative and the Aylesbury Restorative Cautioning Initiative (see McCulloch 1996; Young and Gould 2003 respectively for evaluations of these initiatives).[19] Following significant planning and development work, restorative conferencing became force wide from 1 January 1998 predominantly for first and second time young offenders. What made this case study distinct from those that had emerged up until this point, is that it was overseen by a Headquarters-based Restorative Justice Agency that was set up to monitor standards of facilitator selection; provide high quality training, learning and support; quality assure all processes and data; provide strategic direction to the development of a conferencing programme; and liaise at a force level with partner agencies and voluntary community groups (Pollard 2001). This group comprised officers who were committed to getting restorative justice right and delivering training courses that would meet that goal. Funding was also provided to each of the ten Thames Valley police areas so that they could appoint a full-time coordinating officer as well as a full-time administrator (Young 2003).

Two different types of restorative intervention were primarily available within the Thames Valley approach: restorative cautions and restorative conferences (Pollard 2001). The distinction between the interventions is related to who participates in them. Restorative cautions involve offenders and their supporters (usually parents), whereas restorative conferences include the victim and their supporters as well. All processes used the Wagga Wagga Model and its script so they will not be repeated here. Unlike other initiatives discussed previously, no offences were explicitly excluded from being processed through this new restorative response and so any case that would normally be disposed of by caution was to be dealt with in a restorative manner (Young and Hoyle 2003).

The approach adopted by Thames Valley was evaluated between 1998 and 2001 using an action research methodology so that the police could use interim findings to shape their practice as the research was being undertaken (Young and Hoyle 2003). During this time, 1,915 restorative conferences and 12,065 restorative cautions were delivered by police officers. Before undertaking the empirical research, the research team expected to see conflict between restorative justice principles and police culture, structure and patterns of behaviour (Hoyle *et al.*

2002; Young and Hoyle 2003). The interim evaluation confirmed this suspicion and found that there were a range of practices that could not be considered 'restorative' which included officers: dominating discussions, prioritising their own agendas rather than those of the participants, reinvestigating the offence, engaging in intelligence gathering and behaving as if the offender had to account to them personally, with the other participants reduced to little more than passive observers (Hoyle *et al.* 2002). The researchers viewed this as an implementation issue that needed to be addressed through top-up training and 'a revised script which exhorted facilitators not to pursue a policing agenda within the cautioning session' (Hoyle *et al.* 2002: 14). Although issues remained with practice during the final evaluation, further training and a revised script had the effect of reducing the issues outlined from being present in over half of the cases in the interim study to only a quarter of cases in the final evaluation.

The findings with regards to the procedural aspects of the conferencing/cautioning process were very mixed. Hoyle *et al.* (2002) reported that over a third of the participants were not contacted by the facilitator prior to the meeting which meant that little preparation had been undertaken for when the stakeholders were in the same room as each other. Furthermore, they suggest that victims who chose not to participate cannot be thought to have done so in an informed manner and that the presence of confusion about the purpose and voluntary nature of the meeting highlighted a problem in the way that participants were being informed. Nevertheless, the final evaluation demonstrated that the vast majority of those who went on to participate felt the process was fair, two-thirds reported that they were satisfied with the manner in which the meetings were conducted and that it assisted victims, in particular, to come to terms with the offence.

While meetings were intended to repair the harm caused, the evaluation demonstrated that only in rare occasions was material reparation discussed and present within agreements at the end of the process. Rather symbolic reparation in the form of letters of apology were often included in agreements, although with a mere 14 per cent victim participation rate this was often decided without the victim agreeing to it (Hoyle *et al.* 2002). Where the victim had agreed to some form of dialogue with the offender through the mediator *in absentia*, most were unimpressed with written apologies and would have preferred compensation, further illustrating the lack of focus and preparation involved by the police facilitating the process. In part, the evaluation team explained this by suggesting that police officers saw apologies as inherently 'restorative' and the outcome through which success could be assessed. Unfortunately, at times where apologies were not naturally forthcoming from offenders themselves, they were 'extracted' in coercive ways. Hoyle and Rosenblatt (2016) suggest that 'cop culture' meant that there was ultimately a failure to recognise that reparation was not something to be achieved by officers themselves, but rather something that should be secured to respond to individual and community needs as determined by the participants themselves. A further significant issue that arose was that conferencing was mainly used for cases that would not have been prosecuted

(Hoyle 2002) thus resulting in net-widening that has been absent in most of the case studies up until this point.

By the end of the research project implementation appeared much more in line with restorative justice, although it was often deficient. Nevertheless, the overall impression was that restorative cautioning represented a significant improvement over traditional cautioning, and was more effective in terms of reducing recidivism (Hoyle *et al.* 2002). Furthermore, the practices of Thames Valley Police in the 1990s were the basis for the introduction of restorative justice measures into the Crime and Disorder Act 1998 and the Youth Justice and Criminal Evidence Act 1999 (Hoyle *et al.* 2002; Wilcox and Young 2007). Unfortunately, many of the issues that were raised within the evaluation have subsequently been replicated in other practices. Hoyle and Rosenblatt (2016: 45) argue that while justice is confined to

> the 'shallow end' of the criminal justice system, professional domination, poor victim involvement, and lack of genuine community participation are likely to continue – and facilitators will continue to feel the need to create 'victims' from those unharmed by the offense.

Current restorative policing practice

A survey conducted by Shewan (2010) revealed that 33 out of 44 police forces around England and Wales were using restorative disposals at various stages of the criminal justice process. While no offences are explicitly excluded from restorative justice processing, a stop light system has been established to guide officer discretion (ACPO 2011). Those considered 'green' are the most straight-forward and present no significant implications for any of the parties as such officers are able to facilitate themselves at their own discretion. Those considered 'amber' might include serious offences, but that involve relatively minor individual circumstances. In these instances, officers are encouraged to evaluate the likelihood of recidivism and previous offending history. As such, these may be facilitated by officers themselves or referred on to other agencies. Those considered 'red' require caution and include domestic violence, hate crime and sex offences. It is thought that a formal sanction is necessary for these offences so that a proper record can be made, particularly where there is significant risk of recidivism. Restorative justice training across forces has been implemented at a basic level (which lasts a day) and at a more advanced level (which lasts three days). It is this latter training that is necessary for an officer to facilitate disposals themselves.

Three principal approaches can be outlined where police officers themselves facilitate the process currently in England and Wales, although it should be noted that the vast majority of offences processed via restorative disposals by the police are predominantly low-level crime and anti-social behaviour (ACPO 2011). The first are referred to as Level 1 'instant' or 'on-street' disposals whereby Response Officers or Police Community Support Officers discuss the causes and consequences of the offending or anti-social behaviour directly with the offender (and where relevant, the victim and their parents where this involves minors) shortly after the incident. These are available for relatively minor, first-time offences (such as theft or property damage) and where practical or necessary, an agreement may be made for the offender to repair the harm through some form of symbolic or material reparation (or gesture) to the victim. Such an approach is seen to allow officers 'to deal with minor crimes and incidents quickly and proportionately' (ACPO 2011: 6).

The second are referred to as Level 2 'restorative conferences' which are used when the Level 1 disposal cannot be used or for more significant and, at times, ongoing offences or anti-social behaviour that has an impact on communities (such as vandalism/criminal damage, public disorder offences or neighbour disputes). The process tends to be more involved and time-consuming to organise, with more emphasis being placed on ensuring that affected members of the community are given a voice and are able to influence the outcomes of the conference for the benefit of the community. Given that Response Officers have considerably less time to be involved in longer-term issues, the predominant focus for training has been with Neighbourhood Police Officers and Police Community Support Officers. These officers either arrange and facilitate Level 2 conferences themselves or refer cases to recently developed Community Justice Panels (see Clamp 2014b for further detail about what this entails).

The final approach is a relatively new and innovative experiment that is taking place within some police forces and is referred to as a Level 3 disposal. Here conferences are arranged for persistent and prolific offenders (predominantly adults, but this may also include juveniles) and are primarily used at the post-conviction stage by Integrated Offender Management (IOM) teams. Given that the offender has already received a sentence and is serving a term of detention, it differs from the previous outlined police-led processes in that it cannot run without the presence of the victim and reparation is not the principal objective of the process. Instead, greater emphasis is placed upon the rehabilitation of the offender by enabling them to face up to the consequences of their actions and to improve their prospects of being able to reintegrate into society by increasing their self-awareness of triggers for their offending behaviour.

Regardless of the level at which the case is processed, ACPO (2011) guidance suggests that in order for a disposal to be considered 'restorative', it must comply with the following requirements: the offender must acknowledge responsibility, affected stakeholders must be involved, a meeting must occur which focuses on what happened and what the consequences were, and finally efforts must be undertaken to repair the harm caused. There has been no attempt to ascertain the exact extent of restorative policing practice across the country, in fact to do so might be virtually impossible given the range of informal experimentation that takes place across different forces and how quickly practice might change due to an alteration in local force priorities.

Nevertheless, a number of evaluations can be drawn on to give some insight into the experiences of restorative policing within the last few years. The first is the Youth Restorative Disposal (YRD), which was piloted between April 2008 and September 2009 across eight police forces (see Rix *et al.* 2011). Eligibility criteria included: young offenders aged 10–17 who had not previously received a Reprimand, Final Warning or Caution; both victims and offenders needed to agree to participate; and the circumstances surrounding the case needed to be able to be dealt with 'on the street' shortly after the incident or within a reasonable amount of time thereafter. The research found that 4,355 were issued during the pilot with shoplifting of a low value (52 per cent), assault without causing serious injury (22 per cent) and criminal damage that was largely superficial (19 per cent) being the most common. Seventy-five per cent of cases were dealt with 'on the street' (i.e. instantly) with the most common outcome being an apology. A particular weakness of the scheme according to officers interviewed was a lack of power to enforce outcome agreements, particularly where some form of material reparation was agreed. Nevertheless, officers reported high levels of satisfaction with the process on the basis that it was viewed as the most appropriate response to low-level offences, it was thought to improve public confidence with the police and the process was less time consuming than other disposals. Furthermore, victims and offenders interviewed reported high levels of satisfaction, although it should be noted that the numbers of those interviewed was very low.

The only *comprehensive* evaluation undertaken of the use of restorative justice within a police force to-date was conducted by the Hallam Centre for Community Justice (see Meadows *et al.* 2012), although a number of other research projects and organisational documents may be cited that provide insight into practices in different regions (see, for example, Cutress 2015; Shapland *et al.* 2011; Spruce 2010; Stockdale 2015; Taylor 2008). The South Yorkshire Restorative Justice Programme (SYRJP) was developed by the South Yorkshire Police and the Local Criminal Justice Board in March 2010. The evaluation conducted by Meadows *et al.* (2012) was primarily qualitative in nature and involved a small number of participants in interviews (34 victims, 29 offenders and 10 officers) and an online survey, which yielded responses from 105 victims and 307 officers. While the findings have to be interpreted with this relatively small sample in mind, they do present some interesting insights.

The report shows that from the inception of the programme until February 2012, 3,357 restorative justice disposals were undertaken which involved both Level 1 and Level 2 disposals and a hybrid of the two. Training involved 1,700 officers at a basic level and a further 160 officers at the more advanced level, however, the authors note that relatively few opportunities arose for conferences to be convened. Where conferences were convened, these tended to be for neighbourhood disputes that were not considered criminal in nature. Some issues were highlighted during the evaluation that impeded the use of conferencing: a lack of understanding of restorative justice, how restorative disposals were 'counted' against performance measures, a perception that organising conferences was not an effective use of their time (particularly amongst response officers) and a lack of support by senior staff.

A relatively low number of victims were found to be positive about the process in comparison to other schemes (63 per cent) with only 59 per cent reporting that they would recommend it to others. Of those victims who participated in the follow-up interviews, they reported feeling: supported during and following the event, satisfied with the outcome, empowered by their experience and that the process had a positive impact on the offender. However, a small number of victims reported that they felt pressured into participating in the process by police officers. Offenders were also found to be generally satisfied with the process and in some instances a positive impact was reported by both offenders and their parents as a result of the process. However, interviews with offenders revealed that while they understood that participating in the process would mean avoiding a criminal conviction (and thus formed the basis for their decision to participate), they only demonstrated a modest understanding of what a restorative process entailed. Worryingly some offenders were found to dispute their responsibility for the offence and viewed the victim as equally culpable (although the authors did not view this as problematic given that non-criminal events were being dealt with!) and so there was evidence of hostility between the participants during the conference. The most common outcomes were apologies (85.4 per cent), compensation (11.7 per cent) and reparation (0.9 per cent) although no data is provided about the extent to which these were subsequently fulfilled.

Northern Ireland

The Northern Ireland Youth Justice System was the first deliberately designed system that was based on restorative justice principles and practice. Unlike the New Zealand system, the police were deliberately designed into dealing with conflicts affecting the community through a restorative justice approach themselves rather than referring them to a programme delivered by others (Clamp 2008). Through the Police Youth Diversion Scheme, the police have a number of options at their disposal including the restorative caution (see Figure 3.2 below) and as a result, there has been a dramatic reduction in the amount of cases processed by the courts (O'Mahony and Doak 2009).

An evaluation was undertaken of the pilot of the scheme in Ballymena, which was part of a retail theft initiative and Mountpottinger, which replaced formal cautioning in Belfast from June 1999 to June 2001 (see O'Mahony *et al.* 2002). The scheme involved young offenders under the age of 17 who were diverted from prosecution by way of restorative caution, which did not involve victims, and a restorative conference, which did involve direct and surrogate victims. In order for offenders to be eligible, there had to be sufficient evidence to prosecute the young person, they have to admit to the offence and their parent(s) have to give informed consent for the process to proceed (O'Mahony and Campbell 2006). The evaluation involved a review of other police-led schemes, a review of all cases referred to the scheme during the pilot period, interviews with those stakeholders who took part in

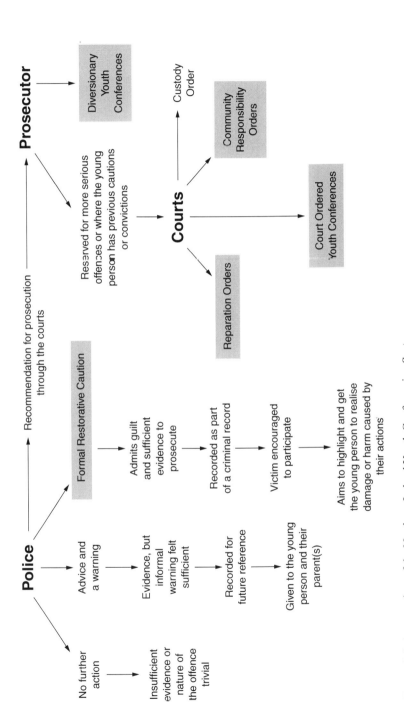

Figure 3.2 An overview of the Northern Ireland Youth Conferencing System.

the process and observations of restorative processes that took place during the evaluation period (O'Mahony *et al.* 2002).

The final report revealed that of the 1,861 referrals received prior to the evaluation period the majority of offenders were male and had typically committed shoplifting and criminal damage, although just under a third were referred for non-criminal incidences (O'Mahony *et al.* 2002). Of that cohort, the most common outcome was advice and warnings (79 per cent, given that these offences were considered to be trivial) and only 4 per cent were dealt with via caution or conference. In Mountpottinger the majority of cases were dealt with through a restorative caution and in Ballymena the majority of cases were dealt with by way of restorative conference. However, the researchers concluded that there was little evidence that cautions or conferences were being used as they were intended, i.e. as an alternative to or in place of prosecution. In fact, the vast majority of offences were first-time offenders who had stolen property to the value of less than £15 and the researchers argued that such practice had the effect of 'net-widening', an undesirable use of police resources given the amount of time spent in organising them (O'Mahony *et al.* 2002; O'Mahony and Doak 2004).

Other concerns included the low victim participation rate (around 20 per cent), the reason for which was attributed to a lack of effort on the part of officers to encourage victims to participate (O'Mahony *et al.* 2002). Shoplifting offences were the most unlikely to attract victim participation either given to the low monetary value stolen or to the fact that the good had been retrieved straight away (O'Mahony and Doak 2009). Where conferences were organised, there was a perceived over-reliance on surrogate victims, who although not directly involved in the particular offence, could talk about the impact of that type of offending due to previous experience (O'Mahony and Doak 2009). Although the use of surrogates had benefits over using other techniques such as written statements from the victim, O'Mahony and Doak (2009) report a number of disadvantages including: the diminished potential for full reintegrative shaming given that offenders did not have to explain their actions to their actual victim and the reduced opportunity for empowerment, dialogue, negotiation and agreement between the direct stakeholders. In terms of outcomes, most involved a written or verbal apology to the victim and where goods were taken, this was returned (O'Mahony *et al.* 2002). Only around 20 per cent of offenders who had been cautioned went on to offend within a one to three-year follow-up period (O'Mahony and Campbell 2006; O'Mahony and Doak 2009).

Of the interviews and surveys conducted in relation to those who participated, a number were uncomfortable with conferences being convened within police stations, the vast majority were appreciative of the preparation that went into the conference in terms of home visits, one victim was very dissatisfied given the offender in question refused to accept responsibility or to apologise (in around 8 per cent of cautions), and some parents felt that conferences were unduly onerous given the type of offence committed. All facilitators were observed to be enthusiastic and committed to restorative justice, although the researchers felt that further training in engaging young people to speak would be beneficial.

Nevertheless, the process was deemed to have distinct advantages over the traditional caution and O'Mahony and Campbell (2006) report that from February 2001 all juvenile cautions were processed as restorative cautions. Unfortunately, there has been no formal research that we could find on the practice since the original pilot study.

From practice to interrogation

The adoption of restorative justice within policing seems to represent a natural progression from attempts to implement a more community-focused and problem-oriented style of policing (Bazemore and Griffiths 2003). Indeed, many of the case studies have reported an explicit grounding in this regard and that restorative justice has been viewed as a mechanism through which the agendas of community policing might be more fruitfully realised. While there were certainly visible developments in this regard, almost all of the jurisdictions, which embraced the Wagga Wagga Model in the 1990s, have subsequently reverted back to their traditional modes of policing. Where possible, we have tried to explain the reasons for this occurrence with any updates in regards to any future potential practice once again emerging. The only exception to this general trend has been England and Wales, and Northern Ireland where police-facilitated conferencing still exists.

While restorative justice has traditionally been thought of and promoted as a mechanism through which to *de*professionalise justice, restorative policing relies on professionals – the police – rather than external and independent agencies to facilitate the process. This review of the Wagga Wagga Model case studies reveals a range of experiences, but for the most part the most significant findings appear to be the fact that those who participated in conferences arranged by police officers were very pleased with the process and that where officers are properly trained and supervised, they can facilitate conferences effectively. This provides some evidence to challenge restorative proponents who argue for a separation of restorative practice from criminal justice and a general deprofessionalisation of the process. Conversely, there have been times where officers have reverted back to their comfort zones and used the process to chastise offenders for their actions – in some instances for very minor infractions thus providing support for a deprofessionalised approach.

These tensions in the orientation of practice which draws on the Wagga Wagga Model and the research findings that have emerged following a period of implementation have divided scholars and policymakers on the potential that restorative policing holds for responding to crime (particularly that committed by youths). The result has been a heated debate between those who view restorative policing as a positive progressive strategy for crime control and those who view policing practice in this area as something to be more wary of. The arguments of each of these camps will now be explored on the basis of the findings of this chapter and that secured from other initiatives that have not been fully addressed in this chapter.

Notes

1 This is a clear break from the values of mediation practices, which emphasise the need for an absolutely neutral facilitator who has developed a trusting relationship with the parties in conflict (McCold 1998: 2).

2 O'Connell and colleagues also reportedly visited South Africa, but there has been no evidence of any training and/or implementation of the model there and so it is not to be discussed in this chapter (see O'Connell 1998).

3 Daly (2001) suggests that a tendency to try to link the history of restorative justice to pre-modern criminal justice is both an error and conveys an exercise in ethnocentrism. She argues that a culturally neutral or appropriate process can be designed without needing to link it to 'indigenous justice' and that the New Zealand Model of conferencing is often linked to Moari culture inaccurately. While the model incorporates 'the features apparent in whanau decision-making processes and seen in meetings on marae today … it also contains elements quite alien to indigenous models'. However, it is also characterised by contemporary bureaucratic forms of justice that are evident within criminal justice systems around the world.

4 However, Moore (1993a) points out that other conferences were held in offenders' homes revealing the offender focused nature of the scheme. This is confirmed further by the low victim participation rates during the early years of the scheme.

5 It is important to acknowledge that the New Zealand system of Conferencing was not entirely devoid of negative effects (see further Maxwell 1999; Maxwell and Morris 1996). Given that this is not meant to be a comprehensive review of research findings on the New Zealand Model, these are not explored here.

6 See Moore and Forsythe (1995) for a discussion of the emergence of community policing in New South Wales more broadly.

7 O'Connell (1993: 223) reports that over a three-year period following the introduction of the Beat Policing programme, four of the five most frequent categories of reported crime committed by youths showed a decrease in incidence. A decline that occurred despite 20 per cent youth unemployment, increasing family dislocation and marginalised youths in Wagga Wagga during that time.

8 Moore and Forsythe (1995) provide further evidence for and explanation of this than is possible here (see their Chapters 1 and 3 respectively).

9 In fact, O'Connell (1998) reflects that in the very first conference, having never observed one before, he arranged for offenders and their families to meet to discuss the incident and then following this invited the victim and their family who were waiting in another room to talk about their experience and to critique what the offender had said. In hindsight, although the conference was deemed a success, he altered this approach.

10 See Moore and Forsythe (1995: 10–11, Chapter 1, and Chapter 2) and O'Connell (1993: 228–232) for details of the initial case studies that were processed and their outcomes.

11 It is interesting to note that a large funded randomised trial was planned to take place in Wagga Wagga in 1995, but just before the evaluation was due to start it was blocked by The Assistant Commissioner responsible for Education and Training, the Deputy Commissioner, and the Commissioner of Police for unknown reasons (see Moore and Forsythe 1995).

12 Moore (1992: 51) cites a number of reasons for this:

> they are cost effective, (2) all but the presiding police officer are volunteers with a vested interest in a successful outcome, (3) the decision to run programmes of this sort is an example of local initiative or 'decentralised decision making', (4) the emerging police role of coordinator between agencies is an example of efficient management, and (5) the extra investment of time and effort on first time offenders represents a saving of substantially more time if recidivism is avoided as a result.

13 Under current arrangements, the involvement of police officers in conferences varies from state to state but may be summarised as follows: in Victoria, South Australia and Tasmania, a police officer must be present at the conference while in the Australian Capital Territory, New South Wales, Queensland, Western Australia and the Northern Territory the police do not need to attend the conference under legislation; and in South Australia, Queensland and Tasmania the police can veto the contents of the agreement reached by the victim and the offender (see further Richards 2010).

14 Although McCold (1998) reports that at the end of 1998 police departments in Indianapolis (IN), Anoka (MN), South Burlington (VT) and Woodbury (MN) all had active training programmes.

15 Perhaps the most punitive outcome from the conferences was 40 hours of community service for stealing a 50 cent candy bar (see McCold 2003).

16 Although the assessment made was more about the nature of offending rather than excluding those with previous records.

17 At Section 4 in the Youth Criminal Justice Act, juveniles are allowed the opportunity for non-court types of interventions if they represent adequate means of holding offenders accountable for their behaviour (see Katz and Bonham 2006).

18 In the UK, given that policing philosophies are to a large extent determined by the senior officers at the top of the organisation, forces vary quite significantly in terms of how they conduct their business. This also means that they are less stable in terms of their operational policies, which are subject to change with a change in force leadership (see further Shapland 2009).

19 The difference between the significance of this approach to the others outlined in other jurisdictions is that a record is kept of the caution which can be used in a decision on whether or not to prosecute should the offender come to the attention of the authorities again (for further detail see Young and Hoyle 2003).

4 Interrogating restorative policing
Cynical and enthusiastic accounts

Introduction

The criminal justice process has often been viewed as a playground for professionals – the judge/magistrate, the defence and the prosecution – who determine
the aspects of the incident that are relevant for discussion and further interrogation. This has produced two losers: victims and offenders, neither of whom is
able to influence the process or the outcome within a criminal justice setting, the
impact of which Umbreit explains as follows:

> Victims often feel powerless and vulnerable ... twice victimized, first by the
> offender and then by an uncaring criminal justice system.... Offenders are
> rarely able to understand ... the human dimension of their criminal behav-
> ior: that victims are real people, not just objects to be abused.
>
> (1988: 86)

A central defining feature of restorative justice, therefore, has been the desire to
'deprofessionalise' justice, or in Christie's (1977) words: to return the 'conflict'
back to its rightful owners. As outlined previously, the key actors in the restorative justice process are viewed as the victim/s, the offender/s and those individuals who may have, in some way, been directly or indirectly affected by what
happened (generally referred to as 'communities of care'). In order to deal
effectively with what has happened and to prevent any future harm from occurring, it is thought that the best approach is to bring these stakeholders together so
that they may discuss the causes and consequences surrounding the incident and
reach an agreement about what actions might be meaningfully taken to repair
the harm.

This has produced somewhat of a conundrum for restorative justice proponents. On the one hand, in order to be true to the core aims of restorative justice,
historically some have called for restorative justice programmes to remain separate from the criminal justice process (see Marshall 1990; Messmer and Otto
1992; Wright 1991). On the other, experience suggests that such an approach
offers very little challenge at all to the *status quo* of how crime is dealt with and
that 'independent' schemes often struggle to attract the referrals that they need to

remain operational (see McCold 1998; Marshall 1999; Miers *et al.* 2001). Restorative justice has thus become increasingly incorporated into the criminal justice response at various points in the process. Two concerns have been raised, in particular, to this trend. First, it is argued that restorative justice programmes, which are based on a progressive philosophy may be co-opted to achieve non-progressive goals (Levrant *et al.* 1999). It should be noted that accusations of co-option do not arise because the criminal justice system has embraced restorative justice, it occurs because it is used as a mechanism through which criminal justice practitioners might achieve the goals of criminal justice rather than as a means of doing justice better as envisaged by restorative justice proponents (Clamp 2016a).

Second, the extent to which programmes are legitimately given the label 'restorative justice' is questioned (Levrant *et al.* 1999). The mainstreaming or popularisation of restorative justice has led commentators to point to a 'misappropriation', 'institutionalisation' or what Umbreit (1999: 213) refers to as the 'McDonaldization' of restorative justice whereby it has been expanded to mean almost anything that departs from traditional sentencing. Within the criminal justice variants of restorative justice, although the right language is used, at times, practice can depart from what restorative proponents would consider to be restorative. For example, the devolution of power down to stakeholders (i.e. victims, offenders, communities) sometimes does not occur, rather professionals continue to dominate proceedings; restorative processes and principles can be used to 'responsibilise' the offender (i.e. to get him or her to acknowledge responsibility) rather than to deal with the underlying causes of behaviour; victims can be used in the service of severity to run the consequences of offending home to offenders rather than to have their own needs met; and supporters can be used to drive home to the offender that the restorative process is a 'lucky escape' and that changes should be made if further and more severe consequences are to be averted (Clamp 2016a). This has led a number of restorative proponents to be highly critical of criminal justice practitioners facilitating restorative processes (see, for example: Ashworth 2001; McCold 1998; Umbreit and Zehr 1996a, 1996b; Young 2001) and they have therefore called for civilians (normally trained volunteers) to facilitate meetings between stakeholders instead.

Nevertheless, others have called for restorative justice to be actively promoted within criminal justice because it is seen as a mechanism through which reform might be secured or where communities might actually co-opt state power (see Alarid and Montemayor 2012; Braithwaite 1994; Vanfraechem 2009). Increased opportunities for offenders to accept responsibility for the consequences of their actions and to take the necessary steps to repair the harm that has been caused to the victim/s at an early stage within the process, means that there are fewer opportunities for stigmatisation to occur because contact with additional criminal justice agents is reduced. The police are seen as pivotal in this regard given that they are the *gatekeepers*: they determine which individuals and actions are diverted away from or into the criminal justice system. Exposing officers to a restorative approach when engaging with victims, offenders and the community – mutual respect, inclusion and open dialogue – is said to hold the capacity to change police culture (Strang and Braithwaite 1998) and thus increase feelings of safety and legitimacy (O'Connell 1996a, 1996b).

As the previous chapter demonstrated, this intense debate has not only occurred within the academic literature but has also had a tangible impact upon restorative policing practice on the ground. This chapter is based on a systematic review that includes the arguments of both critics and advocates of restorative policing. Beginning with the arguments against restorative policing, the chapter then sets out the arguments for police involvement. Whether police conferencing is any more or less constructive than adversarial justice processes – or more or less restorative than other restorative practices – is an empirical question (Braithwaite 1994). As such, reference will be made to relevant research and practice examples throughout to further illustrate what can, at times, be quite convoluted positions and to demonstrate which concerns are based on fact and which are based on conjecture (see also Young 2003) and thus require further study. Before proceeding, it should be noted that there are limitations with this approach. Dignan (2005) warns that it is important to be mindful of the significance of context in relation to positive research findings and equally of the potential of 'implementation failure' in relation to negative findings. Indeed, a number of scholars have raised a number of methodological issues inherent in the research studies that have been conducted on restorative policing. As such, we acknowledge these limitations where they have been raised during the course of our review.

Arguments against police involvement in restorative justice

Concerns about the Wagga Wagga Model relate to the issues of co-option outlined above, but also in relation to the conferencing process itself in terms of its theoretical and philosophical underpinnings and the central role of police officers as facilitators (see Blagg 1997; Braithwaite 1994; Geddis 1993; Minor and Morrison 1996; Polk 1994; Sandor 1994; Umbreit and Zehr 1996a, 1996b). In an early publication on the topic, Moore (1993a) interrogated a number of challenges to the Wagga Wagga Model that encompassed the following concerns: net-widening; that facilitating conferences presented a poor use of police time; that the model blurred the lines between policing and social work; that families were no longer the primary source of socialisation (but rather peer groups and subcultures); and, finally, that the scheme was inappropriate for some young offenders. Shortly after, contributors to Alder and Wundersitz's (1994) collection explored a number of similar concerns in relation to the model which included: ethical and rights issues (see Carroll 1994; Sandor 1994; Warner 1994), net-widening and due process (see Polk 1994; Warner 1994; White 1994), the neutrality of police officers and the potential disconnect of the Model with their perceived role (see Carroll 1994) and the theoretical foundations, procedures and outcomes of reintegrative shaming (see White 1994).

Later in the United States, Umbreit and Zehr (1996a) outlined a number of potential 'dangers' that they thought were posed by the Wagga Wagga Model in comparison to their experience of victim-offender mediation. These included: a lack of adequate preparation of the parties prior to the meeting; the potential for insensitivity to the needs of victims and the potential that they might be coerced to participate; the potential that the process posed for young offenders to feel intimidated by the adults leading the process; a lack of neutrality of police officers which might lead to the shaming of the offender; the inflexibility and assumed cultural neutrality of the process; and, the potential that the process posed for net-widening.

However, it was not until the late 1990s and early 2000s that these concerns and objections were explored on the basis of empirical evidence. In this section, we explore these, and more recent, charges against restorative policing and the counter charges that have emerged on the basis of this subsequent experience. Furthermore, we have attempted to make a distinction between the original design of the Wagga Wagga Model and the subsequent practice that has emerged given questions about implementation failure that have been raised by a number of scholars (see, for example, Dignan 2005; Shapland 2009). For purposes of clarity, we have grouped these issues under broad headings, but acknowledge that some of the themes do overlap and that others have interrogated some of the elements under discussion within one section independently.

The challenge of police culture

Meyer *et al.* (2009) draw attention to the fact that when we think of the police, we do not see them as conflict resolution professionals but rather 'crime fighting' or 'law enforcement' professionals. Brodeur (2010: 104) unpacks this culturally symbolic position in *The Policing Web*, referring to it as the 'police use of force paradigm'. Importantly this paradigm, which originated in the work of Bittner (1970), continues to frame internal and external discussions about state policing in neoliberal countries and is the assumed theoretical framework through which many academics make assumptions about the police role and function in society. In relation to restorative policing, this manifests as a preconception that police officers will be unable to remove themselves from their punitive orientation and criminal justice objectives during the process (Barton 2003; Carroll 1994; Sandor 1994; Sullivan and Tifft 2001; White 1994; Young 2001). The issue that emerges from this line of thinking is that police officers will instinctively co-opt the process to achieve traditional policing objectives (i.e. those of crime control) rather than restorative ones (i.e. those of community control).[1]

As such, a number of scholars have objected to the Model on the basis that an ability for police officers to control the processes of arrest, detention and investigation and then subsequently to also facilitate a case and to oversee its outcomes presents a disproportionate (and worrying) amount of power for one agency (Shapland 2009; Young 2003; White 1994). Some have argued that police misuse of power or 'cop culture' will manifest itself in domination over the conference proceedings; the shaming of offenders; and a prescriptive approach to the contents of agreements without allowing the room for the parties to take control of the discussions and outcomes themselves (Umbreit and Zehr 1996a; Sandor 1994; Young 2003; Young and Gould 2003). This would obviously be the inverse of what restorative proponents and the original architects of the Wagga Wagga Model would view as appropriate for the process, given that it was designed to empower *participants* rather than facilitators. However, Braithwaite provides a challenge to these concerns in relation to restorative policing when he asserts that:

> Well trained and sophisticated community police officers do not seek to maximise control. The prediction that conferences can work with police coordinators is not based on an assumption that police officers are benevolent and non-controlling, but that police are not *stupid*. So long as conferencing is designed so that it is the coordinator who is responsible for ensuring that the agreement reached at the conference is implemented (and taking the matter to court if there is a totally unacceptable breakdown in implementation), the coordinator is foolish to dominate proceedings, foisting an agreement on the parties to which they are not committed. It is foolish because the coordinator risks all the extra work associated with following up an agreement subject to 'chain-dragging' compliance by the defendant and other participants. Coordinators quickly learn that only agreements which the participants own are self-enforcing. It is also true that police are more likely to have to deal with young offenders again as recidivists if, through dominating proceedings, the police officer burdens the young offender with an agreement he or she resents.
>
> (1994: 207–208, *emphasis added*)

Indeed, in our review of the case studies, there was little evidence that police took on the role of 'judge and jury' in the cases that they facilitated (also see reviews by Young 2001, 2003). The temptation to disclose knowledge of the offender and to engage in further enquiries beyond that of the incident under discussion at the conference, to veer away from the conference script and direct proceedings, to limit the full participation of the victim and for unrealistic and unjust outcomes to emerge was certainly evident in *some* instances, but not all (see Chapter 3 this volume). Furthermore, the studies conducted revealed that with proper training, neutral facilities, follow-up and the monitoring of cases selected for conferencing, successful police-facilitated conferences are possible (Hipple and McGarrell 2008; Hoyle *et al.* 2002; McCold and Wachtel 1998a; Shapland *et al.* 2011; Vanfraechem 2009). The script in the Wagga Wagga Model, in particular, is viewed as an essential means through which to restrain police behaviour and to neutralise both the language and the approach that police officers would otherwise take (Vanfraechem 2009). For the most part, this is due to the fact that within the script restoration and participant engagement remains at the forefront of the process rather than allowing police officers to be focused on deterrence and control (although see White 1994 who challenges this).

Some other findings, beyond the 'key' case studies discussed in Chapter 3 have also produced some noteworthy results. While a number of scholars have raised concerns about police facilitation, no research had been conducted on the distinctions between police and non-police facilitation of family group conferences to determine whether the concerns raised were in fact supported by empirical data until the late 2000s (see Daly 2001; Hoyle and Young 2003). The first attempt to decipher any distinctions between police and non-police facilitated meetings was conducted by Paul McCold (1998). In comparing the Bethlehem and Canberra evaluations against the findings of two multi-site studies undertaken on criminal mediation that used volunteers (see Umbreit 1994, 1995, 1996a; Umbreit and Coates 1993), he demonstrated that police-facilitated programmes rated highest overall in terms of fairness against those schemes using 'neutral' facilitators. As such, he argued that what is most important is that facilitators are perceived to be fair rather than as 'neutral'.

Subsequently, Hipple and McGarrell (2008) sought to explicitly plug the research gap by comparing police- and non-police facilitated conferences in the Indianapolis Restorative Justice Project. The authors found that police officers had a tendency to adopt a more *directive* approach than non-police facilitators, demonstrating some support for the concerns raised by critics, but they also noted that officers were more likely to end the session with a reparation agreement to help victims than were civilian-facilitated sessions. This finding was replicated in Shapland *et al.*'s (2006, 2007) review of three restorative justice schemes in England and Wales that produced similar results. The researchers reported that police officers were observed to be procedurally fair, that victims and offenders were very positive about the quality of the facilitation (regardless of the background of the facilitator) and that while observers felt that officers could *sometimes be directive*, they were *not dominant* during the process.

As Umbreit (1988) notes, and as the researchers above observed, a more directive and controlling style of facilitation is not always a bad thing and in some instances might actually be necessary in order to ensure a fair process. On the one hand, one or both of the parties may be so inarticulate or uncomfortable that they are simply unable to engage in any extended direct discussion about the offence or themselves. On the other, one of the parties may be verbally aggressive and likely to intimidate the other party. However, while these instances may require and benefit from a more directive style of facilitation, Umbreit (1996b: no page) argues that a non-directive style of facilitation offers a distinctive key benefit. It provides a stronger opportunity for restorative outcomes to be secured given that the facilitator can effectively 'disappear into the background' whilst still providing direction, leadership and assistance thus resulting in 'a far more empowering and mutually expressive form of interaction'.

Part of the process in adopting a non-directive style involves adequate preparation time being set aside prior to bringing stakeholders together. Indeed, the research findings presented in the previous chapter (particularly the United Kingdom case studies) confirm a range of problems that arise when adequate preparation has not been undertaken. Umbreit (2006) explains that preparation time is necessary for trust to be developed between the facilitator and participants, which increases the likelihood that parties will 'feel safe, understand the process, and talk directly to each other' (Umbreit 2001: 14). A lack of preparation time is certainly a reality when we think about those instances when officers decide to engage in 'street-level' or 'instant' restorative justice disposals. Where police officers bring victims, offenders and their supporters together for a minor incident on the street there will be very little opportunity to speak to each individual separately. It is natural, that in these instances police officers will be more directive than in other meetings that take more time to arrange, however, given the nature of the offences often being dealt with engaging in preparation and delaying the process might be excessive. Furthermore, even where full conferences are arranged for minor to moderate offences, McCold (1998: 6) warns of the potential for participants to be 'over-prepared' so that 'the healthy expression of emotion' no longer features, 'thereby limiting the transformative capacity of the actual conference'.

Nevertheless, it is important to note that when we are talking about directive and non-directive styles, these represent polar extremes along a continuum of mediation styles and in many cases, actual practice may well fall somewhere between these two 'pure' types (Umbreit 1988). Coordinators of youth conferencing in Northern Ireland, for example, reported a range of facilitation styles from already having action plans in their heads prior to the conference to prevent participants getting 'stuck' or as a prompt when they were uncommunicative, while others said they preferred to leave planning as much as possible to participants (Campbell *et al.* 2005: 124). Although not explicitly addressed within the studies that have been conducted on the Wagga Wagga Model to-date, we would expect that facilitation styles would not only conform to the styles at the polar end, but reveal a range of additional styles in between.

Many of the studies on the Wagga Wagga Model have identified officers as being committed to restorative justice values, demonstrating genuine concern for the future welfare of offenders, treating participants with respect and encouraging active participation (see, for example, Sherman and Strang 1997; Young and Gould 2003). To tarnish all officers with the same brush represents somewhat of an injustice. Criticism of police involvement in restorative practice that uses police culture as the frame of analysis struggle to pick up the nuances that emerge from the mixed economy of policing (Crawford 2005). Contemporary policing is resourced via a mixture of traditional reactive police officers who work alongside more community-oriented officers who may be funded by local authorities, private agencies, or those acting as volunteers. Each organisation will have its own distinct working culture and close collaborative working has the potential to produce new hybrid cultures. As such, Young (2003) argues that traditional police culture can certainly pose a challenge to the implementation of restorative policing, but that the evidence suggests that the threat that police will act as 'judge and jury' when facilitating cases might be overstated. A more pressing issue is that senior officers become complacent when implementing restorative practices within their forces, believing that police facilitation poses no problems and can be carried out without the investment of resources. As Sherman and Strang note:

When RJ (or any programme) is rolled out quickly on a wide scale, there is a risk that many conferences will just 'go through the motions' to 'tick off a box', rather than treating each case as a kind of surgical procedure requiring careful advance planning, preparation and follow-up.

(2007: 21)

As research has shown, some officers find the transition a relatively easy one, whereas others are unable to easily grasp the implications of restorative practice for their roles. As such, success in this area requires constant reinforcement through training, monitoring and mentoring. Getting police officers to embrace this role and to understand it presents the biggest obstacle, but involving officers by allowing them to be involved in case selection for the programme and/or observing conferences facilitated by their colleagues has appeared to have a significant impact on attitudes towards the Model subsequently (see Chapter 3, this volume). As highlighted by developmental theorists, notably William James (1842–1910), John Dewey (1859–1952), Lewin (1880–1947) and Piaget (1896–1980), most people learn best through 'doing', which can be fostered by having a support structure in place to facilitate understanding (see Landry 2011 for an overview of police officer learning styles). As such, in many respects, it is inevitable that mistakes will be made and that 'old habits will die hard' until officers gain insight into what is required during the process and hold an appreciation of what it means to act in a restorative way – a radical shift from traditional institutional practice. As Young and Hoyle point out:

[…] it might be an unrealistic expectation to introduce restorative policing that adheres to the principles of restorative justice and mediation before the nature of policing itself is reformed, [but] this comes dangerously close to saying that we cannot change anything until we have changed everything.

(2003: 290)

Shapland (2009) speculates that implementation can have a significant impact on the success or failure of police-led schemes. On the basis of her own experience, she suggests that the best models are characterised by specialised units undertaking restorative justice facilitation on a full-time basis. The importance of this approach is that officers are able to 'up skill' on a continuous basis, they are relatively autonomous and therefore somewhat shielded from the operational pressures experienced throughout the force, they can 'develop and maintain a proper restorative culture', they have sufficient time for follow-up and no conflicts arise in terms of the facilitating officer also being the arresting officer (2009: 128). These assumptions appear to be consistent with the experience of schemes in both Australia and the United States and explain the varied experience in Canada and the United Kingdom.

The challenge of cultural relevance and institutional racism

A number of scholars have been vocal in their opposition of the Wagga Wagga Model on the basis of indigenous justice concerns. These objections are present within the restorative justice literature more generally, perpetuated by an association of the origins of restorative justice with Indigenous justice traditions. For example, Braithwaite (1998: 323; 1999: 1) amongst others (see Johnstone and Van Ness 2007), has claimed that 'restorative justice has been the dominant model of criminal justice throughout most of human history for all the world's peoples', leading some to cite this heritage as a justification for its 'revival' (Mantle *et al.* 2005). However, Daly (2002: 72) describes this position as 'the mythical true story of restorative justice' which she argues presents a 'restricted and modified history'. Sutcliffe (2003) and Richards (2004) further argue that this portrayal of the origins of restorative justice may be considered strategic in terms of promoting restorative justice practice to policy-makers and legislators. In Daly's (2002: 62) words: 'if it can be established that the first form of human justice was restorative justice then advocates can claim legitimacy for contemporary restorative justice alternatives to state-sponsored retributive justice'.

Therefore, Cunneen (2002) and Findlay (2000) argue that restorative justice is nothing more than the colonisation of Indigenous justice practices as a way of securing hegemony over justice and re-legitimating the criminal justice system in the eyes of those it has previously disenfranchised. As Richards (2004: 2) warns these histories – however inadvertently – make restorative justice appear 'natural' and unproblematic, and at times 'miraculous' and a 'panacean' paradigm of criminal justice. In terms of restorative policing in particular, the most vocal critics have been Blagg (1997) and Cunneen (1997) who have pointed to a lack of cultural relevance particularly in relation to notions of reintegrative shaming, the historically tense relationship between police and Aboriginal communities and the over-representation of indigenous people within the criminal justice system. In terms of cultural relevance, Blagg (1997) takes particular umbrage with the assumption that all Indigenous communities around the world are the same. He challenges the view that Australian Aboriginal people live in the 'imagined' community necessary for participation in police-led reintegration ceremonies and that shaming is a central component of Aboriginal social controls. Cunneen (1997: 300) raises additional challenges relating to the assumption that Indigenous cultures operate on confrontational shaming processes, that no disadvantages will emerge due to cultural differences in these supposedly culturally 'neutral' processes and that there is an unproblematic relationship 'between Indigenous communities and non-Indigenous colonial state formations'.[2]

Settler colonialism in Australia was characterised by the use of law to 'legitimize the use of force' and to impose 'a range of cultural, social and institutional values and processes' on Aboriginal communities (Cunneen 2016: 193). Human rights abuses included the removal of Aboriginal children from their families and communities, genocide, dispossession and exclusion. Given that the police were the principal agents involved in dispossession, it is perhaps unsurprising that there is an ingrained sense of mistrust and suspicion within these communities of the police. In contemporary society, Aboriginal people are grossly over-represented within the criminal justice system and the 1989 Royal Commission into Aboriginal Deaths in Custody called on Australia's states to implement strategies to reduce the over-representation of Aboriginal youth in the criminal justice system and increase the involvement of Aboriginal people themselves in justice processes (see further Royal Commission into Aboriginal Deaths in Custody 1991). Given this history, it is perhaps unsurprising that there has been vocal opposition to the Wagga Wagga Model, particularly when the location for conferences has been police stations, a symbol of intimidation, violence and oppression for many Aboriginal people (Blagg 1997).[3]

But, drawing on the preliminary findings of the RISE Experiment in Canberra (see Sherman *et al.* 1997), Braithwaite (1997) argued that the public actually has an opportunity that they would otherwise not have to challenge officers behaviour that is discriminatory on the basis of age, race, income and gender within the Wagga Wagga Model. The Thames Valley research seemed to challenge this, however, given that when offenders did criticise the conduct of police officers, the typical response was observed to be one of defensiveness thus communicating that this type of communication would not be tolerated (see Young 2003). Furthermore, where officers have explained that an unsuccessful resolution of the offence within the conference might result in charges being brought and the case being processed through the criminal justice system (see Young and Gould 2003), it may serve to further dissuade young people and ethnic minorities in particular from voicing any concerns. Worse, it will result in defiance leading to further offending and a recasting of the offender as the victim within the process (Moore 1993a; Sherman 1993).

In a response to some of the other criticisms posed by Blagg (1997), Braithwaite (1997) further explored the importance of police officers as gatekeepers and the strengths and limitations of the process in terms of cultural difference. In relation to the former, Braithwaite (1997, 2000a) has argued that it is important that gatekeepers, such as police officers, embrace values that underpin restorative justice (also see Dinnen 1997; Gould 1999). For the most part, this is due to the fact that:

> If the police do not support conferencing and are not involved and listened to in the development of conferencing policies, then conferencing is not a good idea. This is not just because police resistance will effectively kill the reform. If police do not believe in conferencing and are required to refer young people to someone else to run a conference, they will not refer many cases. Worse, the cases they do refer will be cases they do not regard as serious enough to justify laying a charge themselves.
>
> (Braithwaite 1994: 208)

This position has been supported by a wide range of research studies investigating police decision-making in referring cases to independent schemes. The most common factors cited that influence whether or not police divert cases has included: the seriousness of the offence, offending history and attitude – particularly evidence of remorse and responsibility (see Carrington 1998; Crocker 2013; Doob and Cesaroni 2004; Doob and Chan 1982; Marinos and Innocente 2008; Meadows *et al.* 2012). As a result of these factors, oppressed minorities might benefit less given cultural differences in interaction (police not being able to interpret remorse) and over-policing (and thus prior criminal records).

Furthermore, while proponents of restorative policing have pointed to a decrease in the number of arrests and charges for young people as evidence that the process works, the rate of decrease for Aboriginal young offenders has been substantially lower than that for non-Aboriginals (see Blagg 1997).[4] Thus, the unfettered discretion bolstered by the Model is viewed as particularly problematic given that police-led cautioning can serve to further obscure the over-representation of Indigenous youth within the criminal justice process (Blagg 1997; Cunneen 1997; Warner 1994). The tendency for ethnic minorities to be overlooked as candidates for diversion has not been limited to the policing sphere, however. Research conducted more broadly of restorative justice processes that are housed within criminal justice and controlled by prosecutors and courts has demonstrated that it is often white youths who benefit the most from such schemes as opposed to those communities who have traditionally been subjected to over-policing (see, for example, Clairmont and Kim 2013; Cunneen 2002; Maxwell *et al.* 2004; Stout 2006). As such, in the view of these prominent critics, it is preferred that the power of the police is limited to reduce further opportunities for racial discrimination and oppression to occur.

It is concerning that no discussions occurred within the evaluations on restorative policing in other jurisdictions about the involvement (or lack thereof) of ethnic minorities, particularly in the United States where African Americans are disproportionately represented in the criminal justice system. While proponents of restorative policing in particular, and restorative justice more generally, convincingly argue that the process has been designed to be flexible enough to incorporate a range of traditions and cultures during the process, what is perhaps needed is further empirical research to be conducted on the relationship between restorative justice conceptions of justice and the compatibility of this with other cultural conceptions of justice and of the use of restorative justice mechanisms in response to offending by ethnic minorities. This will provide for a much more informed debate on the topic. Discrimination is present in all criminal justice systems around the world – law is not socially neutral; it affects some social groups more than others and gives legal professionals power over these groups (Moore 1993a). That is not to say that we do not need to safeguard against these injustices or to pose challenges where these injustices might be further ingrained, but rather to stress that this is a systemic issue that needs to be addressed (see also Daly 2000).

However, some have also argued that if the relationship between the police and restorative justice is limited to referral to external and independent agencies, then there is also very little opportunity for any transformation to take place in policing. Braithwaite, therefore, suggested that:

If we think it inevitable that we have police and inevitable that their power is a temptation to domination of the oppressed, then we might be better served with something more than simply circumventing their gatekeeping.... We had better give up on stigmatizing the police as essentially and irretrievably committed to the domination of colonized peoples.

(1997: 503)

One potential untapped (and under-researched) resource within restorative policing is the panel of sergeants that characterised the original Wagga Wagga Model. Such panels may offer a challenge to any discrimination that may creep into case selection, particularly given that their meetings were open to interested parties to attend. Developing oversight mechanisms and encouraging external community participation within these mechanisms may serve to provide an additional set of checks and balances called for by critics and which may also serve to further bolster transformation called for by proponents. Although such mechanisms were not always available in later iterations of the Model (including Canberra), this demonstrates that creative solutions are available and that they can work as police accountability mechanisms too. Moore (1993a), drawing on the Wagga Wagga strategy for implementation, makes an important point that breaks the circularity of the arguments presented here. He agrees that the Model should never be imposed onto communities where it is not wanted or where relations are tenuous. For him consultation with the local community is essential and only once full consent and cooperation is achieved should any scheme be established.

The challenge of the operational policing environment

Police work is generally characterised by an emphasis on 'crime control' and severe time constraints which means that officers who respond to disputes often do not attend to the underlying causes of why particular incidents have occurred (Meyer *et al.* 2009). In this sense, their approach may be thought of as primarily reactive rather than proactive and not sufficiently focused upon problem-solving. The work of Herman Goldstein on problem-oriented policing has been on the police radar for nearly four decades but its implementation remains partial (Goldstein 2010) and its impact 'fairly modest' (Weisburd *et al.* 2008: 5). The operational environment in which police officers work has therefore raised a number of concerns about their use of restorative justice which relate to: the potential that exists for police officers to coerce victims and offenders into participating in restorative disposals and the potential that their involvement holds for net-widening.[5]

A primary principle of restorative justice is that participation should be voluntary for any meeting that takes place between stakeholders (Claassen 1996). Without this, restorative justice scholars question how 'restorative' the process can be. Concerns about the voluntary nature of participating in restorative justice initiatives have not only been raised in relation to police facilitation but in relation to restorative justice initiatives housed within the criminal justice system more generally (see Chapter 2, this volume). Turner (2002), for example, in her evaluation of the implementation of the Young Offenders Act in New South Wales, Australia found that less than a third of participants were aware that they could choose whether or not to participate in a conference. Similarly, Campbell *et al.* (2005) in their evaluation of the Northern Ireland Youth Conferencing System demonstrated that magistrates did not always make it clear that offenders had a choice to participate in conferences thus making participation appear compulsory. Even where this did happen, they argued that the reality is that voluntariness is somewhat illusory given the alternative is to have their case proceed through the formal justice system which may potentially involve more punitive outcomes. As such, the potential for coercion or for referrals to restorative justice schemes to appear mandatory is not limited to the police but rather is an implementation issue for diversion schemes in criminal justice more broadly.

In reviewing the empirical evidence to support claims of coercion in relation to police conferencing specifically, McCold (1998) argues that if police officers were pressuring offenders to participate, these schemes should have artificially high participation rates and that participants would report being dissatisfied with the process. The evidence shows, however, that this was not the case. Many offenders chose to have their cases dealt with through the normal criminal justice process, victims refused to participate and for those who chose to go down the conferencing route reported high levels of satisfaction with the process. In the Bethlehem project, in particular, in the minority of instances where both victims and offenders reported feeling pressured to participate, follow-up interviews revealed that this often stemmed from their family members rather than the police (McCold 1998). There has been no other evidence that we could find that would support the assertion that offenders or victims were being coerced to participate in restorative schemes run by police officers.

Perhaps the most significant charge in relation to the Wagga Wagga model is that it will result in net-widening – something that has been perceived to occur not only in relation to restorative justice initiatives or police diversionary programmes, but in other criminal justice initiatives and processes too (McCold 1998). The central concern about net-widening in relation to restorative policing is that the state is increasing the amount of social control through an intensive system of regulation under an approach that substantially obscures police discretion (Cohen 1985; Pavlich 2001; Polk 1994; White 1994). There is a clear link between the 'professional use of [police] discretion, understood as making appropriate situational judgments' (Marenin 2004: 109), and the broader issues of police accountability and public confidence (or police legitimacy). Police officers decide when to act formally and when to act informally, who to target and who not to target and this leaves them open to accusations of over-policing and under-policing in different areas and communities. Street-level policing often takes place away from the eyes of the general public as well as sergeants and inspectors, which renders much police work invisible and makes it difficult to monitor. The implication of this is that clear and transparent organisational accountability structures are required to maintain public support for the work the police do and, thus, the issue of police officer discretion has been a longstanding contentious area of public debate (Storch 1975; Jefferson and Grimshaw 1984).

The latter part of the twentieth century presented considerable challenges to the authority and legitimacy of the police service within Australia (Chan 1997; Dixon 1997); the United States (Chambliss 2011; Marx 1988), and the United Kingdom (see Dixon 1997; MacPherson 1999; Patten 1999; Scarman 1982). As a result, for the past 30 years varied and various attempts have been made to enhance police accountability to both government and the public which has subsequently led to increased constraints on police officer discretion. Criminal justice agencies in general have increasingly become subject to inspection, audit and evaluation to measure their performance against trends in crime (Pollitt 1986). Reliable data with which to measure performance has become a prime requisite of these processes, and this has generated serious efforts to control the quality, consistency and integrity of recording practices. This has manifested as the *National* Incident-Based *Reporting* System (NIBRS) in the United States and the introduction of National Crime Recording Statistics (NCRS) in both the United Kingdom and Australia.

However, while police performance indicators and league tables sought to provide government and the public with a clear means of measuring the performance of their police force to ensure policing was efficient, effective and equitable a number of unintended negative consequences have emerged. Evidence has shown that the focus on performance indicators drew police officers away from some of their core functions and towards more trivial tasks (Neyroud 2013), thus encouraging a counter-productive emphasis on policing by results and sanction detections. Researchers have identified examples of, on the one hand, the 'cuffing' (hiding) of offences for reasons ranging from work avoidance to a wish to improve the overall clear-up rate (Bottomley and Coleman 1981; Young 1991) and on the other, the recording (amounting to the 'creation') of large numbers of minor offences in order to elevate the crime rate (Tilley and Burrows 2005), for example with a view to supporting a case for more resources. As Moore (1993a: 209) noted, the use of police cautions, in particular, has meant that young people had been coming to the attention of police for 'astonishingly trivial matters'.

In instances where offending is too minor to be pursued further within the criminal justice process, many question whether any intervention should be offered at all. Many practitioners believe that excessive intervention can actually undermine, rather than reinforce individual control (McAra and McVie 2007; Moore 1993a; Young and Gould 2003) despite the prominent political policing discourse focusing upon the necessity of tough and fast intervention (most famously, Wilson and Kelling 1982). In contrast to this public and political debate, there remain many police officers and scholars who challenge the value of an emphasis upon enforcement ahead of diversion to other services for people with a range of vulnerabilities that include age, health and socio-economic circumstance (Paterson and Best 2016; Paterson and MacVean 2007).

While many have raised concerns about the potential for the Wagga Wagga Model to widen the net, Moore (1993a) and O'Connell (1993) state that the

Model was actually designed to *challenge* the prevalence of trivial matters being processed through the system (see further Chapter 2, this volume). The development of the panel of sergeants to review cases that would fall within the remit of conferencing evaluated cases on the basis of which they were serious enough to warrant intervention. The criterion used was the amount of individual and social *harm* caused rather than the type of offence that had been committed. Approaching case selection in this way ultimately led to a reduction rather than an increase in the amount of young people charged and dealt with by the police (Moore 1993a; Moore and Forsythe 1995). In both the Bethlehem study (McCold and Wachtel 1998a) and the original Wagga Wagga evaluation (Moore and Forsythe 1995), it was demonstrated that the number of cases referred to court dramatically dropped following the introduction of police-facilitated conferences. This demonstrates that cases that would normally proceed through the criminal justice process were being effectively diverted rather than officers merely including those offences that they would normally not pursue – a narrowing, rather than a widening of the net.

Furthermore, it must be stressed that the Wagga Wagga Model was not designed to deal with new minor offences, but rather to transform the existing and ineffective cautioning process. The Model fails to function as an alternative when net-widening occurs (such as the case studies of England and Wales and Northern Ireland demonstrate) and can be considered to have been a success in those case studies where the schemes have not been linked to additional funding (such as Australia and the United States) and existing resources have had to be used. If funding is linked to referrals, then there is an impetus for police officers to include an increasing number of cases that would not normally be considered (Bazemore and McLeod 2011 refer to this as 'self-aggrandizement'; also see Sandor 1994). Where existing resources have had to be used, there is very little incentive for officers to include cases other than those that would most benefit from the process. McCold (1998) notes, for example, that the Wagga Wagga Model offers the criminal justice system significant financial benefits given that the only additional outlay that is required is the training of police officers. The operational costs of running these initiatives then subsequently form part of the existing budget given that officers' conduct conferences as part of their normal duties. In Bethlehem, for example, the cost of police-led conferences was less than $60 per case.

Regardless, Weitekamp (1989) refutes the assertion that net-widening effects are always negative by arguing that this is only true when such practice is used to control the public in an intrusive way. The original architects of the Wagga Wagga Model share this view when they argue that the purpose of the scheme is to reduce to the net of 'state control' and to increase the net of 'community control' (see Braithwaite 1993, 1994; Moore 1993a). Moore (1991) suggests that while police officers continue to act as gatekeepers, this role is transformed from one of access to the criminal justice system and instead to that of a social justice system. Nevertheless, Moore (1993a) has acknowledged that the success of the Wagga Wagga Model was largely due to the tight controls placed on the process by those who had designed it and thus warned that if the Model was going to be implemented elsewhere schemes would need to be well grounded in theory and carefully guided and monitored in practice. Polk (1994) has reinforced this view by stating that evaluations of programmes should be determined by the extent to which they meet their original intended goals, something which research has shown the criminal justice system to not be particularly good at (see also Daly 2000).

The allegation of net widening has been valid in the other studies, in part reinforcing the schism between the Models implemented in Australia and the United States and elsewhere. Much of the evidence drawn upon for allegations of net widening in the literature has come from the evaluation of police-led cautioning in Northern Ireland in particular (see O'Mahony *et al.* 2002), in which the researchers found that in:

> [...] some 80% of cases ... examined were for offences concerning property worth less than £15. It was not uncommon to come across cases where a considerable amount of police time had been invested in arranging for a full conference for the theft of chocolate bar or a can of soft drink.
>
> (O'Mahony and Doak 2004: 495)

This raises questions about the potential of restorative justice to enhance police officer discretion in a fair and equitable way, particularly within the current overarching context of austerity measures. Restorative policing has been predicated, particularly within the United Kingdom on the perceived cost savings that it offers to the expensive criminal justice process in the form of reductions in recidivism and processing time (also see McCold 1998). However, the research findings have tended to challenge this assumption. Young and Gould (2003) warned that there has been a tendency to compare reconviction figures that are not suitable for comparison thus over-inflating the perception of reductions in recidivism rates. Furthermore, Hipple and McGarrell (2008) suggested that while conferencing does tend to reveal lower recidivism rates than those of court processes, one needs to account for the type of offenders who opt to participate in restorative justice processes. It is likely that given they are prepared to account for their actions they would have been more unlikely to go on to reoffend than those who decided to have their cases processed through the normal adversarial channels.[6]

As Moore (1993a) noted over two decades ago now, an emphasis on recidivism rates is somewhat of a flawed strategy given that it maintains a link between the welfare and justice traditions. Furthermore, a continued emphasis on reducing recidivism can actually promote an approach by police officers that is concerned with attitudinal and behavioural change that can manifest itself in over-bearing and excessive lecturing, much like the 'old' approach (see Young 2003). If the potential of restorative policing is going to be realised, then the focus needs to be primarily on reducing harm – to both victims and offenders – within a conferencing setting characterized by an open and discursive approach (Young and Gould 2003). This is a radical shift from the zero-sum game (either the victim wins at the expense of the offender or the victim loses so that particular outcomes for the offender might be secured) that tends to characterise the conventional criminal justice approach (Hudson 2003). But one that may be more successful in achieving the cost saving ambitions of policy-makers and criminal justice practitioners in the long run.

Arguments for police involvement in restorative justice

Despite the extensive challenges to the restorative policing model as outlined above, there have been a range of contributions that highlight the perceived benefits of the Model as well. In reflecting on the Wagga Wagga Model while it was still in operation, Moore (1993a) suggested that it presented four particular benefits: crime reduction, a break from the cycle of the escalating seriousness of offending; an opportunity for victims (both direct and indirect) to participate in a process that aims to respond to the harm that has been caused, and a means through which to strengthen communities. Subsequently, Strang and Braithwaite (1998) suggested that given their role as gatekeepers, police are best placed to identify and deal with cases promptly; victims feel more secure because they perceive the police to have their best interests in mind; police-led conferencing lends 'gravitas' to the proceedings; police are more likely to gain compliance with outcomes; the police already have the skills required as part of their duties in community policing; and that restorative policing offers the opportunity to change police culture.

Given his own experience, and perhaps aspirations, Charles Pollard (2001) also felt that conferencing brought a range of qualities to criminal justice, including: a process that benefits victims, offenders and their families; the potential for the policing of nuisance and disorder; interagency collaboration; the increase in offender compliance with the outcomes of conferences; participant satisfaction with procedural justice and fairness; and cost savings. In this section, much like the previous, we have decided to focus on broad themes that encompass some of these perceived strengths of restorative policing. Our approach, as in the previous section, is to begin with mapping out the rationales of our colleagues and then to present evidence, which will either provide further support for or challenge these positions.

The benefits for victims, offenders and the police

Although sometimes discussed as separate issues within the literature, participant satisfaction (or perceptions of fairness) and legitimacy are interlinked. Readers will recall the theoretical reasons and empirical evidence to support this, for engaging with offenders (in particular) in a respectful way: they will be more likely to willingly accept the consequences of their actions and to internalise the experience in a manner which may serve to curb future offending behaviour (see Sherman 1993; Tyler 1990). Furthermore, the blaming, stigmatising and general negative treatment of victims by police officers has been well documented with such interaction being described as 'secondary victimisation' (Maguire and Ponting 1988; van Dijk 2001; Winkel and Vrij 1993; Zedner 1994). The result of negative experiences when interacting with the police has led to decreasing trust and legitimacy. Given the legitimacy crisis being experienced in neoliberal states, it is perhaps unsurprising that so much attention is devoted to this issue.

As Tyler's (2011) work has demonstrated in the United States, Bradford and Jackson's (2010) research in the United Kingdom and Murphy *et al.*'s (2009) research in Australia, perceptions of *fairness* rather than perceptions of *effectiveness* have a more significant impact on how legitimate the public perceive the police to be. For example, Sherman *et al.* (1998) found that police-led conferencing fostered respect for both the law and the police in their evaluation of the RISE project. Thus restorative justice encounters, particularly conferencing, present an important opportunity for the police to increase perceptions of legitimacy amongst the public it serves and there is value in doing restorative justice well. In safeguarding the potential of restorative policing in this regard, it is important for officers to understand that when harm is exaggerated, or too much remorse expected, it can have the unintended consequence of reducing both the deterrent effect and perceptions of legitimacy due to the sense of unfairness that this could generate (see, for example, Young 2003; Young and Gould 2003).

Many have objected to the use of restorative-led conferencing on the basis that it would give officers too much power resulting in a whole host of negative consequences for victims, offenders and communities (see Warner 1994; White 1994). However, the main argument for the use of restorative policing has been that it offers an approach that the community will interpret as both satisfying and fair. In a comparison of police versus non-police facilitated conferences McCold (1998: 9) provided evidence to demonstrate that 'four of the five of the highest rated programs on offender perception of fairness were the police programs'. This, he argues, provides a challenge to those who are concerned that conferences facilitated by police facilitators would not be perceived to be as fair by participants as are those facilitated by 'neutral' volunteers. Rather, he argued, what is needed is not a neutral facilitator, but rather one who is perceived to be fair.

Indeed, all of the studies presented in the previous chapter have spent much time exploring perceptions of fairness amongst victims, offenders and their supporters and the findings have been promising. The RISE experiments produced statistically significant results when comparing interpretations of procedural fairness in those cases conferenced against those cases dealt with in court (see Sherman and Barnes 1997). These findings were replicated in Bethlehem with more than 90 per cent of participants saying that they would recommend the process to others (see McCold 1998; McCold and Wachtel 1998a), in Thames Valley an average fairness rating of 88 per cent was recorded across all participants (Hoyle *et al.* 2002) and more than 90 per cent of participants in the Northern Ireland study felt that they had been treated fairly by the police facilitating their case (O'Mahony *et al.* 2002). In fact, most well-resourced restorative justice schemes replicate these findings.

However, a number of researchers have suggested that caution should be exercised when interpreting promising findings in relation to satisfaction rates or reports of fairness for two reasons. First, Hoyle *et al.* (2002) suggest that victims and offenders may come to restorative cautioning and conferencing sessions with low expectations thus reporting on their *expectations* as opposed to their actual treatment. As such, they argue that we should be far more critical of attaching perceptions of fairness to the conference or restorative justice because often stakeholders do not have a good grasp of what restorative justice is (also see Young and Gould 2003). Second, Young (2003) questions the extent surveys are structured and worded could have on responses. In relation to the RISE study he queries the possibility that legal counsel could have advised their clients that police treatment had been unfair in some respects thus having an impact on their responses. While he acknowledges the speculative nature of his queries, he stresses that interpretations of fairness will be influenced by context and thus our interpretations of research findings need to be conscious of this as well. We would add one further practice-based issue in seeking feedback from participants that relates to when and how their views are obtained. Although positive responses were obtained in relation to Young and Gould's (2003: 98) research on the Aylesbury cautioning process, we would have to question the extent to which the results can be trusted when 'the officer gave all the participants a short questionnaire form seeking the views on the cautioning session'. The extent to which the offender may have given positive responses for fear of reprisals is not clear but perhaps something that is worth further consideration.

The potential for the transformation of police culture

It is important to keep in mind when discussing restorative policing that the policing organisation and policing functions are not one-dimensional. Part of the community policing and crime prevention mandate is to 'keep the peace' which involves responding to incidents, restoring the peace and preventing problems from reoccurring (Shapland 2009). Furthermore, Meyer *et al.* (2009) point out that while police officers often articulate their role as anything but conflict resolution specialists and mediators, the reality of their day-to-day work regularly involves these types of actions (see also, for example, Bittner 1970; van Stokkom and Moor 2009; Vanfraechem 2009; Wood *et al.* 2013). Depending on the situation, police officers will often oscillate between the use of force, arrest and threats and negotiation, mediation and other conflict resolution techniques (Cooper 1997). Increasing police reliance on the latter techniques, Cooper (1997) and can result in defusing tensions from progressing into full-blown conflicts; reducing the threats to both police officers and other community members when particularly difficult incidents arise; reducing police workload in terms of repeated calls to the same location and reducing the incidence of repeated harm caused to individuals.

These are all activities that share much in common with restorative practice as envisaged by criminal justice practitioners. As such, policing scholars challenge the assertions of restorative justice scholars that the policing role can be transformed by restorative justice on the basis that what restorative justice proposes, they have been doing anyway. The tension between the two positions is due to alternative interpretations of what restorative policing is. On the one hand, restorative policing has been viewed as a *tool* for achieving the functions of policing (i.e. working in communities, with victims, investigation and maintaining order). Indeed, Bazemore and Schiff (2005: 289) have suggested that police officers who use restorative justice approaches in their daily work have the potential to develop group competency 'in building relationships or networks for marginalised groups that in turn may also reduce social distance, and ultimately increase social integration'. It is evident that such an approach neatly aligns with the demands made from community policing to engage with communities as well as the requirements of problem-oriented policing to look at the wicked nature of complex policing problems.

On the other hand, a more progressive approach is that restorative policing should be viewed as an entirely different *framework* through which officers serve the community. For example, O'Mahony and Doak (2009) suggested that the more transparent approach offered by police-led conferencing in Northern Ireland provided a bridge between officers and offenders who have traditionally felt alienated and antagonistic towards the police. Similarly, De Blouw (cited in Vanfraechem 2009: 48, emphasis original) suggests that restorative policing should be perceived in a 'broader evolution of *rule of law* towards *rule of engagement*, which frames the daily interactions between people and whereby the police officer starts from the point of empowerment and recognition in order to come to a constructive communication process'. These scholars have been responsible for perhaps one of the most significant, and controversial, assertions that restorative policing holds the capacity to change police culture from 'within' and the potential that this ultimately holds for 'systemic reform' (Hines and Bazemore 2003). This line of thinking has somewhat of a change reaction in mind whereby attitudes and perspectives of some officers will be transformed thus influencing their colleagues and effecting change within the broader organisation as a whole (Hoyle 2007; Vanfraechem 2009).

Thus, what scholars with a transformative view of restorative policing are not arguing for is the integration of a restorative justice as an additional tool or mechanism through which to deal with some types of crime. Rather, they view restorative policing as an alternative approach to perceiving the police role and how they go about fulfilling that role. Pollard (2001), for example, thought that restorative policing schemes could initiate the redefinition of civil rights and responsibilities within communities and a renegotiation of the relationship between those communities and the police in dealing with crime, disorder and fear. Within this new relationship, it is expected that police officers will relinquish their power over order, but retain control over the individual rights guaranteed by the legal system and that citizens will become active rather than passive consumers of police services (see Moore 1993a). If the relationship between the police and restorative justice is limited to a 'tool', then there is very little opportunity for any transformation of this nature to take place. Nevertheless, there are a number of potential obstacles to realising this transformative agenda, most of which relate to the manner in which restorative policing is implemented.

In Wagga Wagga, there was evidence to suggest that cultural shifts were beginning to take place within that force. For the most part, this is due to the fact that the scheme was developed on the basis of a strong theoretical framework with adequate support structures (both within and outside of the force) being built around the philosophy of restorative policing. However, Moore and Forsythe (1995) warned that if police were not significantly involved in the programme there would be little incentive for them to change and if practice subsided, it would be easy for those who had been involved to retreat back into a crime control mode of operation. Indeed, this was the experience in the United States whereby there was little impact on the general policing culture across the force. For the most part, this was due to the fact that the scheme involved only a few officers and while McCold and Wachtel (1998a) reported a shift amongst those officers from a crime control conception of policing to a community policing ethos, they were unable to detect further change beyond the restorative justice facilitators committed to the programme.

Hoyle (2007) suggests that this experience would imply that broader cultural shifts cannot take place unless restorative justice is embraced across an entire force (also see O'Mahony *et al.* 2002; Hines and Bazemore 2003; Paterson and Clamp 2012). However, she draws attention to the failed transformation of policing within the United Kingdom which has adopted a much more inclusive approach to police training and facilitation than experienced elsewhere as a challenge to this perception. While, she argues, it is desirable to expose beat police to restorative values and practices to improve their interaction with the communities it serves, empirical evidence suggests that 'infusing all policing with restorative values is overly ambitious' (2007: 303). However, we would contend that the historical (i.e. Thames Valley) and current approach within England and Wales presents a 'surface approach to learning' (Biggs 1999; Peace 2006). The current police training approach adopted for restorative justice is that it forms but one small (and usually one-off) part of a whole host of different theoretical, philosophical and practical issues that officers are exposed to on their training days. It is understandable that under such a model there would be little impact in effecting substantial and long-lasting change. An exploration of how the transformative potential of restorative policing might be packaged and implemented becomes the focus of the latter chapters of the book, suffice to say here that while such an exercise might be elaborate we do feel that there is value in further exploring how policing might be evolved to become more responsive to the changing world in which we live and to approach conflict in a more just and respectful way.

From interrogation to contextualisation

This chapter has interrogated the restorative policing literature in an effort to consolidate the perceived risks and strengths of restorative policing. The review has demonstrated that the concerns raised in relation to the Wagga Wagga Model in particular, can be observed within those non-police led schemes that are housed within criminal justice. Thus, preventing police officers from facilitating restorative justice processes does not necessarily stop those concerns from being realised. This suggests that there are either inherent problems with conferencing itself, or more likely that the location of conferencing within the criminal justice system creates problems for the realisation of its aims. Furthermore, Young (2003: 198) suggests that part of the problem 'is based on a narrow conception of punishment' and a confusion with conferencing as an alternative to punishment rather than an alternative punishment.

The result has been the emergence of a clear distinction between the original Wagga Wagga Model and later iterations in terms of the outcomes that they yielded thus reinforcing the notion that some less than desirable outcomes could be attributed to differences in both the conception and implementation of the model. In fact, Young (2003: 223) has described the Thames Valley model as a 'watered-down version of conferencing' thus leading him to question how much it has in common with the original Australian schemes. This, he reflects, poses a significant problem for schemes currently emulating the Thames Valley approach. We share his concern and, in fact, are not surprised by the weak transformation that has taken place within forces currently utilising restorative practices in England and Wales. However, we would add an additional obstacle to progressive policing practice moving forward and that is a lack of engagement with the lessons of research that has already been undertaken. We seem to be perpetually recreating the same 'wheel'.

Understanding the 'drift' from the original design is not something that can be discussed in any informed manner by reviewing the restorative policing literature alone. The objections raised in relation to restorative policing are not to be dismissed lightly, but we do not feel that they are insurmountable. The key, for us, is a further nuancing of the contexts into which we are attempting to embed restorative practices. There has been an uneven consideration of the different literatures – restorative justice and policing – when discussing this topic. In fact, the majority of resources available on restorative policing contain only a cursory engagement with the policing literature and we seek to bring the lessons from that literature much more deliberately to the fore in the following chapters. We argue that such an approach is essential in moving the debate on the topic towards a more nuanced discussion about the changes that policing will ultimately need to go through in order to adapt to a rapidly changing social environment given increased levels of migration, multiculturalism and austerity measures.

Indeed, Bayley and Shearing (2001) identified a process of 'multilateralisation', driven by neoliberal shifts in governance, which have led to the emergence of a range of commercial and voluntary policing providers which have very different aims and organisational missions to state police agencies. For Shearing, anyone who is involved in restorative policing contributes to the policing process and should thus be understood as performing a policing function. This includes police officers, statutory facilitators, NGOs and volunteers. This process will be interrogated further in Chapter 5 but, for the moment, we must note that this perspective requires scholars to think about 'policing' as a process, in conceptually separate terms from 'the police' as an institution. When policing agencies, beyond the state police, work together without formal recourse to the law and coercive force, they are increasingly likely to operate as active social agents with distinct operational missions who divert offenders away from formal legal and judicial processes. Because of this, transformations in the purpose of policing need to be understood as being driven by a much broader transformation in the configuration of policing, justice and security. We explicitly turn our attention to this in the following chapter.

Notes

1 It should be noted that issues of co-option are not only evident in policing; there is evidence to suggest that where facilitators are from other professions, their agendas are also present within the conferencing process (see, for example, Maxwell and Morris 1994b; Young 2003). This seems to indicate a disproportionate amount of focus on this agency in particular.

2 For other challenges to reintegrative shaming theory beyond Indigenous communities, see Maxwell and Morris (1994a), Polk (1994), Morris and Maxwell (2000).

3 The objections to conferences being held at police stations has also been discussed beyond the issue of ethnic minorities but without any consensus on the issue. For example, Shapland *et al.* (2006) note that offenders found it a particularly stressful location in their study although Young (2003) reports that the Thames Valley research produced few objections to this as the location for either cautions or conferences. Vanfraechem (2009) notes that in Brussels and Flanders most mediation sessions are held in police stations and that while there may be issues relating to a lack of neutrality and isolation from other services, this location also holds a number of distinct advantages: close cooperation between independent mediators and the police and sensitising the police to alternative methods of resolving minor disputes.

4 Although see Daly (2000) who draws on research challenging the fact that the amount of Aboriginal youth referred to conferences is less than non-Aboriginal youths.

5 See further Braithwaite (1994) for a good discussion about concerns around double jeopardy, concerns with sentencing (i.e. upper and lower limits and consistency) in conferencing and admissions of guilt.

6 However, other research suggests that in certain instances restorative justice may not be an effective crime reduction strategy. Sherman *et al.* (2000) also evaluate conferences for drunk-driving cases and juvenile property crimes. They find no perceptible change in offending for property crimes, and an increase in offending for drunk drivers who attend a conference. In addition, reanalysis of the Australian violent crime data (Sherman *et al.* 2004) finds that, while reoffending might be somewhat reduced among members of a society's dominant racial majority group, racial minorities might not respond similarly. Aboriginals who participated in a conference, generally organised by a white police facilitator and with white victims, were significantly *more* likely to re-offend compared to the control group. These negative findings suggest that restorative justice is not a one-size-fits-all strategy. Individual characteristics, features of the offence, and perhaps components of the conference itself can influence offending.

5 The evolving landscape of criminal justice and policing

Introduction

There has been much focus upon where the police should or should not situate themselves within the context of restorative policing, as well as the potential of restorative policing to drive police reform. From this latter perspective, restorative policing draws police officers closer to their communities but the converse question of how changes to the governance of policing, and more broadly criminal justice, have driven the growth of restorative policing have rarely been explored. This chapter picks up this question and explores changes to the configuration of justice and security networks across the globe as well as their impact upon what Bayley and Shearing (2001) refer to as the 'multi-lateralisation' of policing. Policing has been subject to the same external forces that drove the emergence of restorative justice across neoliberal societies and similar patterns of change and trajectory can be identified. Modern policing evolved out of disparate and informal networks of civic and commercial police and, throughout the evolution of professional policing, the position of state police as the most prominent security node has continued to be challenged, as has its purpose and organisational mission. The challenges that restorative policing encounters within this context are thus cultural and organisational tensions regarding the purpose of both justice and policing that have been accelerated by changes to the governance of criminal justice, policing and security.

This chapter reflects on these changes in the configuration of policing and criminal justice and their implications for the purpose of a plethora of policing agencies. The chapter begins with an overview of changes in the shape and governance of criminal justice before assessing their implications for police and policing. Attention then turns to theories of policing and their attempts to explicate the impact of post-modern cultural, organisational and political shifts for policing and criminal justice organisations. Four areas are identified for further investigation: Changes in interpretations of the police role; the emergence of hybrid policing agencies and collaborations with new purposes and mentalities; questions about the capacity of communities, voluntary organisations and the commercial sector to undertake policing in a fair and equitable manner; and, ongoing diversification and adaptation in the shape of policing.

The chapter concludes with some reflections on the future of policing and the extent to which the aspirations of restorative justice advocates are likely to be met in an operational policing environment.

The shifting sands of criminology and neo-liberal criminal justice

The early history of Anglophone criminology was dominated by a positivist approach which viewed the causes of crime as a consequence of social, biological and psychological influences and a neo-classical perspective which emphasised the Beccarian and Benthamite view that swift and certain responses to crime would reduce the likelihood of repeat offending. While these schools of thought still dominate social and political discussions about crime and criminal justice, the discipline of criminology underwent two major crises during the late 1960s and 1970s respectively which led to quite radical shifts in its thinking about approaches to crime (Young 1988). The first related to what Young (1988) refers to as an 'aetiological crisis'. Positivist perspectives had largely been based on the belief that crime would decrease as post-war social conditions improved. Yet, crime continued to rise and it was not until the end of the twentieth century that crime rates started to decrease. The second crisis was one of 'penality' and was driven by the findings of several high profile criminal justice studies in the United States, which questioned both the effectiveness of the police and the rehabilitative potential of prisons in addressing the problem of crime. These crises found a voice through a pessimism that 'nothing works' in addressing the problem of repeat offending and a subsequent questioning of the capability of sovereign states to manage the problem of crime (Garland 1996).

The Western neo-liberal democracies responded to this crisis with a reform agenda for criminal justice institutions, the promotion of the commercial sector in the 'fight against crime' and the mobilisation of a myriad of non-state mechanisms in strengthening and lengthening the response to crime and other social problems. The responsibility for crime control started to shift away from the sovereign state and towards a new logic of managerialism, the new penology (Feeley and Simon 1992), through which a range of agencies became involved in the technocratic management of crime and other social problems. With informal, non-state agencies, theoretical connections were made between community responses to crime and the concepts of 'social capital' and 'collective efficacy' although this had little initial impact upon criminological conceptualisations of policing which remained grounded in theorisations of the changing nature of statecraft, most notably, the individualistic, free-willed economic visions that underpin neo-liberal thought. It is worthwhile adding a cautionary note here. The concept of neo-liberalism has been applied both loosely and with great frequency since the early 1990s and has a tendency to be operationalised as a blunt denunciatory tool to comment on social and political changes in governance, or the hegemonic order that drives and sustains these changes. The use of the term here refers to a technique of government and, more specifically, 'practices and policies concerned with the construction of market and market-like relations' (Dean 2010: 1) that have impacted upon Anglophone crime control systems since the late 1970s. It is not part of the purpose of this book to critically dissect neo-liberalism in great detail (for further discussion see Dean 2010; Flew 2014; Nonini 2008) but to acknowledge that there are layers of complexity as well as ideological and political assumptions attached to discussions about neo-liberalism which are neither implied, nor should they be interpreted, here.

Growing dissatisfaction with Keynesian economics and the welfare state led to a slow transformation in Western liberal thought about the relationship between states, markets and the social body (Foucault 1991, 2008) which aligned with Young's (1988) identification of an aetiological and penality crisis during the late 1960s and 1970s. Henceforth, the rational economic actor model of human behaviour became the dominant lens of analysis through which crime control was understood at the state level. Although the unevenness and, at times, incompatibility of different strands of neo-liberalism were evident in the simultaneous, and to some degree 'bottom-up', rise in the role of 'victims' and 'communities' within responses to crime. From the 1980s onwards criminal justice became increasingly characterised by an alternative governmentality, the presence of victims and communities in the administration of justice (rather than professionals alone) and a simultaneous politicisation of crime control. The rise of 'populist punitiveness' (Bottoms 1995) generated by the primacy of 'crime' as a subject of public concern led to politicians promoting tough, zero tolerance policies and ever more stringent penal interventions in order to secure public support (Young and Matthews 2003). This governmental shift resulted in increased resources for policing, prosecutions and prisons, but also had the perverse effect of contributing to a heightened fear of crime despite a stable and sustained decline in crime rates from the mid-1990s onwards (Clamp 2010).

This 'crisis of penal modernism' (Garland 2001) meant that previously unchallenged assumptions about the problem of crime continued to be questioned. These assumptions included: the monopoly of state institutions in responding to crime; the dominance of 'professionals' in the administration of justice; and the historical focus on the offender (see Garland 1996). Ideological adherence to a punitive strategy did not produce either greater satisfaction with the criminal justice process or an improved sense of ontological security. Instead, an increase in caseloads of offenders coupled with an absence of faith in the ability of the criminal justice system to deal with crime effectively led to concerted efforts to find new and innovative ways of engaging with offenders, victims and communities that started to reshape the contours of criminal justice. At the same time, post-modern shifts in the media landscape drove an increased awareness of victimisation which led to the promotion of victim advocates who became integral components in the emergence of restorative justice and the philosophy of community policing.

These law and order challenges have been, to differing degrees, reconceptualised since the economic crises emerged in wealthy neo-liberal democracies in 2008. The previously consistent rises in funding for police and penal agencies came to an end and the predominance of economic austerity discourses pushed senior criminal justice officials to intensify their search for more innovative, effective and less costly initiatives to combat crime and disorder as well as frustratingly high re-offending rates. In the United States, this shift in thinking has been most notable in the realm of sentencing, imprisonment and the contracting-out of policing. In England and Wales, the leverage of austerity discourses has driven increasingly radical reform of the criminal justice landscape for the Probation Service and the Police Service. Canada, New Zealand and Australia have felt the impact of the financial crisis to a lesser degree but have all still experienced decreases in funding for criminal justice and policing. In all cases, an initial focus on privatisation, technological development and structural reform has been broadened to embrace consideration of multi-sector collaborations, downsizing and demand reduction. The impact of these high-level changes in governance has been to generate the space at the police and offender management policy level for much more radical thinking about the issues of crime and social justice.

Yet, while grand narrative explanations concerning the governance of security, such as 'the new penology' (Feeley and Simon 1992) or 'the culture of control' (Garland 2001), tend to capture the complexities of governance 'from above' they also have a tendency to underplay the importance of political agency and the way that it operates within structures of governance (Cheliotis 2006). Grand theoretical narratives help us to understand the social, cultural and political conditions that have enabled community-based modes of crime control to rise up the political agenda but they lack a focus on developments at the local level, which can make sense of the messy and uneven processes of policy implementation. This is of particular importance to restorative policing, which is defined by a cluster of local, and often embryonic, projects which tend to have little co-ordinated oversight, accountability and governance. Thus, while grand narratives capture changes in the master patterns of institutional criminal justice, the theoretical frameworks can lose meaning at the micro-level. For example, these frameworks can encourage the development of generic conceptual and analytical constructs such as 'police culture', 'zero tolerance' or 'populist punitiveness', which can be inappropriately applied to local contexts (Campeau 2015). Henceforth, a comparative analysis of case studies provides an opportunity to produce a 'realist' analysis that connects the local with the global and the micro with the macro.

The reshaping of neo-liberal crime control systems has led to contemporary policing structures being made up of an assemblage of disparate policing agencies engaged in a contest for sovereign control over populations at the local, national and global levels. In neo-liberal democracies, this contest continues to be most commonly characterised by attempts by plural policing agencies to align themselves with central or local state governments who have the resources and authority to regulate emerging modes of policing. Recognising this, Bayley and Shearing (2001) laid out a research agenda for policing scholars. This research agenda aimed to capture the full range of agencies that authorise (auspices), and are tasked with (providers), policing roles and functions and to move beyond the research emphasis upon uniformed state police ahead of the multiplicity of non-state policing agencies that the transformations of neo-liberal criminal justice had promulgated.

The police and policing

> [...] the activities that we have come to reference as 'policing' are activities intended to produce interpersonal safety.
>
> (Shearing 2016: 84)

The emphasis placed in this book on restorative policing is but one strand of a process, which Bayley and Shearing (2001) have referred to as the 'multi-lateralization' of policing. This term refers to a process through which a multiplicity of policing agencies have come to challenge the monopolistic position of the state police as providers of security in neo-liberal societies, through a proliferation of both 'auspices' (i.e. those agencies who authorise and regulate the delivery of policing services) and 'providers' (i.e. any agency that provides policing services across the statutory, commercial and voluntary sectors). 'Auspices' of policing include, although are not limited to: government bodies, local authorities, commercial regulatory agencies and voluntary codes of practice. In a restorative policing context, 'providers' include, although need not be limited to, a mixture of police officers, community safety officers, local government, NGOs and volunteers. Use of the term 'the governance of security' generates a picture of top-down governance processes but this terminology also seeks to include security that emerges from below.

It is worth recalling from Chapter 2 that within this conceptualisation of the governance of security, we must think about 'policing' as a process, or a mode of social control, which is conceptually separate from 'the police' as an institution who are responsible for specific policing activities (Bayley and Shearing 2001). The separation made by restorative justice scholars between restorative policing/practice and the broader activities of the police fails to recognise that restorative policing is a separate policing process undertaken by a hybrid collaboration or partnership that has devolved powers from the state to take responsibility for policing processes, most commonly, at the front end of the criminal justice system. Because of this, the emphasis upon police and police culture that is so evident in the current literature needs to incorporate a more sophisticated appreciation of the culture of hybrid agencies and agents and the mission and purpose that they follow. Without this, the literature is destined to remain limited in its theoretical and explanatory value and the potential of a novel normative standpoint may be overlooked.

Furthermore, given the changes to the configuration of policing and security, restorative policing should be understood as just one strand of these processes of multilateralisation that have impacted upon all areas of policing. This includes, the growth of private policing (Jones and Newburn 2002), the intersection between policing and intelligence (Bigo 2000), the enhanced emphasis placed upon partnership and collaboration (Skinns 2008), which increasingly involves NGOs and the voluntary sector (Jones and Newburn 2006). Collectively, these strands contribute to the governance of security although in individualistic terms they represent just one node in a network of security governance (Johnston and Shearing 2003; Wood and Shearing 2007). The governance of security is produced by an increasingly diverse range of 'policing' providers who, in turn, are regulated by increasingly complex networks of governance. While the state performs a reduced role in quantitative terms, it continues to perform a leading qualitative role in constructing policing and security assemblages (Shearing 2016) such as those in the frame of analysis within this book. Analysis of nodal networks of policing unveils a patchwork of security that is similar in its unevenness to that encountered in the case studies of restorative policing investigated here. A neo-feudal (Shaering and Stenning 1983) melange emerges with inequitable access to policing and security. While for many the response to unequal access has been to promote the role of the state (Loader and Walker 2007), for restorative policing, it is at this point that interest in collective efficacy emerges with its potential to generate security from below to build capacity and strengthen weaker security nodes. As such, the work of many restorative scholars is both complementary to and should be informed by the work on nodal governance. With a complementary perspective to that developed by Shearing (2016), Braithwaite (2004) draws on Foucault's metaphor of multiple networks of power to focus upon ways in which those who have security deficits can be nudged into building their capacity (Thaler and Sunstein 2008; Froestad and Shearing 2013). Indeed, these insights will further inform the discussion of implementation issues that appear later in Chapter 7.

Within these regulatory networks, central governments continue to focus upon the provision of punitive sovereign techniques or coercive law enforcement, which seeks to maintain sovereign control of populations and territory (Stenson 2005), whilst new and increasingly disparate modes of policing are undertaken by a range of agencies in addition to the police. In consequence of these developments, the responsibility for regulating interpersonal safety via the spatial distribution of individuals across time and space is sub-contracted to the voluntary and commercial sectors that take on this outsourced, sovereign function. It is as yet unclear to what extent these sub-contracted sovereign functions are different to traditional state policing in mentality, purpose and technologies of implementation. There is a requirement for new research to address the impact of these changes upon those involved in restorative policing, particularly when exploring the impact of culture and ideology upon policy implementation.

The continued restructuring and reshaping of policing across the globe has required police organisations, policy-makers and academics to think about policing and security in new and innovative ways. As contemporary policing agents of sovereign governments struggle to maintain a sense of control over 'problem neighbourhoods' and 'crime hotspots' within a climate of heightened uncertainty regarding the threat of international terrorism and transnational organised crime, state resources become stretched. These enhanced and evolving demands made upon high policing, that are threats to national security, stimulate a need for innovations in low policing, such as the demand for community policing (Brodeur 1983, 2010). Financial constraints lead to security deficits that help to produce new configurations of policing that bubble up in between the gaps left by state institutions. In response to the changes, the early twenty-first century bore witness to a burgeoning of theoretical discourse that concerns 'policing' and 'security', understood sometimes as a public good (Loader and Walker 2007) and, at other times, as a commodity that can be bought and sold (Johnston and Shearing 2003), as well as the implications this presents for contemporary reconfigurations of policing. Most significantly, security is no longer seen principally as the function of the sovereign nation state and traditional large public sector institutions no longer maintain a privileged position in providing security. New security nodes form the voluntary and commercial sectors sometimes display different policing mentalities and can, despite benevolent multi-agency discourses, have divergent purposes to well established criminal justice institutions. It should therefore come as no surprise to find a tension between the purposes of some areas of state policing and the newly emergent nodes of restorative policing.

This challenge to the sovereign primacy of state police institutions was initially driven by new right governments who wanted to decrease the size of the state. From the mid-1980s in the UK, government policy documents, reports by chief constables and political party manifestos indicated that government agencies (including the police) could not, by themselves, succeed in controlling crime (Leishman *et al.* 1996). Much more aggressively in the US, a strong private security industry consolidated its position as a provider of policing services that supplemented and sometimes replaced state policing agencies (Paterson 2012). In Australia, the policy dominance of community policing encouraged new community-based partnerships as the solution to issues of police legitimacy, but the primacy of state agencies remained (Putt 2010). Across each country, and in different cultural forms, a multi-agency approach to reducing crime and social problems emerged that called on a range of policing agencies to understand the social causes of crime and, collaboratively, to implement workable and evidenced-based solutions (for a discussion of evidenced based policing and crime reduction see Bullock and Tilley 2009).

This macro governance perspective highlights the socio-political changes that led to the reconfiguration of policing and which enabled commercial and voluntary modes of policing to flourish. In England and Wales much emphasis has been placed on the need for third sector community-based solutions whereas in the US, the market in security has favoured commercial sector solutions. This analysis helps to explain the more systematic adoption of restorative policing in England and Wales due to an ideological preference for voluntary and NGO-delivered policing compared to the uneven development of restorative policing in the US where the cultural emphasis on law enforcement has favoured commercial solutions from the private security industry that tend to focus on situational crime prevention. In Australia, there has been an oscillation between the service and force ethic of policing and this has presented an obstacle to the extent of reconfiguration in the shape of policing and the development of new partnership models. As Carpenter *et al.* (2016) note, there is limited reference within studies of policing across Australasia to the methods of developing collaborative models of policing with partners from other sectors or evaluating their impact upon crime and disorder. In all instances, the strategy of 'responsibilisation' (Garland 1996) involves the state retaining control of its traditional penal function (through police, courts, prisons) whilst at the same time engaging non-state agencies in the reduction and prevention of crime and disorder.

Despite there being similarities in global shifts for neoliberal states, it is important not to over-estimate or assume similarities in the impact of these shifts due to local differences and their specific political, social and cultural contexts. One specific challenge to the market model of multi-lateralisation is that state agencies in neo-liberal societies continue to perform a more significant and qualitatively different role to other nodes of crime control (Stenson 2005). A competing theoretical explanation concerning changes in policing can be provided through the Foucauldian perspective on sovereign 'biopolitics' (Foucault 1991): how the state seeks to influence the emergence of policing and security networks with the purpose of fostering good social order. Hence, an emphasis upon 'biopolitics' encourages investigation of the complex strategies that link macro-level attempts to manage collective risks to society to micro-level analysis of demands for security that emanate out of communities (Ericson and Haggarty 1997; Stenson 1998). This perspective is particularly useful for understanding restorative policing where success is determined by forces that emerge both 'from above' (i.e. the state) and 'from below' (i.e. the community).

Analysis of the political struggle over sovereignty, policing and security in neoliberal societies should be viewed as a core component of the ongoing struggle for control of territory and populations by a host of informal agencies of governance in civil society. This analytical perspective views the struggle for sovereignty as a set of processes involving a range of rival sites of governance with different conceptions of the purpose of policing, security and interpersonal safety. Rival sites of governance are thus involved in shifting alliances with the state and a plethora of other agencies, or interest groups with the aim of furthering their own interests and values, in alignment with and alongside changes in sovereign law and the reform of state institutions (Stenson 2001). The shape of restorative policing is produced through this process. The state is not passive, it helps to generate the market space for voluntary agents and organisations to enter the crime control system and questions can remain about the capacity of these new agents to deliver sovereign justice without the support of the state. Following on from this argument, while restorative policing is often understood by outsiders as an evolution of community and problem-oriented policing, its successful development is dependent upon the development of a mutual understanding of its role(s) and purpose(s) by state police and associated implementing organisations that are tasked with the translation of restorative policing ideals into effective multi-agency policing practice.

Transformations in the shape and purpose of policing

Post-modern shifts in the demands made on policing organisations have meant that they are increasingly required to grapple with the question, 'what should the delivery of justice entail?' What is, or should, the police role in this process be? As the previous section has outlined, the work of Clifford Shearing and a range of colleagues explores these issues and raises questions about who the most legitimate sources of policing and authority are in post-modern contexts and how should they be organised as part of a nodal structure of governance (Shearing and Johnston 2003). Shearing (2005) bemoans the emphasis placed by scholars upon uniformed state police ahead of broader conceptual notions of policing, which has led to insufficient analysis of new and emerging mentalities, institutions and technologies across the landscape of policing and criminal justice. As the previous chapters have illustrated, restorative policing draws on both new and emerging mentalities and technologies (e.g. conferencing) of policing that are yet to be consolidated and are rarely subjected to detailed inquiry. This raises implementation challenges for the effective working of new hybrid policing collaborations.

It is easy to forget that outside the Anglo-American bubble of wealth and prosperity pluralised forms of policing with an emphasis upon non-state actors still preside due to the absence or unreliability of centralised policing capacity. Taking such a comparative perspective provides a reminder that there is a philosophical assumption underpinning neoliberal policing that the state will take the lead. An appreciation of this assumption is central to understanding the development of restorative policing and explains why there is often public acceptance of police involvement despite the theoretical and ideological protestations of some within the restorative justice community. This challenge is visible in many studies of restorative policing, which remain focused upon front-line police work rather than the broader myriad of agencies and community linkages that facilitate restorative policing. This situation is not new. As we have already noted, the evolution of both community and problem-oriented policing approaches have been plagued by challenges in developing balanced and meaningful partnerships as well as shared leadership across agencies. The historical emphasis upon centralisation and hierarchy means that police leadership, cultures and traditions can act as obstacles to reform and collaboration (Flynn and Herrington 2015; Holland 2007), particularly as one of the central ideological roles of policing agencies is to take control of problematic situations on behalf of sovereign authorities (Bittner 1970; Brodeur 2010). Hence, there is often a cultural challenge to collaboration presented by traditional command and control ways of thinking about and doing policing.

Furthermore, the centrality of crime fighting and law enforcement to perspectives, both internally and externally, of the police has meant that the shifts in mentalities required to support approaches to peace-keeping and community crime prevention have remained incomplete. Thus, policing continues to be categorised by complexity and discordance with regard to both its purposes and its relationship with other organisations. This complexity is augmented by an increasingly risk-conscious and information-rich public, which impacts upon police thinking. Increased investment into, and government control of, policing has inadvertently drawn police agencies away from communities as they have focused upon communities as problems to be solved via improvements in police efficiency and effectiveness. For communities, this has meant that expectations of police organisations have grown and the commodification of police services has led to a cultural process whereby many individuals and communities are increasingly unwilling to address problems of crime and disorder thus generating further expectancy upon the state and reduced capacity within communities. This runs contrary to the aims of restorative justice, which seeks to return conflicts to those involved in an incident and away from the public realm (Christie 1977). It is therefore important to acknowledge that restorative policing raises important political and ideological questions about the administration of policing, security and justice. To paraphrase Moore and Forsythe (1995: 3); is restorative policing a new management tool or a genuine attempt to decentralise, deprofessionalise and democratise community-policing processes?

The deprofessionalisation of criminal justice has directly impacted upon the configuration of police and policing and accelerated growth in civil and voluntary modes of policing. The emphasis placed by proponents of restorative justice upon informal, local dispute resolution is one that would be recognised and supported by many police officers as indicative of traditional policing activities whose loss was bemoaned during the two decades of 'managerialism' and performance targets which dictated police practice but is now heading into a period of retrenchment. Critiques of the performance era now abound (for example, see Eterno and Silverman 2012) and a culture shift is evident within many police organisations that encourages a less technocratic emphasis on crime and detection metrics. In the twenty-first century, a renewed focus on the importance of procedural justice in building public confidence and legitimacy for police actions as well as the central role of police officer discretion in the administration of justice in local contexts has emerged which has helped shape the context in which restorative policing has emerged. Shearing's main interest is the macro level shape and function of the new configuration of policing and, as a consequence of this, the implications for police and societal interpretations of the purpose of policing are not assessed and evaluated in empirical terms at the street-level.

Transformations in the policing of communities

Given that police intervention is always morally problematic there is longstanding agreement that liberal models of policing should be founded upon a principle of minimal intervention (Berkeley 1969) and that, to be just, police action and protection should be distributive rather than allocative. The allocative approach reproduces inequalities, injustice and privilege (Ericson 1982; Manning 2010: ix) when, in democratic terms, each citizen has the same claim to equal rights and protection. Following on from this, Sklansky (2005) notes that as policing itself is a form of social redistribution then democratic principles should be enacted to address any likelihood of the police protective function metamorphosing into something more coercive. This represents a direct challenge to traditional reactive and offender-oriented models of policing.

In a democratic society, the provision of police protection should be underpinned by broad questions of equality, security, opportunity and access to collective goods (Sklansky 2005), which means that wherever the police serve to amplify inequality and insecurity then their role should be minimised. This perspective provides a normative position for the police's public protection purpose whereby all police activity should be subject to the principle of minimal intervention and where police activity is harmful it should be stopped or handed over to alternative agencies that will be tasked with negotiating security and order. Manning notes, following Rawls' (1971) difference principle, that where socioeconomic and political inequality is at its most extreme there should be an expectation that public offices act in favour of the least advantaged in society. This presents a challenge to policing agencies that have historically been tasked with the regulation of the least advantaged and most vulnerable on behalf of the more privileged (Emsley 1991).

Rawls' (1971) provides us with a theory for doing just public protection and policing that is underpinned by an assumption that democratic citizens are rational, reasonable and willing to believe in just institutions. This trust is strengthened when the trust is reciprocated and, through a reflexive and dynamic process, trust between citizens and institutions is built alongside a mutual sense of protection and security. The successes of community policing have often been evidenced in geographical areas where trust and collective efficacy are already high (Skogan 1999), yet in many areas trust and security remain low. It is in these areas that the demand for public protection is often highest and alternative policing strategies are required to address the democratic deficit that is experienced by its citizens. Under these conditions, alternative policing strategies may be required to produce just outcomes and to avoid exclusionary or authoritarian policing (Taylor 2012). The potential of restorative policing as an alternative policing response to security and justice deficits in neoliberal contexts has relevance here.

Thus far, policing has been conceptualised in a top-down manner whereby political and policy elites configure policing on behalf of communities rather than from a more democratic and participatory perspective in which the potential of communities to make decisions on their own behalf is evaluated (Moore and Forsythe 1995; Sklansky 2005). A focus on the reconfiguration of policing and restorative justice has the potential to place 'justice' and the 'difference principle' at the heart of policing philosophies and strategies and to facilitate an understanding of restorative policing as an approach that attempts to address issues of injustice, harm and social reintergration from the bottom-up (Sampson *et al.* 1997; Loader 2006). Within this context, the role of the police remains largely symbolic and recalls the work of Durkheim (1912) on the destabilising impact of modernity and industrialisation and the associated demands for justice and security from the public that accompany this (Loader and Mulcahy 2003; Loader and Walker 2007). There is empirical evidence from restorative policing experiments to support this Durkheimian line of theoretical enquiry, drawing on the work of Sampson and Groves (1989), Moore and Forsythe (1995) and Bazemore (2000a). This line of inquiry has not been picked up, or at least pursued with vigour, by academics for the last 15 years and the remaining chapters in this book attempt to reinvigorate this particular framing of 'restorativeness' within the contours of contemporary changes to the governance of policing and security.

Through analysis of the purposes of policing, restorative policing can be understood as combining both micro-level processes such as conferences and mediation with meso and macro-level policy that prioritises peace-keeping and community crime prevention via formal and informal modes of policing (Bazemore 2000a: 232). This conceptualisation recognises the long held, although much contested, principle that democratic policing takes place with the consent of the policed, the 'willing co-operation' (Peel's third principle) of the public and seeks, as its primary purpose, to address the issue of justice. Therefore restorative policing should be focused on the least advantaged communities that have historically been the target of more coercive strategies and should not, as is often the case, rest on its laurels of public reassurance in, often privileged, low crime communities (Skogan *et al.* 1999).

The preference of the authors for the term 'restorative policing' recognises the central role played by the police in restorative practices that focus on diversion and informal social control in company with an underpinning philosophy that recognises the value of restorative approaches in helping to build community capital that leads to lower rates of offending (Sampson *et al.* 1997; Sampson and Laub 2003). Part of the attraction of restorative justice for individuals and communities is that it re-engages them in the process of justice and attempts to address the harm produced by conflict. In short, restorative justice encourages active citizens to 'do justice'. As justice remains a largely undertheorised aspect of policing it should come as no surprise to find uncertainty and tension amongst both police officers and hybrid policing agencies about the use of restorative approaches as organisational missions and purposes are challenged.

Implications for restorative policing

It is at the juncture between the much investigated formal and less studied informal modes of policing that restorative policing emerges with its myriad of actors that incorporates both the activities of the police plus those of a range of policing nodes or agencies from the statutory, voluntary and commercial sector. Critics of Bayley and Shearing (2001) have argued that their network of policing nodes fails to capture the continued pre-eminence of sovereign states in shaping and delivering policing yet they identified an emergent trajectory through which restorative policing evolved and this has been recognised in more recent work (for example, Shearing 2016). The important role played by the state is evident in the case of restorative policing which, despite its roots in informal social structures, remains delivered through sovereign legal frameworks, and sovereign government auspices, across neo-liberal societies even when the majority of providers are from other sectors (Shearing 2016).

Drawing on Bayley and Shearing's research agenda for this new configuration of policing, questions emerge about new or evolving mentalities, auspices and providers, and their technologies and techniques of policing. Therefore, key manifestations in the reconfiguration of policing and the neo-liberal rolling back of sovereign state functions for restorative policing include: (1) changes in the police role which resulted in an ongoing service-force tension within and across policing agencies; (2) the emergence of hybrid agencies/collaborations with new purposes and mentalities; (3) questions about the capacity of communities, voluntary organisations and the commercial sector to manage new roles and functions; and (4) ongoing diversification and adaptation in the shape of policing. Each of these areas will now be further explored in turn.

The changing police role: service or force?

The ongoing restructuring and rebranding of police forces as police services that are locally-focused, community-oriented and citizen-engaged, highlights the tensions between force and service orientations within police agencies. The cultural responses to this tension are by no means uniform with the United States and the United Kingdom adopting sharply differentiated notions of community policing and the Australian police oscillating between 'force' and 'service' identities. Similarly, police organisations may demonstrate a much more localised and community-oriented nature whilst simultaneously bolstering and centralising their law enforcement policing functions. Despite these differences, the twin drivers for community-oriented reforms across all these countries are a desire to increase public confidence in the police and an acknowledgement of the state's limited capacity to manage problems of crime and disorder by itself. The political emphasis placed upon the importance of 'community' in public policy, coupled with the focus on moral authoritarianism and communitarian values, has helped promote the profile of restorative justice as a facilitator of a service mentality within policing yet there remains much inconsistency in how this is translated into practice. This inconsistency, and the potential for dissonance between values and practice, is characteristic of the broader fields of both policing and restorative justice with their strong cultural emphasis upon localised programmes and the associated difficulties of oversight and quality assurance (Acton 2015). It should be noted that these tensions cannot be simplified into arguments for or against restorative policing. Instead, they represent a manifestation of the contradictory demands placed upon police organisations facing the dual demands of force and service. This is evident in restorative policing practice where organisational demands and an emphasis upon law enforcement can seep into the logic of restorative practice.

The enhanced emphasis placed upon proactive peace-keeping and crime prevention across neo-liberal jurisdictions represents a return to the aims of policing as outlined by nineteenth century police innovators coupled with recognition of the limitations of an over-reliance upon responsive modes of policing and an enhanced focus upon proactive crime prevention. Taking a comparative perspective, it is clear that this situation represents a radical and ongoing transformation for the policing role across neoliberal societies and one that has not yet been clearly articulated in terms of the skills needed to successfully interpret and undertake this evolving role in innovative ways. It is here that there is a disjuncture in the Anglo-American model of policing as police officers are recruited to, trained towards, and acculturated within police organisations that emphasise law enforcement, crime and its control. Police training and education place an emphasis on the law, its application, and self-defence and sends out a message to officers that they should prioritise crime fighting, order maintenance and law enforcement ahead of proactive crime prevention. Thus, it should come as no surprise that attempts to implement community policing encounter significant institutional obstacles. The mundane nature of much crime prevention and peace-keeping work can gather little traction with front line police officers when it is not situated within an overarching purpose or philosophy that elevates its importance for those involved. By placing an emphasis on restoration, as a purpose of community policing, and as the basis for both making and keeping the peace it becomes possible to reinvigorate and reconceptualise Peel's vision of proactive community policing for the twenty-first century.

While peace-keeping is now a term closely associated with international policing initiatives, it has a long resonance within domestic policing that goes back to the academic work of Michael Banton (1964) in the United States and United Kingdom and, conceptually, to Peel's founding principles of 1829 in England and Wales which later influenced professional models of policing in the United States, Australia and Canada. It has been widely acknowledged that the latter part of the twentieth century saw Anglo-American policing agencies drift away from both the preventive mission and the strategy of engaging with the public in a civil manner which utilised minimal intervention (Grimshaw and Jefferson 1987; Hall *et al.* 1978; Sklansky 2005). In the early part of the twenty-first century considerable efforts were put in to addressing issues of public approval and police legitimacy but they continued to emphasise governance strategies that should be done to the public (Bazemore 2000). More subtly, the second decade of the twenty-first century has also witnessed a renewed focus on police officer discretion, civility and the use of soft skills that has been largely influenced by the work of Tom Tyler (1990) and which links neatly to the purpose of restorative policing.

The tension between a police force and service will be ever-present. When contemporary modes of high policing focus upon combating cyber security, counter terrorism, illicit trafficking of goods and people and the causes of crime at the global level this generates further demands for security and community involvement at the local level. While modes of high policing rest within the control of government (Brodeur 1983; 2010), the generation, maintenance and configuration of day-to-day policing and social control is subject to social, cultural and political changes that mould the contemporary networks of low policing that exist at any given time. This is a dynamic and ever-evolving process of biopolitics. A sense of inequity or an absence of trust in police action, governance or accountability in one area generates the space for other, potentially more just, modes of policing to emerge and evolve. Community policing initially emerged against a backcloth of crises in police legitimacy across neo-liberal states and the shift to a service orientation that community-oriented approaches advocate remains incomplete. Furthermore, the local-global interface of individual ontological security and national security places further demands upon the incomplete transition to active community policing and, in resource terms, leads to insufficient capacity for police organisations to respond to these issues which will continue to impact upon the police role.

New hybrid agencies and collaborations

Configurations of policing and security evolve, adapt and mutate within each specific social, cultural and political context. Models of Anglo-American policing emerged from locally focused and administered systems that aligned with the legal, political, socio-cultural and ideological aspects of contemporary liberal democratic society with its emphasis on democratic localism and decentralised accountability. The policing that emerged thus reflected this conceptualisation of democratic politics and its associated modes of generating and maintaining security and order. Until recently, new approaches to crime control in the community would have been considered the province of a state service yet the involvement of locally focused voluntary agencies has accelerated and (re)consolidated itself within a relatively short time. This raises some interesting questions concerning the emergence and ownership of jurisdiction between the state, non-state and hybrid agencies. The development of new modes of policing, including restorative policing, involves complex national and local political struggles and shifting alliances, which influence the shape of new modes of policing.

Policing can be understood both through an analysis of the underlying context which produces and reproduces these networks of policing (an area of inquiry that has been subjected to much research) and through examination of the conditions in which policing takes place (an area subject to much less inquiry). In order to make sense of these processes it is essential to emphasise agency, how actors make sense of the conditions within which they act, and to recognise the conflict experienced throughout the introduction and development of new modes of policing as a contest over who delivers and administers justice. This includes the process of role adaptation and the experience of consolidating new roles. Opposition to new modes of policing arise from a questioning of the legitimacy of voluntary organisations to undertake sovereign decision-making and to engage in new collaborative partnerships. Disputes arise concerning the legitimacy of different organisations to act as sub-contracted providers of policing services and to pursue their own specific organisational goals. As newcomers, practitioners with recently established, evolving or hybrid roles have to build up their professional authority in the eyes of offenders, the more established criminal justice professional agents, and the wider public. While there is much literature documenting debates about the reconfiguration of policing, little discussion has taken place concerning how ideological arguments about the legitimacy of the role of voluntary organisations within new hybrid collaborations impacts upon practical organisational developments. The emergence of new hybrid agents and agencies makes it essential to investigate the situated social practice, or 'habitus' (Bourdieu 1980), of human agents and their new hybrid agencies in different local contexts in order to make sense of the ways in which policy is put into practice. This is an idea that has been explored by Lipsky (1980) who argues that the primary allegiance of public sector workers is to their peer group rather than to the organisation as a whole. The implications of the establishment of new hybrid modes of policing and the requirement for further research is addressed in the final chapters.

Responsibilisation and community capacity

There has been sustained recognition across criminal justice and policing that the purpose of crime prevention can be met with less input from formal state agencies as long as community justice and crime control agencies can be 'responsibilised' to contribute to the management of crime and disorder. The historical dominance of deterrence and rehabilitative models of policing and punishment was unable to address consistent growth in crime rates and an associated expansion of crime control systems throughout the second part of the twentieth century (Christie 1993; Cohen 1985; Simon 2006), which became economically and ideologically unsustainable when faced with the financial challenges of the early twenty-first century.

There are clear and distinct commonalities that exist within contemporary political discourse in the fields of restorative justice, criminal justice and policing surrounding active citizen participation, social inclusion, community cohesion and improved informal social controls that ultimately aim to foster more civilised, self-regulating conduct amongst citizens. Attempts to promote greater citizen participation in policing are just one component of broader attempts to reassert the central role of the community in policing and to recapture the essence of Peel's enduring principles of a 'civic' police. One of the benefits of the burgeoning research on non-police policing has been recognition of the key role the police play in developing new policing or security assemblages (Ericson and Haggerty 1997; Brodeur 2010), often under the slogan of community policing. Hence, state police agencies in neoliberal states continue to play a central role in the coordination of policing services but they no longer necessarily occupy the Hobbesian position as governors of security despite occupying the symbolic and cultural ownership of this position.

The conceptual links between policing and good order hark back to the work of La Mare (1722) in France who conceived 'police' as being generated by local and central government alongside civil society with all three nodes demonstrating collective responsibility for the generation and maintenance of good social order. This concept of 'police' is much broader than many contemporary commentators acknowledge. Thus, an emphasis on policing as peace-keeping has been historically grounded in a bottom-up process through which trust in policing and other modes of social control are built up in societies (Loader and Walker 2007). Following on from this, the basis for the emergence and success of any formal or informal policing structure is trust in impersonal authority (Manning 2010: 9) and institutional structures that credibly maintain the public peace as well as symbolic and cultural capital (Loader and Mulcahy 2003). From a restorative policing perspective, the political question that emerges in response to this is which structures, rather than public officials, will best enable communities to make decisions about the governance of justice and security (Moore and Forsythe 1995). Any form of police or policing will be challenged when there is a failure to build trust in this process.

Communities have enormous potential to generate and sustain social capital with leadership that draws the relevant components from local economic and cultural capital together (Bourdieu 1980; Sampson and Graif 2009). When strong neighbourhoods emerge within cities, they can create networks of information that hold influence over neighbourhoods in surprising ways (Johnson 2010). Shearing points to the extent of dispute resolution that has always taken place in the shadow of the law at the local level and without formal recourse to police interventions (Bayley and Shearing 1996: 586). This work recalls that of Nils Christie (1977) with his emphasis upon the informality of everyday order maintenance. Therefore, with restorative policing the objective is to push forward a shift in both power and responsibility towards neighbourhood groups who are tasked with policing functions. Police officers play a key facilitative role in this process but there remains much uncertainty, amongst police and communities, about the extent to which this shift in power and responsibility can be achieved.

The potential of diversion, particularly for low-level, first time young offenders, has become increasingly embedded within thinking about community crime prevention, as has the perspective that victims should have a voice in the processes of justice (Moore and Forsythe 1995). Within this context, the idea of restorative justice, as a structure for the bottom-up governance of security, has become increasingly popular, although it has often been digested, and regurgitated, via the top-down offender-focused philosophies of criminal justice professionals rather than concerns that emerge out of communities. This is particularly evident in restorative policing where an emphasis upon preventing crime is central to the symbolic police role and manifests itself in the police use of discretion to regulate the gateway to criminal justice rather than building community capacity to manage problems of crime and disorder.

Because of this, there has been much fragmentation and unevenness in restorative policing projects that do not have central coordinating drivers. In England

and Wales, this is partly a consequence of the cultural and symbolic value of constabulary independence and the localised nature of policy implementation across 43 separate forces. This geographical unevenness is even more evident in the US where the use of restorative justice is sporadic and spread across 18,000 separate police forces, thus inhibiting the potential for coordinated political support. The inconsistency emerges out of the differentiated emphasis placed upon community-oriented initiatives, often due to the different modes of funding as well as existing ideological and organisational affiliations with problem-solving approaches.

Ongoing diversification and adaptation

According to Neocleous (2006: 17), 'most research on the police has eschewed any attempt to make sense of the concept itself or to explore the possible diversity of police powers in terms of either their historical origins or political diversity'. Because of this, there is often an absence of recognition of the historically plural nature of policing. The emergence of Peel's professional police was, at least in part, a response to anxiety from the privileged classes about the failure of those plural networks of policing to manage working class criminality and associated ontological insecurity. Similarly, the rise of commercial crime prevention during the post-Second World War period, and then more rapidly from the early 1980s, was a response to public and political dissatisfaction with the police's response to three decades worth of rising crime (Jones and Newburn 2002). The 2008 economic crisis stimulated further re-evaluation of the configuration of policing as the impunity of the financial elite was followed by a run of scandals involving politicians, the media and police officers and a questioning of the police's suitability to investigate crimes of the powerful. These examples support Liang's (1992) assertion that democratic police are both moulded and restrained by a combination of competition from other modes of policing, citizen resistance and social change.

Yet, most of police history from the twentieth century was grounded in state-centred models of professional policing that regarded nineteenth century developments as either a civil and organic response to the problem of crime and urbanisation or attempts to control an increasingly politicised and unruly working class. Both Colquhoun (1796) and Bentham (1791) envisaged a new administrative science of deterrence by surveillance as part of the civilising process of urbanising societies. This thinking had significant influence over the formation of the professional police in England and Wales in 1829 and diffused into the other models of Anglo-American policing that emerged during the nineteenth century. The question of how best to sustain order in societies was broached from a more insightful sociological perspective by Durkheim (1893: 193) who, similarly, saw the breakdown of traditional models of community surveillance taking place as a response to urbanisation but, in an important differentiation, also acknowledged the requirement for different mechanisms of maintaining order as an ongoing and ever-evolving challenge for societies. Thus, Durkheim provides us with a framework for a much more dynamic criminological appreciation of the changes that helped establish professional police agencies but which continues to evolve, with state-centre policing as but one point in a long history of the governance of security.

In twenty-first century democratic societies order maintenance is the responsibility of an increasingly broad array of nodes acting under the conceptual auspice of policing. This includes, formal police agencies, commercial security, local government officials, charities, pressure groups and voluntary agencies, amongst many others. This perpetual state of networked policing flux has been recognised across a range of recent reports that drew inspiration from the 1999 Patten Report on security governance in Northern Ireland and which include the Canadian Report on the Future of Policing (2014) and the Stevens' Report (2013) on the future of policing in England and Wales. The political question raised by these reports is 'how can public authority's best co-ordinate the policing resources that are available to them to generate good order, and who should fund this?' These reports draw on Shearing's challenge to the social and cultural misnomer that the police are policing and that they alone hold a monopoly over coercive force.

In direct opposition to this monopolistic perspective, the police are subject to the same market forces as any other economic object and may grow, whither, centralise and fragment at any given point. If state police do not provide a service that fully meets the aims and purpose of policing then other new modes of policing will emerge. The question of who helps to generate good social order is therefore political, ideological and economic and subject to change at different historical points. The purpose of policing is not to reproduce order (Ericson 1982) but to redistribute social order with an emphasis on equity and social justice. It is this latter issue that is most challenging and problematic for plural mechanisms of policing as distributive and restorative approaches to maintaining order tend to be regarded, at least by those who govern from the top-down, as a democratic luxury rather than as an essential component of the governance of security and order.

Notwithstanding these challenges, restorative policing and other partnership problem-solving strategies help us envisage the continued diversification and adaptation of problem-oriented policing strategies whereby responsibility for informal social control is increasingly devolved back to individual citizens, local communities and voluntary organisations in a multitude of different ways where the research evidence supports such an approach (Crawford and Clear 2001). This latter part of Goldstein's problem-oriented argument is often underplayed – that he saw problem-oriented approaches as embracing a multitude of organisations that would contribute to the resolution of crime problems both in partnership with the police and on behalf of them. Goldstein remained frustrated at the partial implementation of problem-oriented policing and the failure of police organisations to fully embrace, in ideological terms, the approach that he was advocating (2010: 13). The simultaneous growth in evidence-based thinking, if not yet always practice, across neoliberal states seems to indicate that this trajectory towards greater diversification and adaptation will continue as police agencies assess, evaluate, monitor and modify strategies and tactics that have been used for many years. It is at this point that our interest turns towards how these changes will influence the possible futures of policing.

Mapping the futures of policing

The post-modern focus on harnessing informal social controls and communal bonds helps us to foresee a future landscape of policing in which active citizens play an enhanced and more dynamic role in the policing of social order. This vision of policing represents a partial shift in thinking back to pre-modern societies in which systems of informal social control dominated at the local level prior to the establishment of a professional police. However, this vision can also incorporate other judgements on the future shape and prospects of policing. The recognition of the limits of sovereign states in twenty-first century societies and the new modes of governance that it produces encourages us to think about what future shapes and configurations of policing could look like. In his 1998 book, *Understanding Crime Prevention*, Gordon Hughes (1998) identified three possible futures for crime control in societies experiencing post-modern changes and a shift to active citizenship at the same time as an increase in demand for policing resources amongst an anxious and uncertain populace. This section uses Hughes's crime control vision as the parameters for three separate models of the future of policing. The section adapts and updates Hughes's three futures, using an approach previously used by Paterson and Pollock (2010), to situate them in their twenty-first century policing context.

Fortress cities and exclusionary policing

Mike Davis's (1990) 'City of Quartz' remains the most vivid exposition of the threat of exclusionary developments in policing and crime control. Davis's depiction of crime control in Los Angeles revolves around the militarisation of urban policing in a 'fortress city', characterised by 'privatism and social exclusion' (Hughes 1998: 138). In the fortress city, those who have wealth have the power to use exclusionary techniques against 'others', as they create safe and secure private enclaves in suburban areas that are policed by private security personnel. This removes financial support for community policing strategies and encourages urban policing strategies that focus on the management and containment of risks using militarised forms of policing.

Aspects of Davis's Los Angeles have become part of the architecture of crime control in other neoliberal states. The exponential growth of new policing and surveillance technologies, initially in the United Kingdom during the 1990s, but in the United States, Australia and Canada after this, embodies Davis's fear of urban areas becoming characterised by security strategies which focus upon those deemed to be most at risk (Lyon 2003; Zureik and Slater 2005). In this exclusionary future, private modes of policing have become dominant, security has become commodified, and the wealthy purchase security whilst the poor are left exposed to the consequences of crime and disorder. Davis's Neo-Marxist perspective foresees future cities being characterised by a comprehensive architecture of policing and security that is embodied in security patrols, omnipresent surveillance of the kind uncovered by Edward Snowden, and carceral urban design for the poor and 'other', whilst the rich are socially segregated and live in secure gated communities.

In societies that are experiencing a rapid growth in the amount of repressive policing hardware available for the governance of its citizens it becomes increasingly important to defend the need for equal justice and to understand the mechanisms that drive growth and change in policing, in particular the influence of the private security industry. It is clear that unregulated growth in commercial policing presents a potential threat of inequitable policing provision whilst restorative policing represents a potentially more just response to security deficits. By outsourcing or contracting-out services to the commercial sector central government is able to expand the crime control system, and thus meet the political demand for enhancing security, whilst also deviating around economic and fiscal restraints. Nevertheless, there are alternative strategies of governance available which are explored in the next two sections.

High trust active communities and authoritarian communitarianism

Although much has been made in criminological and policing literature of the restructuring of policing it is important not to overstate the extent to which the role of the public police has diminished. State police agencies remain distinct from other policing providers because of their legal powers to use coercive force and their central cultural and symbolic function in the maintenance of social order that separates them from policing agencies from the voluntary and commercial sectors. Both Beck (1992) and Giddens (1990) argue that late modern society is characterised by risk, an absence of trust and ontological insecurity. This presents a challenge to the concept of active citizenship as it points to the detachment of individuals from their community and the breakdown of social ties. Therefore, instead of an active community with strong informal social controls, Beck and Giddens help us to imagine a potential future where communities are supported by a strong authoritarian state, which enforces social control. From this perspective, authoritarian policing reinforces the collective values of active citizenship, which aims to restore order in fractured communities where the informal social controls and traditional social ties that are central to the active community are missing.

Instead of the active community we have 'high trust authoritarian communitarian societies' (Hughes 1998) and strong moral communities supported by a strong authoritarian state. This perspective is tied, in theoretical terms, to Wilson and Kelling's (1982) 'Broken Windows' thesis as it foresees the police retaining a central and symbolic role in the maintenance of social order, much as they have done for the past 200 years, but alongside a multitude of other policing providers. From this perspective the police act as a symbolic authoritarian body that re-asserts the hierarchical and disciplinary nature of society; enforcing social norms where they are perceived to have broken down. In this instance, the hyper-reality of post-modernity means that images and public discourse about policing continue to focus on the important sovereign function of the state and to influence how state institutions and politicians interpret and shape their responses to crime.

Thus, debate about restorative policing initiatives recalls longstanding international debates about democratic policing and the fair and equitable use of police discretion (Grimshaw and Jefferson 1987; Haberfeld and Cerrah 2008; Manning 2010). On one hand, critics target its 'soft' interpretation of the purpose of policing and, on the other hand, proponents support its emphasis upon the creativity and innovation that can emerge from the professional use of police discretion and the 'responsibilisation' of communities. Contemporary discourse in policing promotes the idea of reinvigorating police discretion to free officers up to engage with communities and place less emphasis upon performance targets. This is an approach that is supported by many front-line police officers, but it represents a challenge to the training and development of a generation of police officers whose professional knowledge has been immersed in a target driven culture. A shift from a process-led perspective to one focused on outcomes is commendable yet it runs contrary to police training methodology, which focuses largely on police procedure (Peace, 2006). The cultural shift required here should not be under-estimated and is addressed in detail in Chapter 7. Furthermore, it is important to restate the conflict perspective on the potential pitfalls of too much police discretion. As a consequence of the conflict and violence that lies at the heart of the police role, the history of police–community relations across the globe is littered with social, political, ethnic, racial and gendered conflict (Chan 1996; Haberfeld and Cerrah 2008; Hall *et al.* 1978; Loader and Mulcahy 2003; Manning 2010). This turbulent history indicates that unregulated discretion may lead to restorative policing having an uneven impact across different communities and different sociopolitical contexts as the punitive and authoritarian demands of communities and police officers seep into operational practice and interpretations of community-oriented initiatives.

Towards civic and inclusive restorative policing

Restorative approaches place an emphasis upon the democratic potential of partnership strategies, particularly in terms of building pressure to address crime problems through radical political, social and economic changes that empower citizens and encourage their involvement in policing. This perspective views the processes of globalisation as generating a renewed focus on local community engagement and the creation of 'civic and inclusive safe cities' (Hughes 1998: 146) that is exemplified by the evolution of restorative policing. The drivers here are a desire to increase community confidence in the police, stimulate informal responses to crime problems, reinvigorate police discretion and reduce costs as part of a tacit acknowledgement of the state's limited capacity to manage problems of crime and disorder by itself. This policy focuses attempts to improve police legitimacy through the enhancement of democratic structures that rebuild what Durkheim (1893) referred to as organic solidarity but which many contemporary scholars explain through the more complex discourse of social capital and collective efficacy. Rebuilding and maintaining organic solidarity is much simpler in small communities where community capital remains high but it is much more challenging in complex and diverse urban settings where the majority of police resources are focused.

There is strong evidence that community involvement in the process of justice aids public confidence in the police (Bazemore 2000a; Rix *et al.* 2009) and that restorative policing strategies will free up police officer time to provide a more visible presence on the streets. Restorative policing can thus save substantial resources that will allow police organisations to enhance visibility while improving public confidence through a greater emphasis on procedural justice and positive community engagement. This raises questions, once again, about the future shape of policing. Evidence has demonstrated that the public are supportive of the police role during restorative processes yet police officers are recruited, trained and acculturated to very different styles of policing. Given their sovereign position, questions remain about the extent to which the police will be willing to delegate key duties to other agencies and the capacity of those agents in responding to this challenge. The rest of this book addresses this challenge by identifying clear conceptual and theoretical links between restorative justice and policing (Chapter 6) and assessing their implications for the implementation of restorative policing (Chapter 7).

From contextualisation to transformation

Core elements of restorative policing continue to recall Sir Robert Peel's ninth principle of policing; 'the test of police efficiency is the absence of crime and disorder, not the visible evidence of police action in dealing with it' (Reith 1948: n.p.). While contemporary historians have challenged Peel's authorship of the policing principles[1] this nineteenth-century preventative vision of the police officer role remains woven into community policing philosophies despite cultural challenges from the divergent emphases upon national security, complex global crimes and local crime recording practices. The development of community policing and problem-oriented policing philosophies and strategies has encountered significant ideological and organisational challenges, yet they have slowly seeped into the working ethos of police organisations and paved the way for the more radical changes involved with restorative policing. This may not always have been done in the way Goldstein (2010), or many restorative justice advocates may have imagined, but the perception of police officers as collaborative problem-solvers of micro-crises has become commonplace.

These changes have been an essential response to questions surrounding policing, democracy and social justice (Sklansky 2005; Manning 2001). The historical absence of emphasis upon repeat victimisation had left a range of vulnerable populations with a security deficit yet policy trajectories across criminal justice systems increasingly emphasise victims' interests and the emotional and psychological benefits of victim-oriented policy. Clark (2005: 650), from a United States perspective, refers to 'victim-centred policing' as 'law enforcement and community based practices, which prevent primary or secondary victimization, and which reduce the effects of victimization upon the community'. Alarid and Montemayor (2012) identify clear links between Clark's description of 'victim-centred policing' and Bazemore and Griffiths's conceptualisation of restorative policing via the enhanced emphasis placed upon

> the tools or levers for building social capital and efficacy around the direct response to specific incidents of crime, conflict and harm … *(and)* at the case level a decision-making role for citizens in formal sanctioning and the effective resolution of individual incidents of crime.
>
> (2003: 337)

Thus, any understanding of restorative policing should be underpinned by an appreciation of crime as both a cause and effect of weakened relationships and informal social controls that can be addressed when interested stakeholders meet with the intention of addressing the harm caused and resolving conflict. For police officers, this represents an inversion of their traditional adversarial role as it is members of the community who will lead any restorative intervention. Police officers are therefore required to act as change agents (Wood *et al.* 2008) who endorse diversion from formal criminal justice processes; this is a process, which requires a fundamental shift in the meaning of police work for many organisations, but this is a shift that is already emerging through innovative police practice in a number of areas. Challenges in interpreting the purpose of restorative policing remain and present obstacles to effective implementation. As such, we seek to further consolidate and further develop our conceptualisations of restorative policing in the following chapter.

Note

1 These were most likely to have been written by Richard Mayne, or his co-commissioner Charles Rowan, and were first published by Charles Reith in 1958. Despite this, they are still known as Peel's principles of policing (Lentz and Chaires 2007).

6 Towards a 'transformative' vision of restorative policing

Building social capital from 'within' and from 'below'

Introduction

This chapter further develops and grounds restorative policing within the context of the changes that have been outlined in the previous chapter in two ways. First, restorative policing is viewed as a new mode of governing crime, which Garland (1996) refers to as a 'responsibilisation strategy', which seeks to stimulate new forms of behaviour and to halt negative ones. Second, restorative policing is viewed as a framework through which to further develop the function of the police as a social agent that is increasingly reliant on partnerships to more effectively prevent and respond to crime (Faulkner 2003). As such, we view restorative policing simultaneously as a criminal and non-criminal method of intervention that seeks to promote beneficial forms of *social capital*. In seeking to further articulate our vision, we acknowledge the limit of what can realistically be achieved within an increasingly 'bifurcated' criminal justice approach (Bottoms 1977).[1] However, we also perceive such a context as providing an opportunity for criminal justice agencies (such as the police) to devise creative ways in which they can respond to both the legitimacy and resourcing deficit that characterise criminal justice systems in contemporary neoliberal societies more broadly (Cavadino and Dignan 2007).

In conceptual and theoretical terms this requires scholars of policing to explore and interrogate new ways of thinking about policing for the twenty-first century that extend beyond the traditional police use of force paradigm that has dominated police scholarship for the last half century (Brodeur 2010; Manning 2010). While we are making a case for quite a radical transformation of policing, we do acknowledge that a range of justice practices are needed to respond to the complex and varied problems that police officers face. We are certainly not suggesting that officers should divert all cases to a restorative process, nor that officers themselves will always have the necessary skills needed to deal with the complex social issues that underpin some types of offending (also see Vanfraechem 2009). We do believe, however, that it is necessary for the manner in which officers conduct their role at the 'shallow end' of criminal justice to evolve to ways that could be described as 'democratically participatory' and 'restorative'. Such a transformative project will involve not only additions to the 'tools' that are available within the policing 'toolbox', but also a much more radical reframing of the ways in which we construe crime problems and our 'conceptions of what constitutes a good solution' (Johnstone 2008: 60).

The basic argument of this chapter is that we need to reconnect with one another and so the purpose is to unpack how restorative policing might facilitate this. We begin by exploring what social capital is and what it's associated strengths and weaknesses are perceived to be. Next, we investigate how social capital has been used as a driver for criminal justice reform, particularly in relation to the development and adoption of community policing and restorative justice. Finally, we make a case for a more transformative vision of restorative policing that takes its ultimate aim as the development of social capital and outline what this would entail.

What is social capital?

First emerging within the work of Pierre Bourdieu (1985), the concept was expanded by other sociologists (such as Loury 1977 and Coleman 1988a, 1988b) before gaining significant popularity within public policy discourse as a result of the work of political scientist Robert Putnam (1993, 2000). Bourdieu (1985: 249) focused on the instrumental value of the concept wherein he argued that the benefits that individuals experience as a result of group membership are directly the result 'of the solidarity which makes them possible'. While Loury did not go on to develop the concept in any significant detail, he did suggest that the social context in which one lives has a significant impact upon the aspirations held by individuals and the potential for realising those aspirations leading to further work on this issue (Portes 1998).

In fact, Coleman (1988a) subsequently expanded the meaning of social capital on the basis of Loury's work by introducing the concept of 'closure', which described the existence of sufficient ties within a community to guarantee the observance of norms. In these contexts, the threat of exclusion or negative consequences remains the glue that binds people within the group together and ensures that all members abide by the norms of the group. As such, social capital has also been linked to informal social control and sociologists have viewed social capital as inherently relational. It concerns the ability of individual actors to secure benefits by virtue of membership in social networks or other social structures (Portes 1998: 6), which is distinctive from human capital (i.e. education and skills) and physical capital (i.e. physical objects) (Coleman 1988b; Kurki 2003; Putnam 2000). For example, Coleman (1988b) gives a range of examples whereby children were engaged in intellectual discussions at a young age by family members and these discussions have underpinned their success in school and beyond. For him, it is the investment of time and interaction (i.e. the relationship) that is the social capital rather than the knowledge (i.e. human capital) of their parents.

However, in his seminal publication *Bowling Alone*, Putnam (2000) expanded the concept by making it communal. In other words, he applied the concept to explore the level of 'civicness' in communities such as towns, cities, or even countries and argued that where a community has social capital, people tend to do things for each other.[2] He defined social capital as 'features of social organisation such as trust, norms and networks that can improve the efficiency of *society* by facilitating coordinated actions' (1993: 167, *emphasis added*). So where communities are thought to have high social capital, they will also be characterised by high social control, which renders formal or overt controls unnecessary. Where communities are thought to have low social capital, they will also be characterised by low social control in which formal or overt controls are required (Coleman 1988a; Kurki 2003; Portes 1998).

Putnam's work (1993, 2000) further conveys the complexity of social capital by outlining that it can be both a private good and a public good, and that it can have both positive and negative consequences. It is a private good (or what Portes 1998 refers to as having an 'instrumental motivation') in that the networks we seek out have some form of tangible benefit to our own lives. It is a public good (or what Portes 1998 refers to as having a 'consummatory motivation') in that the social networks that develop amongst people can have broader positive consequences for others. Networks depend upon mutual obligations and thus foster a culture of reciprocity. Reciprocity can be specific where transactions take place between individuals (you do this for me and I will do that for you) and general (whereby people help others because they know that acts of kindness or altruism will be forthcoming for them in the future). According to Putnam (1993, 2000), societies characterised by general reciprocity are more efficient and they are more trusting because not every act of kindness or altruism is expected to be accounted for immediately. Thus, Putnam views trust as an important form of social capital because it facilitates interaction (also see Coleman 1988b).

However, while networks and associated norms of reciprocity are generally good for those inside the network, social capital can also have a number of negative consequences for those outside of networks (Portes 1998) and be directed toward malevolent, antisocial purposes (Putnam 2000). Organised crime, mafia families, youth gangs, prostitution and gambling rings, and corrupt officials are examples of how embeddedness in social structures or high social capital can be turned to less than socially desirable ends (Brannigan 2007; Portes 1998). Putnam (2000) suggests, therefore, that attention should be given to thinking about how the positive consequences of social capital – mutual support, cooperation, trust, institutional effectiveness – can be maximised and the negative manifestations – sectarianism, ethnocentrism, corruption – minimised.

These ideas have had a significant impact on a range of policies including education (see Coleman 1988b) and criminal justice (see Rose and Clear 1998) and spawned a flurry of academic research which has sought to apply and test the concept in a range of settings (see Schafft and Brown 2003). The result is that the development of a working definition of social capital is extremely difficult (Settles 2009). As the following section will show, social capital has transcended the original meaning of 'interaction' to social engineering in the form of 'community-building' within criminal justice. It appears that a misunderstanding of the original precepts of social capital have led to criminal justice strategies that often do not work.

Social capital and criminal justice

According to Faulkner (2003) ideas of citizenship, social capital and community have been developed quite prominently as themes for public policy, which promote social responsibility, mutual respect and support, reciprocity and local initiative. Within criminal justice settings, Bazemore and McLeod (2011) suggest that social capital takes two forms: social control and social support, which are often mobilised through social relationships (Bazemore *et al.* 2000). Both social control and social support have been inversely associated with crime in a variety of empirical studies; however, it is the former that has received the most attention within criminal justice policies rather than the latter. We agree with Cullen *et al.* (1999: 189) who argue that such a strategy presents a significant hindrance to tackling crime and enhancing social capital because it 'ignores the softer side of human relationships' and does 'not lead easily to progressive crime policies'. Typically, these strategies have been predicated on 'what works' rationalities and require interventions that are done *to* people rather than *for* people.

Hunter (1985) has distinguished between controls imposed by the families ('private controls'), those imposed by community institutions such as schools and churches ('parochial controls') and those imposed by the state ('public controls'). While it is important to note that each of these controls can be discussed in conceptual terms independently, they are interdependent in reality. It is a widely held assumption that where controls are inadequate, crime and disorder will flourish but where controls are effective at each level, crime and disorder will be minimal (Rose and Clear 1998). Typically there has been a lack of consensus about the type of control that is important in tackling crime – some emphasise formal controls (i.e. public controls) whereas others stress the importance of informal social controls (i.e. private and parochial controls) (see further Cullen *et al.* 1999).[3]

Social support, on the other hand, has been defined by Cullen *et al.* (1999: 190) as 'the provision of affective and/or instrumental resources' which 'are motivated by unselfish motives and conduct' (1999: 191). The authors draw upon the general theory of Gottfredson and Hirschi, Hirschi's social bonding theory and a wide range of research to demonstrate that supportive relationships are important components in the process of crime control and prevention (see, for example, Sampson 1987, 1988; Sampson and Groves 1989). Disorganised communities are typically characterised by a lack of community interaction and strategies to tackle common problems, whereas organised communities are characterised by integration and strong ties between members, which increases its capacity to self-regulate (see Rose and Clear 1998; Sampson and Groves 1989). A number of early intervention programmes have developed across neo-liberal states to respond to a lack of support that 'at risk' youths might be experiencing, however, this forms a smaller component of the criminal justice landscape than those characterised by social control as outlined above.

The basic impetus for a focus on social capital within the context of criminal justice relates to the belief that governments are unable to deal with the crime problem on their own (Crawford 2008; Garland 2001). In an acknowledgement that criminal justice agencies need the public, a number of strategies involving the withdrawal from reliance on the state or on central government (bolstered by the 2008 global financial crisis) and some redefinition of the relationship between the state and the individual has emerged (Brannigan 2007; Faulkner 2003). Strategies have included: seeking ways of 'privatising' justice through a process of multilateralisation characterised by privatisation and volunteerism (Bayley and Shearing 1996); developing collaborative relationships with communities so that they can increasingly become responsible for managing local community problems (Settles 2009), and emphasising the responsibility of citizens in preventing both disorderly behaviour and more serious crime (Faulkner 2003).[4] However, in an increasingly isolated and fragmented society, many families and neighbourhoods are unable to effectively respond to the gap left by reduced government spending (Brannigan 2007; Kurki 2003; Miller *et al.* 2013).

So while research has established the connection between collective social organisation and crime, governments have been unable to provide an effective strategy for creating and increasing positive interaction, social capital and support, and informal control in neighbourhoods (Kurki 2003: 308). Part of the reason for this has been a result of tensions in ideological standpoints as outlined above. In attempting to develop social capital, there needs to be an acknowledgement that relationships matter and strategies need to foster buy-in from families and individuals within communities. Unfortunately, our regulatory institutions have mostly assumed that individuals are solely motivated by self-interest, which has meant that rewards and punishment have been the dominant mode of regulation (Morrison 2001). Indeed, neo-liberal states often emphasise the responsibility of citizens in supporting the criminal justice system in confronting offenders and 'stamping out' anti-social behaviour, rather than promoting more considerate behaviour in the first place (Faulkner 2003: 296). As such, government rhetoric around the development of communal bonds can largely be seen to disguise the true aim of participation in regulatory frameworks: the development of individual responsibility (Morrison 2001).

Public controls that operate without regard for private and parochial controls (particularly in relation to the increasingly interventionist strategy of the state in the form of diversion programmes) are perceived to have the effect of exacerbating problems that underpin crime because they can impede private and parochial controls and thus undermine local social capital (see Bazemore *et al.* 2000; Rose and Clear 1998).[5] Thus, both Coleman (1998b) and Morrison (2001) have suggested that formal institutions must assume some responsibility and leadership in developing positive relationships that will foster social capital within communities. Two strategies that have attempted to do this (albeit with mixed results and not in any systematic way) have been community policing and the integration of restorative justice initiatives within the realms of criminal justice. Each of these will be briefly discussed in turn.

Insights from community policing

The upsurge in complexity of the police role has been increasingly recognised by police organisations across the globe. Strategic developments in areas such as public reassurance, procedural justice and the pluralisation of service provision demonstrate a continued shift of the role and function of policing agencies beyond reactive functions and towards problem-solving and interactive community crime prevention. This is based on recognition that the effectiveness of policing rests on community support, the perceived legitimacy of policing activities and an ongoing negotiation with professional and community groups at a local level. The argument for the conscious integration of social capital policies that would further inform policing strategies within communities, which are socially deprived, is based on an acknowledgement that, while criminality may be perceived to be ingrained, developing ties within the community and linking 'at risk' individuals with particular service providers to respond to socio-economic deficiencies that are stimulating criminal activity is a far more effective strategy than criminalisation (also see Loury 1977). Such an approach requires early intervention and diversionary strategies that are supported by multi-agency working and partnership approaches and, as Rosenbaum (1998: 14) notes, the identification of creative ways to 'help communities help themselves'.

Within the community policing literature, it is argued that the police and the public 'are more effective and more humane co-producers of safety and public order than are the police alone' (Skolnick and Bayley 1988: 1). As such, community policing sees a transformation of the policing role from that of crime 'fighter' to 'service provider' (see Skogan 1998), which aims to facilitate positive interactions between the police and community. Thus, police officers no longer are solely responsible for guarding the gates of the criminal justice system; they are expected to initiate referrals to other social and community agencies that can respond to the needs of individuals as well (Goldstein 1990). However, as Robinson's (2003) research demonstrates, the social capital that police officers experience in their working relationships can have an impact on the extent to which they are effective in their roles. For example, drawing on the work of Miller (1999), she demonstrates that neighbourhood police officers who developed strong relationships with beat officers were able to secure acceptance and cooperation from their colleagues for community-policing activities. Robinson (2003) also highlights that strong relationships with supervisors can have a significant impact on the extent to which community policing activities are successful, particularly given that it is the type of initiative that is not wholeheartedly accepted within police subculture (see further Miller 1999).

Bayley (2003) draws attention to the fact that community policing has tended to work least in areas characterised by high levels of crime, unemployment and transience, and low levels of income and education. For the most part, this is due to the fact that such communities lack the 'social capital' to create effective institutions of local government and therefore require concentrated commitments in terms of resources and sustained efforts in the generation of social capital from outside sources. However, in reality, programmes are often short-lived; the relationships between local residents and government agencies are often tenuous; and a range of infrastructure, bureaucratic and organisational cultures do not lend themselves towards true partnerships between them and communities (Kurki 2003; Rose and Clear 1998). For example, Rose and Clear (1998) suggest that although in 1996 President Clinton announced that community policing would receive federal funding this was accompanied by pre-identified strategies for revitalising the community – neighbourhood watch schemes and foot patrols. The problem with this strategy, as they rightly point out, is that what is often called 'community-based' are merely a front for 'top-down' policy models (see Chapter 7 for a further discussion of this) that assign particular activities and modes of regulation for local actors to impose on its members (Rose and Clear 1998: 447). The result is that local residents are rarely empowered and collaborative relationships seldom emerge (Kurki 2003).

The difficulty for police organisations is that although police officers draw on different policing styles in different contexts, they tend to favour one particular approach, which is linked to their own personal values and interpretation of the purpose of policing. For example, Mastrofski *et al.* (2002) examined police encounters with 3,130 suspects and identified four community policing styles, typifying where individual officer preferences about the purpose of policing lie. The study identified: *professionals* who adopted the latest innovations and applied them in practice; *reactors* who preferred traditional response-style policing; *tough cops* who viewed policing solely through the lens of crime-fighting; and *avoiders* who were generally content to do the minimum required to get through the day. This typology suggests that different police officers tend to drift towards one particular interpretation of the purpose of policing, albeit not exclusively, ahead of others and this cultural predisposition has implications for how community policing is interpreted and implemented at the street-level. Mastrofksi *et al.*'s (2002) typology identified the ideal type for community policing as *professionals*. Although professionals only made up 19 per cent of the officer cohort they were the most proactive and willing to engage in long-term, sometimes problem-solving, strategies aimed at addressing the long-term impact of crime on the community.[6]

Further evidence from the United States (McCold and Wachtel 1996; Bazemore 2000b), the United Kingdom (Foster and Jones 2010), Australia (Moore and Forsythe 1995) and experiments in the global exportation of community policing (Brogden and Nijhar 2005; Wisler and Onwudiwe 2007) point to similar findings which present a structural and cultural challenge to the incorporation of community policing into day-to-day police activity. For example, Willis *et al.*

(2010) further outline that policing priorities are an important factor in the extent to which community policing can become embedded. Their research from the United States demonstrated that the decentralisation and officer flexibility argued for by community policing reformers only rarely becomes manifest on the front-line with sergeants focused on the more immediate demands of responding to 911 calls. There are similar findings from England and Wales where Foster and Jones (2010) summarised the views of police officers on community policing as being 'nice, but not essential' – once again, secondary to the primary purpose of police organisations which is responding to 999 calls and dealing with what Brodeur (2010) refers to as 'microcrises'. These views recall Bittner's wonder-fully enduring conclusion that policing is fundamentally focused upon 'something-that-ought-not-to-be-happening-and-about-which-someone-had-better-do-something-now' (see Bittner in conversation with Brodeur 2010: 107). It is therefore unsurprising that analyses of police culture do not identify a pre-dominance of police thinking that emphasises and advocates for approaches that actively engage and make communities responsible.

To be clear, the authors are not stating here that community policing does not exist, that there have not been successful community-oriented developments (see, for example Darcy 2005; Skogan and Hartnett 1997), nor are we taking the neo-Marxist position that 'community' represents a rhetorical trope which seeks to mask exclusionary strategies (although it sometimes does). Community polic-ing clearly does exist at the strategic level in police organisations but through the messy process of policy implementation and cultural interpretation it can become secondary to other more immediate priorities. For this reason, it is the conclu-sion of these authors that community policing remains an abstract and analytic-ally cumbersome term for police criminal justice and criminological scholars that encourages a superficial discourse about how the work of the police is con-ceptualised. The loose and lazy use of the term 'community' leaves the purpose of the community policing philosophy unclear, leading to more divergence than convergence on the substantive content of community policing reform. As such, communities continue to have consultation, engagement strategies and, in some places, exclusionary policing strategies done to them under the over-arching banner of 'community policing'. The community is rarely 'active' in community approaches and police organisations remain wary of active civic engagement and more comfortable with their traditional reactive domain.

Nevertheless, individuals and communities have enormous potential to generate and sustain social capital with leadership that draws the relevant com-ponents from local economic and cultural capital together (Bourdieu 1985). When strong neighbourhoods emerge within cities, they create networks of information that may not be visible to public officials but which hold influence over communities in often unexpected and differentiated ways. Because of this, there is rarely an appreciation of social capital at the neighbourhood level – a factor that can lead to implementation failure (Sampson and Graif 2009). As a consequence, where engagement with the community is superficial there is likely to be little real or sustainable change. A focus on social capital places analytical emphasis upon the social ties between the people and positions that structure local communities (Bourdieu 1986). Sampson and Graif (2009: 1580) develop this idea further by stating that neighbourhood social capital can be 'profitably conceptualised in terms of the differential ways in which communities are socially organised'. Thus conceptualised, it is possible to place further emphasis upon the prospects of democratic participation via assessments of neighbourhood-level variance and its likely impact upon policy development.

Yet, organisations and services that only use the reactive without building social capital beforehand are less successful than those that also employ the proactive. As such, Kurki (2003) suggests that restorative justice will work better in generating social capital than community policing efforts because its processes rely on the direct participation of members of the community; it is based upon dialogue and consensus decision-making; it involves making specific plans to address concerns; it reveals additional concerns within the communities in which participants live; offers tangible support to participants; and finally, it reduces the distance between varied groups of people (victims, offenders, their family members, community members and criminal justice professionals). Engaging in such problem-solving interaction, she argues, offers an opportunity for the creation of new relationships – something that many community policing efforts overlook.

Insights from restorative justice

In many respects, restorative justice is more compatible with notions of social capital. For the most part, this is due to the fact that criminal justice approaches tend to leave relationship building to chance, whereas restorative justice begins and ends with a focus on social relationships (Bazemore *et al.* 2000a). The application of social capital within the restorative justice discourse relies on a broad definition of the term as 'anything that causes or results in collective action, even when that collective action is limited to those affected by a criminal episode' (Settles 2009: 286). Wachtel (2013) suggests that where social capital (in the form of a network of relationships) is already well established, it is easier to respond effectively to wrongdoing and restore social order – as well as to create a healthy and positive organisational environment. But even where these networks are not strong, Bazemore and Stinchcomb (2004) suggest that restorative justice processes (such as conferencing) can be viewed as components to building social capital because it 'fosters discussion about minimum community standards and promotes the strengthening of local networks' (Moore and O'Connell 1994: 63). Thus, according to Bazemore and McLeod (2011), where restorative justice processes are facilitated by the state it may lead to improved private and parochial controls within communities.

A common aspect of Putnam's (2000) work that is often drawn upon by restorative scholars is his distinction between 'bonding social capital' (the building of bonds and networks *within* groups) and 'bridging social capital' (the building of bonds and networks *across* groups). In a conference, victims and offenders draw on family and friends to provide support to them during the process and they might be thought of as their 'bonding social capital' (Huang *et al.* 2012; Shapland *et al.* 2011). The discussions (resulting in increased understanding and the breaking down of stereotypes) and plans (providing reparation and dealing with triggers for offending) that emerge as a result of participating in a conference then form the 'bridging social capital'. Shapland *et al.* (2011) perceive facilitators as providers of the bridging social capital given that they can link victims and offenders with support agencies that they otherwise would not have had access to. For this reason, they argue that facilitators do need either some experience of the criminal justice system or access to others who can guide them toward relevant provision.

In relation to crime control, restorative justice has been predicated on the fact that the dominant models of justice in common law jurisdictions have reduced the ability of those most affected to deal with the consequences and, instead, replaced their 'ownership' of crime with a retributive form of justice that is both ineffective and alienating (see Christie 1977). Restorative justice conceptions held by criminal justice practitioners have therefore been characterised by attempts to involve the participation of the 'local community' in responding to youth offending. However, Settles (2009) suggests that such an approach has not sought to give conflicts back to those most directly affected, but rather limited restorative justice to an extension of the punishment process. As such, the potential of improving social capital, reducing the negative effects of offending on victims and reducing recidivism by offenders is said to be limited. Two particular aspects of criminal justice approaches to restorative justice can provide further illustration of this position.

First, many questions have been raised in relation to the meaning and relevance of community (see further Hines and Bazemore 2003). Within criminal justice, a common approach has been to define community on the basis of geographic location, but as Settles (2009) notes, this is often unsatisfactory in restorative justice terms since it has tended to lead to reliance upon 'victim surrogates' rather than an identification of those most affected by the incident in question. What matters most to restorative scholars rather, has been 'communities of care' or 'micro-communities', which consists of those individuals who know the victim and/or the offender and are able to provide support and guidance in overcoming the causes and consequences of the offence (McCold 2000; McCold and Wachtel 1998). In some respects, this approach has been driven by the time constraints associated with criminal justice processing of cases. Real victims may require more time than criminal justice will allow, practitioners may feel out of their depth when dealing with victims when they have traditionally focused on offenders and a lack of understanding of restorative justice may all contribute to the lack of victim participation. This tendency for low victim participation in many programmes (see Chapter 4, this volume) has the adverse effect of reducing the potential for developing social capital.

Second, research conducted by Huang *et al.* (2012) revealed that communities already characterised by high social capital – those that had high levels of trust and viewed collaboration to tackle mutual problems as rewarding – were more likely to be supportive of restorative justice initiatives. Conversely, traditional or conservative attitudes (i.e. concern over moral decay and fear of victimisation, as well as punitive attitudes to offenders, the poor and those who deviate from social norms) were seen widely as an obstacle to the spread and appeal of restorative justice. These findings provide some insight into why restorative justice tends to succeed in those areas where it is least needed. But Brannigan (2007) cautions that communities are often ill equipped to respond to crime because they are unable to effect larger social changes that may underpin offending behaviour regardless of the strength of relationships (social capital) within those communities. As such, he is wary of the potential of restorative justice to develop social capital where it is most needed – within communities.

While strong social capital is thought to be good for reducing crime and it has influenced a number of policy initiatives that seek to develop strong communities (Crawford and Evans 2012), only minor attention has been given to developing what social capital means and how it might be achieved within a restorative policing context. From our perspective, a reconceptualisation of restorative policing offers a bridge to some of the limitations of community policing and restorative justice outlined in this section. In the following section we, therefore, further theorise the potential of restorative justice for policing organisations through the notion of social capital. This requires a significant redefinition of the policing role given that advocacy and relationship building are 'not part of the job description of the average professional' (Bazemore *et al.* 2000: 15). In order for this aspiration to be realised, there is a need for community and problem-oriented policing strategies and restorative practices to dovetail into a more comprehensive strategy for the prevention of crime and the development of social capital and support. In the words of Bazemore and McLeod (2011: 166), we call for the empowerment of 'the community while using government/professional resources to facilitate conflict resolution and build community capacity'.

A transformative agenda for restorative policing: changing lenses

While the original architects of restorative policing in Australia have argued for a shift in discourse away from it as a form of 'restorative justice' to a form of 'transformative justice' (see Moore 1993a, 2004; Moore and McDonald 2001), they did not engage with the fact that the restorative justice literature contains transformative conceptions as well and should not necessarily be considered as something distinct from restorative justice (as originally highlighted in Chapter 2; also see Clamp 2014, 2016a, 2016b, 2016c). Harris (2008) helpfully restorative justice proponents into four categories on the basis of their views about the compatibility of transformative justice and restorative justice. First, there are those who feel that they are distinct processes primarily because they have different orientations – restorative justice is backward-looking because it seeks to restore and that transformative justice is forward-looking in that it prioritises change at a structural level. While some argue that this backward-focused interpretation of restorative justice is inaccurate (see Llewellyn 2007), there is a tendency within the restorative justice literature to link restorative justice to reparation and restoration, without giving adequate attention to how the process and outcomes may lead to transformation.

As such, the transformative value of restorative justice within the conventional literature has often been limited to an inner change that occurs within stakeholders as a result of participating in the process. On the one hand, the victim is transformed from a position of powerlessness to one of power by being able to confront the offender and let go of the incident through a process of forgiveness (Zehr 1990). On the other, the offender is transformed through a realisation and acknowledgement of the impact that his or her behaviour has had on others (Zehr 2002) through a process of reintegrative shaming (Braithwaite 1989). However, the extent to which such a process has a longer-term impact beyond the process in terms of self-preservation, empowerment or crime prevention in relation to victims; and desistance in relation to offenders, and the mechanics of that change are left largely unexplored by the literature.

The second camp claims that restorative justice creates spaces for transformation to occur over time, but the two camps remain distinct because restorative justice does not deal with any structural dimensions of conflict. As Zehr points out:

> Crime ... is at its core a violation of a person by another person, a person who himself or herself may be wounded. It is a violation of the just relationship that should exist between individuals. There is also a larger social dimension to crime. Indeed, the effects of crime ripple out, touching many others. Society too has a stake in the outcome and a role to play. Still these public dimensions should not be the starting point. Crime is not an offence against society, much less against the state. Crime is first an offence against people and it is here we should start.
>
> (1990: 182)

This has resulted in some critiquing restorative practice for predominantly focusing on resolving incidents and specific issues rather than addressing the contexts that are giving rise to the behaviour and/or victimisation in the first place (Dyck 2008). David Dyck (2008) draws on the work of both Harry Mika (1989) and Marie Dugan (1996) to illustrate how current restorative practice involves a 'surface-level' approach to conflict resolution that actually reinforces the status quo. He argues that this occurs because restorative justice practitioners are trained to focus on the interpersonal dimensions of crime. As such, they inadvertently 'cover up deeply rooted dimensions of conflict in favour of an "ideology of harmony" which suggests that shared feelings create empowerment' (Dyck 2008: 527).

A third camp sees restorative justice as occupying a middle ground between criminal justice and transformative justice, thus while they remain distinct we can say that they work in a complementary capacity. Harris (2008: 562) explains that in this view, transformative justice is perceived as building on the 'ideas and practices associated with restorative justice beyond the micro-level of specific disputes to the macro-level where the values can be applied to any problem or conflict'. The processes and values associated with restorative justice are perceived as a useful way of designing responses that will allow for the realisation of transformative aims. Restorative justice, in other words, provides a mechanism whereby transformative activities may be decided upon, but this camp does not see restorative justice processes as bringing about that change.

Finally, a small cohort (which includes the authors) views restorative justice and transformative justice as interchangeable – 'a set of values and positions to guide choices made by citizens, governments, nation-states, organisations and groups' (Harris 2008: 563). Sullivan and Tifft (2001) argue that at the most elementary level a restorative response to harm grows out of a needs-based conception of justice, and if attended to, will ultimately lead to transformation. Perceiving restorative justice as transformative justice has implications for its use in response to offending behaviour. No longer can we view restorative justice as a mechanism that will address incident-specific issues. Rather, it becomes a long-term, sustainable process embedded in society that seeks to address the class, race/ethnicity and ideological causes of crime and conflict.

However, this cannot be achieved if we do not design processes that encourage and indeed are reliant upon the active involvement of broad segments of the population. Our current short-term view of conflict resolution is perpetuated by our perception that conflict is somehow abnormal – a temporary disruption of a normal state of equilibrium and harmony – and a bad thing (Froestad and Shearing 2007). Rather than trying to solve offending, perhaps what is needed is for us to learn that it is a feature of daily life and that a more effective use of our energy might be in trying to develop capacity to deal with it more effectively. This is quite a step away from the neoliberal version of restorative justice that dominates current practice, with processes occurring within specified time frames and being generally limited to a single meeting. In further developing how restorative policing might be more transformative and used to secure social capital within communities, we use Howard Zehr's (1990) metaphor of viewing restorative justice through a lens. Our transformative reconceptualisation calls for a 'broadening' and 'lengthening' of the lens through which we view restorative justice when applying it to operational policing environments.

Broadening the restorative policing lens

Up until now, restorative policing has tended to focus primarily upon the conferencing *process* and achieving outcomes for *individuals* (i.e. participants). Within our transformative vision for restorative policing, we suggest that such an approach is limited because the transformative potential restorative justice holds for both policing organisations and communities remains unrealised. As such, we argue for a broadening of the lens by thinking creatively about ways in which restorative justice principles and processes might be used to improve and evolve both vertical relationships (i.e. between organisations and individuals) and horizontal relationships (i.e. between individuals and between organisations). Such an approach can only be realised if accompanied by a dramatic change in perceptions of the causes of crime and the policing role as well.

Some have suggested that crime can be thought of as 'counter violence' in response to 'social-structural violence' that prevents individuals from realising human needs that is (mis)directed at others who may at the same time be victims of social-structural violence (see Gill 2006; Katz 1988). Viewed in these terms, Johnstone (2008: 73) suggests that restorative justice is merely 'seeking to improve and humanise "repressive social-structural violence" because it deflects attention from and helps to legitimate the initial social-structural violence'. In other words, the tendency to define crime in terms of its relational implications rather than in terms of its structural causes (Clamp 2014, 2016b) means that it covers up the underlying causes of offending through a process which aims to generate positive feelings and the belief that this will result in changed future behaviour (Dyck 2008). On this basis, a number of scholars have criticised restorative practices for leaving the broader structural factors or to use Gill's terminology the 'structural violence' that underpin offending intact (see Cunneen 2010; Stubbs 1997).

In order for the transformative potential of restorative justice to be realised, it is important that we move our conceptions of restorative justice beyond a process through which to respond to crime and instead, to a framework through which to further build social capital and to transform structurally violent, unjust societies (Johnstone 2008; Sullivan and Tifft 2006b). While Bazemore (2000b) suggests that macro-level applications of restorative justice initiate a move away from a sole concern with individualised objectives to a focus on collective outcomes, we question whether the outcomes achieved are collective enough. From our perspective, restorative policing offers a far more grand opportunity for police officers to take a much more proactive role in seeking to tackle the structural causes of offending in two important respects.

First, there have been a number of reported cases, particularly those involving long-term community-based disputes, which have been resolved effectively by police officers arranging a restorative conference. As Schnell (see Mirsky 2003) notes, for example, in one incident the police had been called out to a particular community experiencing a number of quality of life issues 40 times in a period of 60 days. Clearly the traditional policing manner in which these incidents were being dealt with was not working. What resolved the underlying issues was a two-hour community conference in which those involved and affected by the ongoing conflicts were engaged by the police in discussing their community and how they would like it to change (also see O'Connell 2008). This empowered those involved by evolving discussions from who did what (the blame game) to setting out standards of behaviour that everyone would be expected to abide by. Through such a process officers could also initiate 'bridging capital' whereby victims, offenders and their supporters could be linked to other agencies and support organisations that will further assist them in dealing with both the causes and consequences of the offending where this is warranted (as promoted by community policing advocates – see Goldstein 1990). The conferencing model for restorative policing is perceived to be an ideal mechanism through which to identify the causes of the breakdown of family and community controls and to initiate efforts to restore social bonds (Moore 1993a), however, the model is less effective in addressing wider issues of inequality and social vulnerability (Polk 1994). What we are suggesting here involves a more deliberate approach to generating more creative and meaningful outcomes from the conference that will assist in achieving these ambitions.

The justification for this, as pointed out by Bazemore *et al.* (2000), is that offenders often require the development of skills and social capital to develop and maintain strong, positive relationships and connections that can lead to both social and occupational benefits. One potential strategy is for offenders to be involved in community projects or reparation activities that not only draw or build upon the skills of the offender, but which also demonstrate that these skills have meaningful contributions to the common good or to individuals in need (Bazemore *et al.* 2000). Such an approach, argue Bazemore *et al.* (2000), sends a message to the community (including the victim) that the offender is worthy of support and investment and to the offender that he or she has something of value to offer to others. This provides an important cycle of reinforcement in attempts to generate social capital that are often missing from reparation activities that are designed to get offenders to atone for their behaviour in restorative justice agreements within criminal justice diversion schemes.

Second, police officers could harness a crime prevention orientation by altering the way that they interact with victims once a crime is reported. They could achieve this by not only asking questions about the incident itself, but also by exploring the impact of the offence which provides an opportunity to discuss and empower victims to become proactive in their crime prevention strategies (see, for example Mirsky 2003). Police officers could also subsequently track and make connections between trends in offending and their causes across cases that fall within their specific beat or jurisdiction that they dealt with in a restorative way. This would then initiate opportunities for further interagency collaboration in terms of developing services to respond to functional and structural deficits that exist within communities and which provide a trigger for crime.[7] This role transformation harks back to the Peelian principles outlined in Chapter 1 whereby the primary objective for police officers is the *prevention* of crime and further harm. Such proactive strategies are expected to have important positive consequences for communities, particularly those characterised by social disorganisation where access to much needed services are not always available. This may then contribute to increases in the perceived legitimacy and efficacy of state agencies. As outlined by Rose and Clear (1998: 465), while government agencies are typically present in these communities, the state is most likely to be encountered as a coercive agent of control rather than an agent of 'justice'. We agree with the authors that due consideration needs to be given to the *quality* of relationships (also see Robinson 2003) among the different forms of control, rather than the *quantity*, so that each might be made more effective.

A particular obstacle to our proposed reorientation for restorative policing is the manner in which restorative policing has been implemented within policing organisations (see Chapter 3). Ultimately, there has been insufficient stimulus for a change in the paradigm of policing (i.e. crime control). As a result, conferencing has merely become another 'tool' in the policing 'toolbox' at the shallow end of the criminal justice system offering little challenge to the *status quo*. As Kurki (1999) notes, the challenge is not how to do things differently, but rather to get the criminal justice system and its agents to change their thinking. Where this does not happen, all initiatives tend to return to the same *modus operandi* whereby government agencies or experts establish guidelines, standards and requirements for programmes reflecting their missions and values, thereby bureaucratising them and once again 'stealing conflicts' from communities.

In functional terms, the mission of restorative policing should emphasise peace-making, peace-keeping and proactive community crime prevention orientations. For this transformative potential to be realised *within* policing organisations, a cultural shift needs to take place throughout the police hierarchy. This is one that will be inherently more difficult for the majority of police officers who favour an 'order maintenance' or 'crime-fighting' approach and perceive intervention, authority and action to be core elements of the police role. Pollard provides further explanation for what this transformation entails:

> Restorative justice provides the sort of rational, problem-solving response to social conflict that is highly resilient to the demands of different policing situations, and promotes more of the human, face-to-face contact with victims and offenders that so many officers intuitively recognise as essential to rebuilding social capital and community confidence. Restorative justice is not just about new approaches to juvenile justice… it is also about shifting police culture towards a more problem-oriented, community style of policing; bridging the gap between the criminal justice system and the caring agencies; developing new ways of resolving conflict more amicably and sensitively in civil society in schools and the workplace; and, most importantly of all, providing new processes and mechanisms to help strengthen communities, rebuild emotional and physical landscapes fragmented by crime, and improve the overall quality of life.
>
> (2001: 166–167)

Such a perception of restorative policing has a number of implications for the policing role as well as the structure of the policing organisation as a whole. While it is acknowledged that many beat police or community/neighbourhood policing officers are aware of and closely involved in the problems that affect their 'patch', they often lack the resources and support within the organisation and from their colleagues to deal with the problems effectively (van Stokkom and Moor 2009). This can lead to feelings of frustration and the eventual abandonment of proactive approaches over a period of time. But as Jackson *et al.* (2012) note, research has demonstrated that the police can have a significant impact on the extent to which individuals engage in criminal behaviour, informal social control and the co-production of social order. Underpinned by notions of trust, legitimacy and the quality of relationships between the police and the public, this implies that the role of policing extends beyond crime control. In fact, by embracing more respectful and collaborative ways of working, the police are able to instil in the public that obeying the law is morally just.

In a previous publication, we argued that restorative policing, with its emphasis upon bottom-up leadership, inverts the traditional police hierarchy and positions street-level police officers and communities as key sources of organisational learning, leadership and decision-making (Clamp and Paterson 2013). In this context, the restorative policing 'expert' becomes the frontline officer and the role of the broader organisation should be to support the frontline officer in using his or her discretion to respond to the needs of the community. This shift is challenging for police organisations and officers that do not value community policing roles and functions and do not empower front-line officers with a framework in which they have the flexibility and discretion to make decisions that help to engage communities. A vital aspect of restorative policing, and a linear development of the community policing model, is recognition of the skills and attributes of police officers to engage with and stimulate community connections and capacity.

Lengthening the restorative policing lens

Drawing on the work of Bazemore (2000b), we make two suggestions in terms of how the restorative policing lens might be 'lengthened'. First, sustained citizen involvement needs to be stimulated in order to activate social control and social support. Where public controls serve to undermine the private and parochial controls within communities, public controls have to alter their course to regenerate community capacity by incorporating local actions into a broader anti-crime effort with success being measured in terms of increases in quality of life (Rose and Clear 1998). According to McCold and Wachtel (1998b: 76), harnessing informal social control mechanisms that exist within the community are particularly important for a number of reasons: often these are the most effective means for dealing with the issue; doing so reinforces the capacity of the community to govern itself; and finally, this is often the least restrictive and intrusive approach and thus fits neatly with the neo-liberal democratic model of policing. As outlined previously, social capital stems from a sense of trust and obligation. Restorative justice principles provide an important resource for guiding these types of interaction and restorative processes (such as conferencing) provide an ideal forum (as outlined previously) for generating social capital amongst those who are in conflict.

Second, institutions of deliberative democracy need to be established so that further understandings about the structural and functional deficiencies that are affecting local communities can be made explicit (Bazemore *et al.* 2000). Given that crime is perceived as a cause and consequence of weak relationships, efforts to develop ties between private and parochial groups is an important reintegrative and preventative strategy (Bazemore and McLeod 2011). As the number and strength of informal opportunity networks increase, it is thought that they will build social capital for social support at the neighbourhood level (Bazemore and

McLeod 2011). Our model thus specifies a reciprocal relationship between public social controls (i.e. the police), private controls (i.e. the family) and parochial controls (i.e. local institutions) through a community restorative policing approach. We argue that this would involve a community policing approach where specific officers are tasked with one beat so that they can get to know community members as well as the issues that affect them.

Where communities are unable to develop links and ties with the police due to high staff turnover, we would argue that these conditions would both decrease the ability and willingness of individuals to report incidents to police officers and for police officers to overcome hostility or mistrust between different groups residing within the community (Tyler 2011). As highlighted earlier, an important form of social capital is trust (Putnam 2000) and, particularly important in disorganised communities which may be characterised by high levels of distrust, strategies need to be devised that can increase trust. This can only happen when relationships are developed and nurtured with experience showing that the police are indeed trustworthy. Bradford and Jackson (2011) suggest that by acting in a way that signals to the community that the police are invested not only contributes to increases in perceived legitimacy and trust, it also means that they are engaged in acts of social control that link formal and informal mechanisms and thus the social production of order.

An increased visibility of police officers and their associated integration within the daily life of a community, it is argued, would result in diminished calls for more punitive action given that issues that drive fear of crime will be effectively addressed (Weitekamp *et al.* 2003). Weitekamp *et al.* (2003) argue that by perceiving the police as a necessary and important partner in dealing with crime and by harnessing a restorative approach in facilitating interaction between these stakeholders, it further holds the potential to increase trust and communication between citizens and the police (thus realising the goals of community policing). Meyer *et al.* (2009) have also suggested that a restorative approach to police engagement with communities will increase cooperation, the more communities trust the police, the more likely it is that crimes will be reported and individuals will become more actively involved in policing their own neighbourhoods (see an example of this in action in the next chapter, Darcy 2005). Furthermore, the benefits that police officers could gain in terms of developing their conflict resolution skills include an opportunity to:

> [...] improve their ability to consider alternative courses of action, display resourcefulness and imagination, and establish satisfactory relationships with others by being self-confident, knowledgeable, amenable, decisive, but flexible.
>
> (Volpe 1989: 232)

This requires the adoption of non-judicial approaches, such as conferencing, largely due to the fact that criminalising behaviour often contributes to, rather than eradicates weak informal social controls (see Clear 2007; Rose and Clear

1998). Concentrating efforts in generating engagement and reciprocal relationships between residents of a community can result in an increased understanding of the challenges that they face, what residents fear, and potential strategies for tackling this. Rose and Clear (1998) suggest that successful examples of this involve finding supports for neighbourhood systems of self-regulation, such as embracing non-judicial responses to low-level offending or anti-social behaviour and working with parents in terms of finding ways to change this behaviour informed by the theory underpinning conferencing approaches.

For example, Coates *et al.* (2006) reflect on a number of case studies whereby restorative dialogue has been used to address hate crimes. One case study, in particular, offers further insight into the approach that is being proposed. A school in Minnesota was plagued by racial tensions that reached breaking point when five white boys wielding a baseball bat assaulted a young African-American youth. Although he was not seriously injured, his parents complained to the authorities about the perpetual acts of violence and intimidation against their son. In response, the school engaged in awareness campaigns that included educational programmes and guest speakers, however, this did little to assuage tensions. In fact, they escalated into the community and a variety of agencies became involved, including a community mediation team to assist in resolving underlying issues.

After three weeks of preparatory work by the community mediation team, 150 individuals gathered at the school for the conference. While several incidents were identified, no single incident or group of victims/perpetrators formed the basis of discussions that allowed for a broad range of experiences and perspectives to be shared. In instances involving such large numbers of people it is difficult to follow a particular script, and in some respects such situations force ownership and control out of the facilitators' hands and into those of the community. Preparing key participants prior to the conference and carefully planning the structure and process is obviously important. Organisers in this case asked that everyone identify themselves before speaking, set the tone of the meeting with the statements prepared by initial speakers, limited comments to two minutes so that many voices could be heard and encouraged respectful interaction.

In this context, bridge building is the principal aim rather than 'restoration' or 'reparation'. In order to break down barriers, Coates *et al.* (2006: 17) argue that it 'requires persons threatened by conflict to get to know one another which in turn requires face-to-face sharing of personal experiences'. This long-term perspective of conflict resolution is important in contexts where crime may have been a normal part of the communal landscape. Dialogic attempts to reduce prejudices take place over multiple occasions and as Coates *et al.* (2006) point out, some facilitators work on cases for many months, certainly as long as the stakeholders need them to. In the traditional policing response, officers may be successful in disrupting the dispute from escalating; however their presence and the associated threats of penalties do not *resolve* the conflict between the parties. Conventional applications of restorative justice initiatives deal with conflict *within* the micro-communities that exist within conferencing processes, but there is often a lack of positive or reconciliatory engagement *between* those communities. This can result in reignited conflicts between different groups that reside within the same community. As Moore explains:

> Ideally, mechanisms that can re-establish effective – and just – community control need to be developed. The family group conference is considered to be just such a mechanism. Of course, no forty-minute session – no matter how powerful or transformative – can solve problems caused by years of abuse, injustice, neglect, incompetence or just bad luck. It can, however, act as a 'circuit breaker' or 'shock treatment' to stop further deterioration. It can identify some of the family and social problems that may have encouraged delinquent behaviour.
>
> (1993a: 211–212)

However, restorative justice is often reduced to a process that includes 'victims' and 'offenders' or to a particular outcome such as 'reparation' or 'an apology', thus losing its problem-solving quality that is so necessary for breaking down stereotypes. In many respects, the use of labels and processes to generate 'solutions' appeals to our human nature, our desire for accomplishment, so that we can see that something has been done. However, as Christie warns us:

> [...] it is important not to presuppose that conflict ought to *be solved.* The quest for solution is a puritan, ethnocentric conception.... Conflicts might be solved, but they might also be lived with.... Maybe participation is more important than solutions.
>
> (1982: 92–93, *italics original*)

Learning to live with and accept difference is perhaps even more pressing where communities have regarded each other with suspicion for significant periods of time and committed harms against one another (Clamp 2014a). Adopting such a stance would result in a 'lengthening' of the restorative justice lens whereby one incident and one meeting is traded for discussions of broader experiences over a significantly longer period of time, contributing to the rebuilding of trust between communities by creating the space where empathy may develop (Fletcher and Weinstein 2002). Drawing on the work of Christie, Froestad and Shearing (2007) argue that conflicts should ideally give rise to a more protracted 'political' debate, in which the whole community participates and in which there are no exclusionary rules preventing people from introducing facts and arguments that they consider relevant. One potential way of evaluating such an approach would be:

> [...] to ask whether the intervention process, and subsequent follow-up steps, created or strengthened relationships; increased participants' sense of capacity and efficacy in community skills in problem-solving and constructive conflict resolution; promoted individual awareness of and commitment to the common good; and expanded informal support systems or 'safety nets' for victims and offenders.
>
> (Bazemore and McLeod 2011: 162)

From transformation to implementation

Restorative justice (including restorative policing) has traditionally been thought of and implemented in a programmatic, rather than a systemic way (see also Bazemore 2000b). As such, the debate so far in relation to restorative policing has been about its value as a diversion process or programme rather than its value on the basis of the role of the community and police in the socialisation of young people. The thrust, in other words, has been about its role as a mechanism of state intervention. We have argued that this as a particular limitation in the restorative policing experiment thus far given that it confines restorative justice values, principles and processes to the margins of police work thus having minimal impact on the sociocultural meaning of policing and on communities as a whole. We do not perceive restorative policing to be yet another one of these programmes. It certainly can be (and the Northern Ireland experience and, to some extent, the Thames Valley experience have confirmed this), but it does not have to be. Rather, we agree with Kurki (1999: 3) who argues that a true integration of restorative justice requires a fundamental evolution in agency missions and that restorative programmes should be about 'a new way of thinking, not just another way of doing'.

Given the perceived limited agenda of restorative policing, this chapter has sought to demonstrate how we might adopt a more expansive approach through a transformative view of restorative policing that seeks to develop both local (i.e. between family members and their immediate social networks) and public (i.e. networks that bind individuals to government institutions such as the police) social capital (Miller *et al.* 2013). The key argument has been that restorative policing can be viewed and practiced as both a criminal and non-criminal method of intervention. Where the criminal justice process has to be engaged the purpose, wherever possible, should be to promote beneficent forms of social capital (i.e. to rehabilitate offenders and provide support for their families and for victims). It should not have the effect of weakening them, or of creating relationships or networks that are socially destructive (Bazemore and McLeod 2011; Rose and Clear 1998). What we are suggesting requires a shift in thinking from the individualistic paradigm that dominates contemporary thought about crime and crime policy and the application of restorative processes (such as conferencing) beyond the constraints of individual cases. We suggest that such efforts would need to involve strengthening the interaction between private, parochial and public controls to develop and maintain safe and engaged communities.

We acknowledge that there will be opposition to our vision, but we encourage our colleagues to engage in a debate about the extent to which restorative justice can and should be 'broadened' and 'lengthened' to deal with the social and structural factors that perpetuate crime. In sticking with the *status quo*, many of the criticisms levelled against restorative justice – that it does not challenge the structural causes of conflict, that it serves merely to legitimise the agendas of government officials and criminal justice practitioners and that it is insensitive to context (Cunneen 2008) will continue to ring true. Good restorative practice must allow the underlying causes of conflict to be framed within the broader macro-causes of conflict, and the political, social and economic factors that underlie and sustain criminal and anti-social behaviour (Eriksson 2009). We agree with Bazemore and McLeod's (2011) vision that it should be restorative justice principles, not the programmes and system-driven policy that must guide efforts to strengthen community responses to crime.

This strategy requires a dramatic shift for officers from perceiving themselves as a primary stakeholder within offending behaviour to facilitators (Settles 2009) and as equal partners in increasing public safety, preventing crime and responding to crime-related problems (Kurki 1999). This means that discussions about local injustices must 'bubble up' from below to inform policy-making debates (Braithwaite 1994, 1998; Braithwaite and Parker 1999). However, all of this remains abstract unless there is a means through which such change might be activated. This involves a significant transformation in the policing role and the policing agency mandate (Bazemore and McLeod 2011). In the final substantive chapter of this book, we seek to further explore how such a transformative vision of restorative policing might be implemented.

Notes

1 Cavadino and Dignan (2007: 28) define such an approach as

> a dual-edged (or twin-track) approach to punishment: differentiating between 'ordinary' or 'run of the mill' offenders with whom less severe measures can be taken on the one hand, and on the other hand 'exceptional', 'very serious' or 'dangerous' offenders who can be made subject to much tougher measures.

2 However, as Portes (1998) notes critics have questioned the extent to which civic virtue is on the wane as claimed by Putnam or if it has just assumed alternative modes to those outdated versions outlined by him.

3 Parochial controls, in particular have been demonstrated to have a significant impact upon behaviour from offending (see Sampson *et al.* 1997) to dropping out of school (see Coleman 1988b).

4 A number of scholars warn of the potential negative effects of such strategies. Brannigan (2007), for example, highlights a range of issues with assumptions held about community and social capital, particularly in relation to the fact that the social structures and identities of people within a community may be an outcome of historical forces, including capitalism and colonialism. Portes (1998: 21) is similarly wary of increased social ties and warns that while it can bring about greater control over wayward behaviour and provide privileged access to resources; it can also restrict individual freedoms and bar outsiders from gaining access to the same resources through 'particularist preferences'.

5 For example, Rose and Clear (1998: 442) argue that in high-crime neighbourhoods, a concentration of police efforts removes large numbers of residents from the neighbourhood but that this can damage local control because it disrupts local networks leading to increased frayed relations between residents and the police.

6 This study focused on just one police department but its findings on community policing have been replicated on sufficient enough occasions to suggest they indicate trends that are replicable in other contexts (see Trojanowicz 1994 for an overview).

7 Such an approach resonates with Goldstein's (1979) aspirations for problem-oriented policing as well as his critique of its partial implementation.

7 Initiating change 'from above' and 'from below'

Towards an implementation strategy for restorative policing

Introduction

Bazemore and Griffiths' (2003: 340) review of police involvement with restorative justice in the United States bemoaned the absence of a 'systemic vision' for restorative policing. While they called for the institutionalisation of restorative practices within police organisations, they stopped short of articulating how this vision could be realised. This standpoint has become commonplace in the restorative policing literature whereby obstacles to change have been identified, but often without transformative solutions that are likely to be credible in operational policing environments. The sheer scale of change management required means that questions remain about the extent to which restorative policing can become embedded in an operational policing environment unless it is accompanied by a significant shift in the sociocultural meaning of police work as well (Clamp and Paterson 2013; also Chapter 6, this volume). Viewing restorative policing in this way requires not only substantially more commitment to developing more meaningful partnerships with communities, it also demands a radical shift in traditional policing practice – a shift that creates a number of tensions at the implementation level.

We view the true potential of restorative policing as lying not in a single programme contained within the usual business and structures of policing organisations, but rather as philosophical framework through which to guide police interaction with the community it serves (see also Hines and Bazemore 2003; also Chapter 6, this volume). Thus conceptualised, restorative policing can be understood as a vehicle for delivering high quality community policing. As such, we suggest that in order for meaningful and sustainable organisational learning and change to take place, a twin-track approach is needed whereby leadership 'from above' is informed by a restorative philosophy that not only allows, but also actively encourages transformation from the 'bottom-up'. In what follows, we develop our ideas within the context of the work already undertaken in relation to community policing.

The reasons for this are twofold. First, community policing and restorative policing overlap in terms of their broader philosophies and strategies (as we outlined in Chapter 1). This means that rather than reinventing the wheel, we are further developing thinking about policing that has been in existence across neo-liberal societies for over three decades. Second, restorative policing offers front-line staff the tools to both bolster and structure their discretion (which has been largely missing from the literature on community policing) in terms of dealing with problems affecting local communities. From this perspective, we seek to draw out ways in which police officers can use their discretion to view offending (particularly by younger offenders) on the basis of its structural causes and to develop strategies (i.e. by withholding punishment and enforcement) to deal with this in a more restorative way. While this approach demands creative thinking around how officer discretion might be responsibly enhanced, we also argue that if policing organisations are to implement restorative justice in a sustainable way, then both frontline staff and communities need to be involved in the design, implementation and monitoring of local initiatives (Kurki 1999). Drawing on the policy implementation literature, this chapter explores what this strategy would involve and makes suggestions for how such an approach might be realised.

However, a number of caveats need to be drawn before we proceed. First, it must be acknowledged that there are a number of limitations to the community policing literature and restorative justice literature when it comes to implementa-tion. Often there has been little understanding of the community's role and gen-erating citizen participation has commonly been found to be a difficult task (see, for example, Clamp 2014b). Furthermore, priorities and routines vary across police forces within a country (and across countries) and the approaches and rationales underpinning crime control can vary greatly. For example, within the United States, Leena Kurki (1999: 6) notes: 'some efforts rely on heavy street-level enforcement, while others emphasize citizen involvement, better quality public services, delivery of community-based treatment, or diversionary policing that withholds enforcement as a way to build relationships with communities'. This creates a challenge in terms of developing a strategy that can be adapted according to the specific context and challenges faced by *different* policing organisations.

Second, there has been little attempt to measure the extent to which the rhetoric of community empowerment, involvement and partnership building becomes reality, and where efforts have been made, the results that have emerged have not been particularly encouraging. Many applications of community policing and pro-secution are not fundamentally different from traditional approaches, although they may shift control to local levels and include the community in law enforcement efforts. In fact, Kurki (1999) suggests that at times, community policing strategies can actually result in a more punitive response to crime because it takes so ser-iously the types of behaviour that affect quality of life within communities. We further acknowledge that the reality for restorative policing is the same and that there are proponents who, like us, call for the integration of restorative justice values and processes within policing organisations and those who are vehemently against it (see Chapter 4, this volume). For many critics of police organisations, the combination of increased community involvement alongside enhanced police discretion raises fears of democratic authoritarianism.

These caveats aside, we do believe that even though the emergence of truly 'restorative' policing organisations in neo-liberal countries is highly unlikely, exposing police officers to restorative justice can motivate and facilitate change (i.e. by giving victims a greater voice, securing an element of social justice and increasing relationships between people) amongst those who work within communities. In an attempt to identify ways in which such a strategy can be realised, our argument will be structured as follows. We begin by outlining top-down and bottom-up approaches to policy implementation, discussing the strengths and weaknesses of each. Next, we provide a discussion of how to build support for restorative policing. We then make a case for a framework that integrates the strengths of these approaches to produce a strategy for the successful implementation of restorative policing. In the final section, we map out the key elements that we view as central to such an approach, both from the top-down and from the bottom-up. Throughout, we offer a number of examples of good community justice and restorative policing practices and suggest how positive outcomes might be further enhanced.

'Top-down' versus 'bottom-up' policy implementation

Research on public services and, more specifically, criminal justice professions highlight how the objectives of policy-makers, managers and those working at the 'street-level' often diverge (Ianni and Ianni 1983; Lipsky 1980). Manning (1984) and Cordner (1997), for example, have proposed four factors that can account for the success, or otherwise, of community policing projects. Manning (1984) introduced four meanings, which he characterised as ideological, programmatic, pragmatic and organisational. Cordner (1997) similarly identified four dimensions: the philosophical, the strategic, the tactical and the organisational. These concepts were used to define a basis for a quantitative analysis of success factors and a matrix for assessing the suitability of community policing that is adaptable to the context of restorative policing. A similar approach to multi-dimensional modelling has been adopted by Williams (2014) who distils the above and concludes that analysis of ideological, socio-cultural, political and legal factors are the most common characteristics addressed during the process of policy transfer and implementation. These factors should be incorporated into any audit or assessment of the conceptualisation of restorative models (i.e. their appropriateness for any given context) and reviews of their implementation.

The social and ideological context relates to the environment in which restorative policing is implemented and the mentalities of the communities and local organisations that are engaged within a project. An important consideration here is the extent to which understandings of 'community' and 'policing' can be connected, whether there is community support for such an approach, and the expected impact upon neighbourhood issues of crime, deviance and disorder. Organisational culture refers to the police agencies that are facilitating or implementing a programme whereas political and legal frameworks refer to the wider set of conditions that reflect how local and national political hegemony may, or

Table 7.1 Thinking about policy implementation

Ideological	Organisational
Political	Legal

may not, embrace restorative developments and whether the legal context proffers appropriate flexibility to utilise discretion in a creative manner.

The ability of governments to effectively implement their programmes has often been limited, largely due to the fact that 'local actors often deflect centrally-mandated programs towards their own ends' (Sabatier 1986: 22). In attempting to understand and further develop strategies for the implementation of restorative policing, these factors provide an important framework for the further interrogation of both 'top-down' and 'bottom-up' approaches to developing restorative policing and other community-based initiatives. Such a lens of analysis needs to incorporate both a macro-focus on legislation, politics and policy and a micro-focus on local organisational cultures and ideological dispositions that includes agencies implementing the initiative and the community. This form of analysis highlights the way in which the police and other agencies interpret the role and function of restorative policing initiatives as well as the contested notions and understandings of 'community' that exist at the local level and which influence policy implementation (Moore and Forsyth 1995).

Initiating change from the top-down

In top-down approaches, justice initiatives are designed (in terms of their delivery and parameters) and driven (in terms of their agendas) by the executive of a particular organisation. Hann and Mortimer (1994) suggest that while such a strategy produces a plan which is corporate in scope, it amounts to a leap of faith whereby initiatives are introduced without a strong assessment of internal capability, marketplace credibility or cultural fit and, perhaps most importantly, it does not engender community buy-in. As such, Cunneen *et al.* (2016) suggest that this strategy represents a lost opportunity for organisational learning and partnerships that other more democratic strategies might offer and instead can be seen to most closely conform to ideas around 'governing at a distance' and 'government through community' whereby engagement with communities is largely about implementing what has already been decided (see further Chapter 5, this volume).

In practice, there appears to be a tendency for such strategies to involve the transplantation of largely successful local initiatives that have been developed in a grassroots way by senior criminal justice bureaucrats. These strategies often result in failure because they are repackaged, expanded and then imposed upon frontline staff and communities without due regard being given to the nuances of different locations and the varied problems they face. Two examples can be referred to here. First, as Chapter 3 demonstrated, policy-makers and police executives sought to further embed the community-policing mandate by implementing Community Justice Forums across Canada. Their strategy involved investing considerable resources in the training of frontline staff (and other community-based organisations and members) and devising communication strategies that demonstrated support for restorative justice at the highest levels. However, implementation challenges were presented by cultural perceptions of restorative policing as a soft and difficult to quantify measure which led to resistance from all points of the police hierarchy and, despite extensive training, the programme did not build up sufficient support to become self-sustaining. There was little evidence of a clear implementation plan which aligned restorative justice with other police imperatives and an absence of hard data on reduced recidivism, coupled with the centralising instincts of senior leadership, led to the programme's closure (Duekmedjian 2008). Ultimately, the initiative did not attract the levels of success that bureaucrats were looking for at the grassroots level and so funding was ceased and their attention was focused elsewhere.

Second, in 2005 Community Justice Panels emerged in Chard and Ilminster (a small town in England) as a local response to the absence of accountability structures for low-level offending in the community (see further Clamp and Paterson 2011). An inclusive training programme was essential in developing buy-in, not only from police officers, but also the (relatively homogenous) local community of the value of the approach. The success of the model soon garnered the attention of counsellors in other areas and a pilot was subsequently set up to implement the model (with a range of additional criteria being added) in Sheffield, a location substantially larger and containing a significantly more diverse and transient population. No consultation was conducted with the local police or the community and, as such, the scheme continued to be viewed as peripheral to the day-to-day concerns of the force and its officers (see further Meadows *et al.* 2010). These case studies indicate the importance of meaningful engagement at the local level and the limitations presented by the exclusive adoption of top-down implementation strategies in certain contexts.

Initiating change from the bottom-up

Conversely, bottom-up approaches begin at the local level whereby policy priorities, linkages and service delivery models are determined through community decision-making and negotiated with different levels of government (Cunneen *et al.* 2016). Hann and Mortimer (1994) argue that a particular strength of this approach is that it draws on the creativity of staff, creates ownership over strategies and ensures that plans are consistent with customer needs and expectations. As such, this approach involves a more participatory democratic approach to determining, prioritising and delivering public policy and services (Cunneen *et al.* 2016). However, bottom-up approaches have been considered to be limited in that they can allow inexperienced individuals to influence strategic directions without a sufficient understanding of both internal and external business environments (Hann and Mortimer 1994). Furthermore, bottom-up approaches raise organisational capacity issues such as the availability of police officers with the relevant skill sets to drive the development of restorative policing from the bottom up. While there are countless examples where local partnership innovation has occurred, these initiatives often have a short life span and offer little in the way of sustained organisational learning.

As a consequence of these challenges, restorative approaches are easier to embed in organisations that already demonstrate a philosophical approach that encourages conflict resolution and community engagement. Resistance can be expected in police organisations that are wedded to crime fighting and law enforcement approaches or which are not attuned to local innovation. Yet, while there is much evidence of resistance from police officers and organisations towards the use and implementation of restorative justice in the academic literature, there are fewer acknowledgements that many police officers agree with the values of informal conflict resolution and diversion – albeit as interpreted through the lens of police discretion. The timing and context of change is all important although rarely acknowledged by critics of criminal justice and policing reform.

The majority of literature on police, and criminal justice, cultures focuses upon the macro- and meso-levels of policy development and implementation. This has largely been informed by Schein's definition of organisation culture as the 'deeper level of basic *assumptions and beliefs* that are shared by members of an organisation' (Schein 1985: 6, *emphasis added*) which encourages a structural interpretation to change and police reform. A distinct conceptual model has emerged more recently which focuses upon micro-cultural analysis and the role of the rank and file as police change agents (Campeau 2015; Sklansky and Marks 2008; Wood *et al.* 2008). These perspectives place an emphasis upon the role of officer agency, creativity and discretion and the capacity this holds to drive forward police reforms. This bottom-up perspective helps explain the unevenness in experience of restorative policing as a consequence of the key role played by individuals and small groups of officers in influencing how restorative approaches are translated into police practice.

A good example of such a strategy involved the efforts of a Police Commander to initiate a community policing response with limited resources in Woolloomooloo, a socially disadvantaged inner-Sydney suburb in Australia (see Darcy 2005, what follows is a summary). Woolloomooloo is based in Kings Cross, a challenging area for police services given its extremes of social disadvantage and affluence uniquely blended in the most densely settled residential area in Australia. In 2001, Superintendent Dave Darcy began exploring the local area to get a sense of the problems that were present and talking to local residents and community service providers about their day-to-day experiences. Not unlike a number of similar suburbs: youth offending, street-level drug dealing and theft from motor vehicles were particular issues blighting the community, local residents did not have a relationship with the police and therefore did not report crime, service providers were ignoring the area (particularly those responsible for lighting, garbage collection and graffiti removal), homelessness was rife and there were no forums through which the police and community members could communicate about local issues.

Within his Local Area Command, he found a generalised disdain for the area by some officers, that the amount of full-time officers stationed at Woolloomooloo had over time reduced to four officers (although they were often required to work elsewhere), and those who were on shift in the area tended to stay inside the station completing paper work. As such, there was little understanding of local challenges and no connection to the community, which provided local 'crooks' an upper hand in terms of getting away from officers when they spotted engaging in criminal activities. Furthermore, a generally negative attitude to all youths in the area meant that community attitudes towards police deteriorated rapidly. Interagency cooperation had completely fallen by the wayside with relationships between the police, the local school, Department of Housing and the Department of Community Services virtually non-existent.

In his attempt to reinvigorate community policing, to reduce the likelihood of social injustice from occurring and to respond to the concerns outlined by the community, Superintendent Darcy engaged in a number of specific practices which included: selecting the right people and expanding the number of officers dedicated to the area; communicating clear objectives to these officers which included strategies through which they could be realised; the establishment of a Community Safety Officer role to develop sustainable social development strategies; and the re-establishment of the Woolloomooloo Police-Community Consultative Committee. Within six months the strategy had paid off. Community-police relations had improved dramatically, interagency cooperation had resumed, the homeless had been relocated and services signposted for them, crime had reduced and both officers and the community alike became unwedded to the perception that the legalistic approach should be the first option. Rather, both were able to appreciate that investing time and resources in responding to the environment in which crime was taking place paid significant dividends.

The case study is an example of how conferencing can, if employed frequently enough (even inadvertently), build capacity in participants to apply the process on their own. As such, the bottom-up approach involves an appreciation of the complexity of community contexts and shared, even ambidextrous (March 1991), leadership that is driven by police-community collaborations rather than the traditional mechanics of command and control (Flynn and Herrington 2015; Herrington and Colvin 2016). Although the themes of partnership and collaboration have dominated government and policing policy for three decades, the extent to which this policy translates into just policing or inclusive partnership practices remains subject to much debate and is manifest in uneven and inconsistent experiences of both community policing and restorative policing (Paterson and Clamp 2012). From a policing perspective, much of this challenge lies within the organisational structure of policing where extensive discretion for front-line police officers encourages a culture of innovation which is rarely captured and shared within or across police organisations and leaves them subject to the ebbs and flows of changing visions from senior leaders (see also Shapland 2009).

Building support for restorative policing

It is perhaps unsurprising then, that contemporary approaches to policy implementation are rarely enacted exclusively from the top-down or the bottom-up (Hann and Mortimer 1994). Generally a hybrid approach exists whereby particular policy directions might be devised at the top, but the implementation strategy for those policy directions are informed by advice and further contextualisation from the bottom-up. Gilbert's (2012) research on place-based initiatives within indigenous communities in Australia indicates that they can have a significant impact in facilitating change, but that they require deep-seated reform on two fronts. First, government agencies have to become much more collaborative in delivering services to communities, and second, they have to become much more consultative in setting priorities with those for whom services are being devised. In sum, the challenge is that governments are required to adopt less familiar methods of working which are 'characterised by networks, collaboration, community engagement and flexibility ... in order to alleviate long standing disadvantage' (Gilbert 2012: 2).

Dandurand and Griffiths (2006) summarise a number of key factors that promote the successful implementation of restorative justice in particular. First, much like restorative processes themselves, successful initiatives involve collaboration between all stakeholders – not only the police and communities, but also the other agencies that will affect the remit of the programme, such as the prosecutor's office or the court. Second, they have effective communications strategies that disseminate the role and purpose of restorative justice in such a way that it fosters support from both officers and the community. Third, consultation has often been undertaken with stakeholder and advocacy groups within the community. Fourth, the eligibility criteria are clear and understood by those who refer cases to restorative justice initiatives. Fifth, all stakeholders, but victims in particular, are informed about the process which allows them to make a truly informed decision about whether or not to participate. This process involves addressing issues such as confidentiality, the strengths and weaknesses of the approach in comparison to other options, information about legal counsel, the support resources available and access to the facilitators' credentials. Sixth, clear training standards and oversight of facilitators is effectively implemented. Seventh, a strong evaluation strategy is in place – this is important not only for measuring how successful the programme is, but also as a basis from which to evolve practice. Finally, a realistic assessment of the resources has been made to sustain programmes beyond the initial pilot phase.

The original Wagga Wagga Model provides the best example of such an approach. This is largely due to the fact that the impetus for change was derived from the top-down by senior bureaucrats; proposals received endorsement from all departments and were then passed onto those with the greatest local knowledge for implementation (i.e. Terry O'Connell and Kevin Wales, see Chapter 3, this volume). The distinctiveness of the approach emerged out of the canvassing of both the community and frontline staff to assess the likelihood of the successful implementation of the proposals as well as the means through which implementation strategies could be devised. Furthermore, the selection of a small group of officers to identify cases to be dealt with through conferencing generated capacity and knowledge of the process amongst key staff before extending training to others, thus limiting the burden of significant levels of frontline discretion. This process allowed front-line staff who was resistant to this philosophical approach to observe the process from start to finish via a slow transformation of the traditional cautioning process to one of conferencing. This meant that positive outcomes from the process were embedded in local police culture and retold as 'war stories' which helped build acceptance from colleagues (Moore and Forsythe 1995: 12). Most importantly, the process was voluntary for stakeholders, which helped generate a sense of ownership from police officers rather than a feeling that they were responding to edicts from above. In short, achieving buy-in was a key element of the implementation process from the beginning.

The importance of culture and the social-cultural meaning of police activity are felt amongst small groups and this is notable in the development of the Wagga Wagga Model. Bazemore (2000a: 232–233) outlines how this approach functions for those involved and mobilised by their experience of conferences which exposes them to an emphasis on reparation and collective outcomes ahead of traditional offender-orientations. This represents a dramatic change for police officers, communities and the offenders and victims who engage in restorative processes. Many of the challenges faced by restorative initiatives during the first wave of programmes during the 1990s emerged due to an underestimation of the impact of this change for all those involved in these processes (see case examples from Chapter 3, this volume). As such, we suggest that the transformation demanded by a move towards a more restorative approach needs to take place through a process that helps police officers to identify the benefits of restorative approaches, to develop the appropriate skills and attributes (such as communication, problem-solving, leadership and relationship-building) and to consolidate organisational knowledge and learning.

In Canada, Marinos and Innocente (2008) have identified several factors that influence police support for informal resolutions such as restorative justice. These include the flexible use of discretion to interpret legislation and guidance, the use of restorative measures for first-time offenders, and for relatively minor property offences and assaults. Officers have also cited the significant influence of an offenders' attitude as a determining fact on whether or not they would be selected for diversion. Abramson (2003) has also identified significant barriers to the use of restorative justice in a separate Canadian project and that involves an unwillingness to use informal resolutions for anything but the most minor offences. Therefore, while there may be slight differences in views on appropriate offences, there is a clear synergy across the literature on restorative policing projects about the value of discretion for low-level offences with individuals who demonstrate contrition and accept culpability.

It is also important to identify offences that are deemed to be appropriate for a restorative response and the extent of appropriateness is ultimately determined by the support of local agencies and the wider community. One example of this is the San Francisco 'Resolve to Stop the Violence Programme' (RSVP) where, immediately after the arrest of a domestic violence perpetrator, a victim advocate is introduced to assess the victim's needs (i.e. security, psychological) and to take a formal statement (for more, see Alarid and Montemayor 2012). The victim advocate works within a victim assistance unit that has the chief purpose of supporting and protecting victims (as opposed to securing a conviction) and assessing whether victim-offender mediation is appropriate for each case. This approach is underpinned by research that demonstrates that significant numbers of domestic violence victims are less likely to experience further victimisation after the first call to police when they have had the opportunity to drop charges and proceed with an informal judicial route (Guzik 2008). This requires an appreciation of a broader policing role from one that is primarily concerned with keeping the peace to a role that proactively makes the peace (Meyers *et al.* 2009). It is also essential, given the sensitivities of domestic violence cases, to ensure that the victim advocate role is professionalised via the development of minimum standards of practice, appropriate qualifications and good quality training (Choi and Gilbert 2010).

Aertsen (2009) has suggested that one of the reasons for the popularity of restorative justice within police organisations is that it is flexible enough to be moulded to fit the multiple agendas that make up policing. He elaborates by highlighting that restorative justice is

> not only about delivering a service to the public, or narrowing the gap between the justice system and the public, or even improving the image of the police within society, it is also part of a crime control strategy and to some extent a sanctioning mechanism.
>
> (2009: 79)

As such, it is important for due consideration to be given to the objectives, principles and values as well as the nature of partnerships and the roles of actors within restorative justice initiatives. He points to three strategies that should be adopted: the active involvement of the police in developing restorative justice (in whatever form) should be encouraged; an integrated approach should be adopted whereby the community is consulted and restorative justice is conceived in partnership with community members to avoid over-institutionalisation and to garner support; and finally, mediation and other restorative justice practices at the level of the police should be given 'sufficient autonomy', as it is defined in the Council of Europe Recommendation R (99)19 with respect to the position of mediation services in the criminal justice system.

By way of example of the 'lessons' outlined above, David Hines, a former Lieutenant at the Woodbury Police Department (see further Chapter 3, this volume) provides a good account of his initial reaction to restorative justice and what it involves to successfully implement programmes based on this philosophy (see Hines and Bazemore 2003). He suggests that initially he was very sceptical and that he did not invest time in the practice until nearly two months later. Part of the reason for this was that the idea seemed disconnected with the realities of policing – something that seemed more aligned to social work. The impetus for the change in this perception and the start of the transformation project within Woodbury Police Department was a realisation of the important role of the community in responding to crime effectively and its central place within restorative justice practice. As such, the approach adopted was underpinned by the belief that it could only work if the community was central to both the design and implementation of the model – the police would have to deliberately seek to engage the community in further strengthening and building on the experience of the model wherever it could. Thus, restorative policing became associated with an effective partnership with the community in Woodbury, not something that could be achieved by the police alone, and the key factor to the success experienced within this force (Hines and Bazemore 2003).

In relation to policing, in particular, Hann and Mortimer (1994: 157) suggest that obstacles to effective policy implementation include 'poor training, inappropriate planning methods, inadequate communication, lack of information, and resistance to change'. Building on these lessons about what is involved in successfully implementing restorative justice projects, we seek to develop a framework for policing organisations that can lead to significant and sustainable change.

Towards a framework for change

The successful adoption of restorative policing requires a significant shift in the sociocultural meaning of police work that not only highlights the benefits of restorative policing for street-level police officers, but also how this might alter their role within the communities that they serve (Clamp and Paterson 2013). There is wide recognition of the importance of police culture in analyses of restorative policing although there is also a tendency to interpret culture in an overly structural manner and to underplay agency-oriented perspectives. This is largely due to the well renowned foundational studies of street-level police culture (for example Grimshaw and Jefferson 1987; Reiner 2010; Skolnick 1968) taking structural perspectives that envisaged police officers as obstacles to reform. These structural perspectives have since been updated and adapted with an increasing focus upon police as potential agents of social change (Campeau

2015; Chan 1996; Wood *et al.* 2008) and recognised within police organisations that are increasingly aware of the need to build in appropriate approaches to recruitment, training and leadership development to harness this potential.

Policing systems that embrace active citizenship, community engagement and proactive community crime prevention tend to be more comfortable with the sociocultural meaning of restorative policing. Drawing on his experience from the field of victim assistance, Aertsen (2009) argues that orienting daily police work into a new direction requires a shift in professional culture, ongoing support and guidance at the local level, and the availability of time and human resources. Using the conceptual work previously undertaken on police culture as a basis, theoretical models of organisational development with multiple cultural layers were proposed as far back as 1993 by Manning. He suggested that there are three key subcultures of policing – senior command, middle management and the rank and file – which can be used as analytical sites for investigation when implementing policy. Manning's (1993) conceptual separation of three subcultures helps us to interpret the organisational emphasis on values and ethics at different levels of the police hierarchy; it also explains police resistance to new initiatives that do not sit within the framework of existing police (cultural) knowledge. Thus, rather than understanding police culture as static and mono-lithic, it is more helpful to emphasise the importance of the social, legal and political sites in which policing takes place.

Stockdale (2015) uses Manning's model to explore how rank and role affects police interpretations of restorative justice. Her findings suggest that street-level police officers interpret the purpose of restorative approaches as primarily a *process* through which to repair the harm caused, middle managers view it as a *practice* through which to give victims a greater voice, and senior command per-ceive restorative justice as a *philosophy* through which to influence and secure more effective responses to crime. Thus, the different sociocultural sites of polic-ing mean that restorative initiatives are interpreted in very different and poten-tially competing ways. This is not surprising. Chan's work on police culture emphasises the importance of 'the interaction between the socio-political context of police work and various dimensions of police organisational knowledge' (Chan 1996: 110). This framework draws on the work of Bourdieu (1980) and provides an acknowledgement of multiple police cultures that operate both hori-zontally and vertically as well as across time and space, and helps to explain the multiplicity of responses to restorative policing from different areas of police organisations.

As such, in order to develop a sustainable and meaningful position for restora-tive values within policing organisations, change is required across all three cul-tural sites of policing (Chan 1996; Heslop 2011). This cultural and organisational perspective opens up the possibility of change and the incorporation, or translation, of restorative values into contemporary thinking about policing. Attempts to imple-ment restorative policing must bridge all three cultural arenas otherwise policy implementation is likely to fail and the focus on restorative approaches is likely to be usurped by more traditional punitive policing strategies and tactics used by fellow officers (Mastrofski and Ritti 2000). The work of Holland (2007), Skogan (2008) and others has demonstrated that the process of reform (i.e. the way in which it is enacted), in particular the central role played by middle-level trainers and leaders, is as essential for success as the activities of senior leadership.

We suggest that the transformation demanded by a move towards a more restorative approach in policing needs to take place through a process that provides police officers with the necessary skills, alongside strategies that will facilitate buy-in from frontline officers so that they may adequately adapt to this new way of fulfilling their daily tasks. Priorities among the lower ranks within police forces are generally operationally focused (Pearson-Goff and Herrington 2013). As such, processes and practices which align with their perceived purpose and function are far more likely to be embraced than those that veer too far away from traditional role interpretation. Because of this, any significant reform or change to police practice has to be cognisant of cultural reactions to that change, particularly where the reform involves a significant shift in policing philosophy.

Drawing on the lessons from the discussions in the previous sections, we make a case for transformation in a number of key areas. Given that our position is that both top-down and bottom-up strategies are essential, but need to be reconsidered in their current guise, we discuss these areas in relation to both top-down and bottom-up strategies. While the concept of police culture is useful in understanding the obstacles and boundaries that may impede police reforms it does not provide a constructive way forward for policy-makers and practitioners who are tasked with policy implementation. The combination of analysis of law, politics, organisational structure and ideology alongside an understanding of the process of knowledge translation at the macro, meso and micro levels can help to generate a more multi-dimensional framework for change.

In the next section we, therefore, identify and further unpack four key areas that we perceive to be crucial in attempts to drive change: leadership, organisational structure, training and education, and empowering the frontline. These factors have already been identified as important in the existing restorative policing literature, but they have often been interpreted and analysed through the overly structural lens of police culture. As such, we attempt to further develop analysis by undertaking a more appreciative approach that utilises concepts of social capital to assess the potential for change in each of these four areas. The implementation science literature is clear that the process of change is unlikely to be either a simple or linear experience and that the 'wicked' nature of the problems being addressed means that a long-term commitment to change may be required.

Leadership

The hierarchical nature of policing with its quasi-militaristic structures means there is a tendency to interpret leadership exclusively from a top-down perspective. This interpretive instinct is evident in police training manuals and leadership courses from across the globe. Yet, we argue that this approach overlooks the work conducted by individuals in non-administrative positions and overemphasises the impact that leadership from the top has on the rank-and-file. In order to illustrate this position, we suggest that leadership can be discussed at two levels in respect of the implementation of restorative policing from the top-down as well as from within the organisation.

The first is the way in which we would traditionally think of leadership for organisations, which involves those at the top of the hierarchy. The role of senior police officers is to provide a vision and a sense of mission for the force and their orientation will naturally affect the areas that are prioritised and resourced (Skogan and Hartnett 1997). This extends to setting the tone of what policing in their force involves, how officers should practice it and the political support on offer to accomplish it (Robinson 2003). A good example of where restorative policing has been driven from the top-down through a clear mission statement and with adequate resourcing took place within Thames Valley in England (see further Chapter 3, this volume). Charles Pollard was the Chief Constable at the time and was able to initiate change in existing procedures and the sociocultural meaning of community policing. Moreover, his influence in government had broader implications in terms of prompting the development of national restorative justice legislation for the youth justice system (Hoyle and Rosenblatt 2015).

The second way to think about leadership is more closely aligned with the other restorative policing experiments that were initiated in Australia, the United States and Canada. The pioneers in these areas did not hold the same governance positions within their forces and were not able to create a radical shift in the focus of the force in terms of its overall priorities and resourcing. Rather they were members of the meso-level mid-upper ranks, well respected and perceived to have a particular skill set that could help to initiate change as part of a specific reform initiative housed within the force. While their duties and responsibilities were considerable, the overall impact on the force was limited given that their work formed an isolated subset of other departmental priorities and was not aligned with broader force and governmental imperatives. As such, these initiatives were much more susceptible to changes in the priorities of the force that took place at an executive level. Hines and Bazemore (2003) suggest that incident-driven and case-focused policing limits strategic thinking or reactions that would normally focus on long-term solutions. This is largely due to the fact that the traditional criminal justice system generally (and policing specifically) is designed to *remove* problems, not *fix* them. As such, the general trend has been for restorative justice programmes to be implemented by one key professional in a criminal justice agency and only that individual needs to be converted to the philosophy underpinning it.

These observations have also been made in relation to the implementation of community policing practice. Robinson (2003), for example, in her study on the implementation of community policing in Indianapolis and St Petersburg, suggests that an important factor in the extent of change that occurs relates to how those initiating change translate philosophy into practice. In both sites, Chiefs were appointed because of their support and promotion of community policing, but they varied in how they translated this into practice. In Indianapolis, the

Chief sought to reduce fear of crime by increasing the use of stops, arrests, searches and seizures; interpreted partnership as staff members attending community meetings; and created a section of Crime Bill Officers who worked together on community projects. The effect was that community policing was assigned to a few officers within the force and collaboration with the community did not feature. In St Petersburg, however, the Chief focused on problem solving by encouraging community partnerships; community officers worked with patrol officers as a team to resolve issues confronting local areas; and performance appraisals were altered to reflect the position that community policing was the responsibility of all officers. Through this process, the community policing approach became embedded into organisational structures and thinking.

While it is evident that top-down implementation is important in initiating and providing political support for change programmes within policing organisations, Robinson (2003) also demonstrates that leadership is limited in what it can achieve. While police leaders provide the impetus to expose their forces to restorative policing and drive forward changes in the approach to dealing with crime at a frontline level, following their retirement their legacy tends to wither and normal policing styles resume. In many respects this is unsurprising. The role of senior police officers is to provide vision and a sense of mission for the force, however, 'vision among the lower ranks is more operationally focused' with officers reluctant to change their approach and practices unless such change also suits their perceived purpose and functions (Pearson-Goff and Herrington 2013: 19). In many respects then, the initial 'boom' of restorative practice within police forces can be attributed to subordinate officers following orders, while the subsequent collapse provides evidence of a veneer of change rather than a meaningful shift within the sociocultural meaning of police work at the local level.

In order for restorative thinking to become a central part of the policing response, steps need to be taken to reinvigorate innovation and leadership at all levels of the police hierarchy. The organisational constraints generated by an emphasis upon hierarchical control and administered via a quasi-militaristic structure have the potential to stifle officer discretion, street-level leadership and inadvertently encourage risk-averse behaviour rather than strengthening officer capacity to enact change. Some have suggested that the key to longer-term change lies in a move from a transactional leadership style to a transformational leadership approach. The former, said to be a traditional or conventional approach to managing forces, involves the leader specifying not only the expectations of subordinates but also the conditions under which such expectations should be met and the rewards and penalties on offer (Engel and Worden 2003). In the twenty-first century, the transactional approach has increasingly fallen into disrepute and transformational leadership styles which emphasise 'participation, consultation and inclusion' in a bid to get subordinates to buy into the 'vision' that is being proposed (Silvestri 2007: 39) have become increasingly popular.

Here, we take the argument a step further and suggest that the required style of leadership must attempt to engage not only street-level police officers but also the public who are required to actively engage, rather than simply support, the changes in policing. We therefore argue that restorative policing can only work if the myriad of cultures, values and practices that it exhibits secures the full appreciation of both the police and public and builds their capacity to work in collaboration. This requires transformational leadership from senior police officers and managers who use their positions to change the way police organisations think about its mission and purpose (Burns 1978). A clear vision of local police leadership needs to be articulated and consistently practiced by police leaders via participative and open management styles that engage police officers (Alarid and Montemayor 2012) and generate sustainability by sharing leadership throughout the organisation and into the community.

Restorative justice, at its core, is a participatory process and it is likely to gain further purchase where its values inform senior police leadership and management styles. As such, we argue that leadership must be coupled with the structural changes needed to support officer engagement in restorative policing. To date this has not occurred. We call for a long-term view of effecting change within policing organisations and for leadership styles to be built around this strategy. Timing is important to this process. Police leaders need to recognise emerging trends resulting from social, economic and cultural change and to predict how this will impact upon future police-community engagement and surrounding structures. It is then changes to organisational structures that embed sustainable change and impact upon officer behaviour in the long term (De Jong *et al.* 2001; Trojanowisz and Bucqueroux 1998).

Organisational structure

An important dynamic in the successful implementation of restorative policing is the micro-level bonds and structures that tie people, groups and institutions together (Hirschi 1969) as well as the macro-level social ecology that either helps or hinders social organisation (Sampson and Groves 1989). Restorative policing seeks to mobilise action at the micro-level, via the sustained engagement of individual officers with communities to strengthen existing linkages and build citizen-institution partnerships, which perform, where appropriate, both activist and mentorship roles in communities. The process is built from the micro-level upwards by relationships between small groups of police officers and communities that are consolidated at the meso- and macro-levels. The challenge herewith is the extent to which communities have the capacity, or collective efficacy (Braithwaite 1989; Sampson *et al.* 1997), to engage in such processes and to use them to strengthen relationships between at-risk individuals and groups within the wider community.

As the community policing case studies in this chapter have shown, geographic permanence is essential for success largely due to the fact that it promotes ownership, responsibility and a sense of political support among police officers for what happens on their beats and because it allows mutual relationships characterised by trust and accountability to develop between police and community residents (Trojanowicz *et al.* 2002; Paterson and Best 2016). Permanently assigning officers to a particular area, as Darcy's (2005) experience demonstrated, allows officers to develop a local understanding of the particular issues confronting that community and to develop links with service providers for that area in developing a more effective service. Responding to these issues is important for improving quality of life which can result in a reduction in crime, so although police officers may not see these issues as falling directly within their remit, they certainly do have an impact on their job (see Darcy 2005; Gilbert 2012). Furthermore, officers assigned to those beats can collaborate with more reactively focused officers to develop creative solutions for working together to resolve problems.

In seeking to further effect change for the long term, an additional strategy would be to further decentralise police organisational structures so that specific police officer roles draw on differentiated approaches to recruitment and training. This would encourage organisations to develop specific policing roles, styles and strategies based on the characteristics and needs that the communities they serve require. In this manner, local responsibility and authority is structured throughout the organisation rather than operational priorities and strategies being uniformly set for the whole force regardless of 'local fit'. This change would assist police officers in adopting a leadership position in the communities in which they are based and place specific requirements to develop trust with senior command and local communities, to assess community capacity, to view themselves as community leaders, and to develop and implement community-policing projects in conjunction with all stakeholders.

'Community capacity' models provide a framework to map both individual capacity and the socio-environmental conditions of a community that enable or inhibit local capacity (Jackson *et al.* 2013) to understand the extent to which there is capacity within a community to generate assets that can be drawn on to improve the well-being of local people. These models are appropriate for restorative policing as it then provides a mechanism for identifying where the development of restorative policing is likely to be supported by community structures rather than by decisions made by public officials at a distance from the community. Analysis is provided of social networks that are understood as 'conditions' that may facilitate or hinder social integration. These conditions can help build a map of supportive linkages for individuals that can be addressed through the processes of restorative policing to help support positive collective outcomes. The processes of restorative policing thus serve to strengthen individuals (working at a procedural level) and families, to build connections within communities, to re-enforce community values, and mobilise action to address crime problems (Stuart 1997). There is much potential here to address the longer-term impact of crime upon individuals and communities although it is important to be cognisant of the challenge of central authority narrowing the administrative focus of restorative policing and not engaging with these linkages. Therefore, the aim is to explore not only the capital, talents and skills of individuals, but also the community conditions that can be manifest in structures and processes as exemplified in the Wagga Wagga example (Moore and Forsythe 1995).

However, Hann and Mortimer (1994) warn that devolving power down through the policing hierarchy to achieve more participatory, community-based and locally responsive approaches is something that police administrators need to prepare the organisation for, particularly if they have been used to a top-down management style. They point to four obstacles: first, there needs to be a robust training strategy in place for operational managers; second, strategies need to be put in place to overcome the reluctance that middle and senior management may pose (see also Skogan 2008); third, it needs to be acknowledged that the skills set of officers may not be what is required by the change in approach (see also Paterson 2011, 2016); and finally, exemplars of 'best practice' are needed for operational staff to refer to. It is also essential that the right members of the community be recruited, which means those who demonstrate the appropriate values for doing restorative work. Hines and Bazemore (2003: 421) allude to these values, which include 'respect, responsibility (account-ability), acceptance of others, safety (or security), nonviolence, [and] working together to solve problems'.

There have been objections to such a strategy of devolution within the crim-inological literature, however, largely due to the fact that it creates the poten-tial for 'postcode lottery justice' (Crawford and Clear 2001; Acton 2015). The concern is that some areas will be exposed to law and order styles of policing with substantial numbers of youth and ethnic minorities (in particular) being processed through the criminal justice system whilst relatively affluent areas benefit from more democratic and community-oriented responses. Yet, Shap-land *et al.*'s (2007) research from England and Wales has already identified two key factors which are essential to avoid this unevenness with restorative policing. These are selection of police officers with the relevant skill sets, not least the ability to empathise with a multitude of viewpoints, and the provision of relevant and operationally useful training that links restorative justice to other proactive, problem-oriented policing strategies. Holland's (2007) ana-lysis of diversity training has raised similar points, in particular the central role played by trainers and leaders, in facilitating policy and systemic reform that requires a reconceptualisation of traditional values, roles and expectations.

We argue that under a restorative justice framework, police officers no longer act as authoritative figures responding to disputes, conflict and crime but are rather required to engage with communities in ways that are determined as much by the community as the officers themselves. This presents a significant chal-lenge for the development of new skills, attributes and organisational capacity, a dramatic change not only for police officers, but for communities as well. It is clear that law, politics and organisational structure provide a platform for the development of restorative policing but it is training and education that addresses ideological issues and the social-cultural meaning of police work for police offic-ers and communities.

Training and education

Victim-oriented strategies, such as restorative policing, require police officers: to demonstrate attributes such as empathy; to relate to both offender and victim; and, to have the courage to intervene in complex situations without strict legal guidance. Approaching policing in this manner requires a training and education system that does more than set core competencies and which focuses on officer capability to learn in the job, supports risk-taking and feeds new knowledge into mechanisms of organisational learning which can be shared with colleagues. Subsequent developments in restorative policing need to be embedded at the street-level via police officers with relevant skill sets to integrate restorative practice into day-to-day policing and to build the social capital of police-community networks. These changes recognise the value of organisational learning as a process through which officers throughout the police hierarchy challenge 'old ways of thinking, overcome defensive routines, and engage in incremental change' (Alarid and Montemayor 2012: 458). It is widely acknowledged that the approach to training, which is currently used in the United States, Australia and England and Wales, does not currently do this although there is growing acknowledgement of the limitations of an overly legalistic approach (Flynn and Herrington 2015).

Restorative forms of policing require officers to act as community leaders in addressing the harm caused by offending behaviour; to use their discretion in such a way that prioritises problem-solving ahead of conflict management; and to see the community as partners in responding to and managing conflict within the community. This transformative change requires a distinct shift in the socio-cultural meaning of police work for those involved in restorative programmes. This transformation crucially needs to take place through a process that provides police officers with the necessary skills to adapt to such a dramatic change in their role and questions remain about the available organisational capacity to upscale restorative policing in this manner. Addressing organisational capacity requires assessment of opportunities for training and development, support from senior officers, and police officer attributes and skill sets to determine whether the timing is right to introduce a new initiative.

As we have highlighted in previous chapters, Mastrofskis *et al.*'s (2002) typology of community police officer in the United States pointed to the continued structural and cultural dominance of reactive law-enforcers within police organisations and the secondary positioning of community-oriented endeavours to response work in other jurisdictions (Foster and Jones 2010), particularly for those working in urban areas. This cultural and organisational position is unsurprising given the relatively slow pace of change to police training which means that modes of training continue to focus upon the law and core competencies rather than the deeper learning required for complex problem-solving (Cox 2011; Paterson 2011). Once again, this picture is uneven both within and across countries.

There are a number of issues that should be given due consideration in training officers to effectively deliver restorative processes and in adopting restorative justice principles to inform their approach to working with members of the community. First, there needs to be adequate training in the principles and prac-tice of restorative justice (Dandurand and Griffiths 2006). In fact, Aertsen (2009) suggests that restorative justice should not only form a part of officer training, it should become a permanent fixture in all police training. It is impossible to expect anyone to truly grasp what restorative justice means for themselves or for others (such as victims, offenders and the community) if they do not understand what restorative justice is, what it involves, its benefits and limitations and what it means to work in a restorative way. Second, there needs to be a clear articu-lation of, and training for, the techniques and skills required by a restorative response to conflict. In both of these instances, it would be beneficial to involve policing staff in restorative processes to allow them to observe what happens from the beginning to the end of the process. In some respects, this may chal-lenge the temptation to continue with business as usual.

Training and education is essential in developing ideas around what the police do and how they should interpret their roles. Yet, current teaching methods for new police recruits do not offer the opportunity for officers to interpret their role in flexible ways (Neyroud 2013). Furthermore, training for officers on restora-tive justice is often limited to one-off sessions that expose them to the broad ideas contained within the restorative justice literature or only marginally more substantial training in what conferencing looks like. Given the complexity of restorative justice as a concept, the radical shift that it requires from traditional police responses to crime and the enhanced skills required to deliver restorative processes in an effective way it is clear that there are plenty of examples of train-ing on the topic that are not fit for purpose.

The ongoing philosophical shift to community-oriented policing continues to encourage a shift from a technical focus on competencies towards a more reflex-ive appreciation of the complexity of the police role and officer capability within changing contexts. This process mirrors long-established developments in the fields of medicine, law and social work where officers are recruited and trained with the critical thinking skills to challenge managers and existing ways of doing things. Critical thinking skills encourage flexibility in orientation to competing demands whilst also generating transferable skills that help individuals to develop competence in a number of areas (Jaschke and Neidhardt 2007). Teach-ing officers how to operationalise their values and beliefs in a way that co-exists with the different values and beliefs of other citizens is a formidably complex challenge, particularly in an organisation that can resemble a paramilitary insti-tution during times of social conflict (Waddington 1998). International evidence indicates that giving priority to an educational and training focus on critical thinking alongside an emphasis on law and control can aid the development of more flexible value-systems suited to the demands of community-oriented polic-ing (Paterson 2011, 2016).

There is some evidence that higher education is likely to have a positive impact upon the delivery of community policing, such as college educated offic-ers receiving fewer complaints than their colleagues with less education (Kappe-ler *et al.* 1992). Experience is also an important dynamic here with De Jong

(2004) noting that female officers improved their responsiveness to members of the public as they got more experience. In both these instances, harnessing the benefits of training and experience can benefit public trust in the police via the more professional use of discretion – that is making appropriate situational judgements about how, why and whether to apply the law – and its impact upon public accountability and police legitimacy.

While all officers can be involved in restorative policing at the point of diversion it makes pragmatic sense to only involve those who embrace restorative values in conducting mediations or conferences. This would mean that all officers needed to be provided with grounding in restorative practice, but only those who engage in the more specialised work would be required to attend to the more complex conceptual and theoretical issues and their implications for practice. These officers would be able to lead partnership strategies and restorative practice that takes place in neutral facilities without imposing themselves on facilitative arrangements. As part of capacity building in this area these officers should also be involved in case monitoring and programme evaluation (as in Wagga Wagga, Bethlehem and Thames Valley). The involvement of these officers in the mutual development of research and evaluation programmes will ensure that knowledge of restorative policing is embedded within police organisational knowledge via action learning methodologies.

The recruitment and training of community members, which embraces restorative values is equally as important as the recruitment of police officers. This process needs to operate at the local level, as has been demonstrated in case studies from New Zealand and Australia, where policy was developed via collaboration of local community stakeholders and included training for victim advocates. Those whose views may diverge need to meet up at an early a stage as possible to ensure that the meaning of restorative justice is not co-opted by one agency (Schwartz *et al.* 2003). Restorative approaches require the active input and support of the community, but building community buy-in and developing this critical partnership requires much initial work and constant reminders to citizens and community groups of their importance while keeping them involved in a meaningful way. Police must also be willing to share what they are doing and to discuss this with the community. Having community volunteers requires a commitment to recruit, train and 'maintain' them.

In Woodbury, for example, a structured training and development programme in restorative processes was established for volunteers to ensure sustainability and support for the programme. The programme emphasised the development of key volunteer skills for conferencing efforts and the central role of members of the community in overseeing conferences where there had been a significant impact upon the community. Through this process, members of the community were able to establish norms that represented their community during the conference (Bazemore and Schiff 2002; Karp and Walther, 2001) and to provide support for victims. Collectively, the approaches outlined above helped to build a sense of co-ownership of programmes as well as an infrastructure for developing key skills. These processes enabled those in front-line positions to invest in the programmes yet for these approaches to work in other contexts analysis is required of the assumption that officers and communities are provided with the appropriate socio-legal context to do this work. While we have already addressed issues related to leadership, organisational structure, training and education via analysis of a mixture of political, ideological and organisational factors, the final section incorporates a much more prominent focus on the legal aspects of implementation to complete our four point analysis.

Empowering the frontline

Restorative policing, with its emphasis upon bottom-up leadership, inverts the traditional police hierarchy and reconceptualises street-level police officers and the communities they work in as key sources of agency, social capital, decision-making, leadership and organisational learning. This process requires the empowerment of front-line officers through support for risk-taking and the creative use of police discretion to work alongside communities that are used to the police taking sovereign responsibility for breaches of the law and social order. There is a clear tension here particularly during the absorption of restorative thinking into police environments which can lead to unexpected outcomes as new ideas are rapidly consumed, digested, and adapted by strong local occupational cultures. As we stated earlier, Chan (1996: 100) sees this as an organisational issue, as new initiatives are culturally translated through the 'socio-political context of police work', but it is equally applicable to individual officer agency and the networks of political and legal knowledge that inform the practices of small groups. Thus, clear and consistent organisational support is required to build a culture of innovation, leadership and creativity in which police officers' utilise their discretion for progressive purposes.

Empowering the front line in an effective manner has the potential to further empower and engage individuals and communities. As Gehm (1998) acknowledges, police officers play a crucial role in ensuring victim participation and require an emphasis upon their position to empower victims by encouraging their role in restorative processes. Police officers perform a key community leadership role in recognising threats to an individual's safety and reinforcing a victims' sense of their right to occupy space (Erez and Ibarra 2007: 103; Taylor 2012). In their Buenos Aires case study, Paterson and Clamp (2014) noted that whilst traditional criminal justice agencies remain stakeholders in victim-oriented initiatives an emphasis is placed upon the role of the individual as the active decision-maker. This challenges traditional conceptualisations of policing roles further and delineates this approach from community and problem-oriented policing strategies, which remain embedded in offender-oriented conceptualisations of the purpose of policing.

The emphasis placed on individual well-being, positive social identity and interpersonal relationships avoids disempowerment and emphasises the role of a victim as an active social agent. In these instances, the police officer role is focused upon facilitating peaceful outcomes rather than being a sovereign arbiter. At the same time, this transformed role needs to remain grounded within the myriad of demands that are made on police officers. Restorative policing, with its emphasis upon victim-oriented policing should also be aligned with other policing demands such as order maintenance and crime fighting. Hines and Bazemore (2003) draw on their Woodbury case study to note that restorative policing did not stop officers from using more traditional crime-fighting approaches in other areas and that arrest rates, detection rates and convictions remained high, which ensured continued support from the judiciary and prosecutors. Wood *et al.* (2008) also acknowledge that successful change programmes must be aligned with street-level reality and the experiences of front-line police officers. As such, through these processes restorative policing becomes recognised as an approach that can be drawn upon at the appropriate time.

The concept of police leadership can be stretched and applied to the front-line officer involved in restorative policing who can build legitimacy for their role from objectives set in collaboration with local communities. Police officers will subsequently be encouraged to question traditional thinking about offender-victim dichotomies and the role of the formal criminal justice process and to seek resolutions to problems from within active communities. This process requires police officers with flexible value systems that actively engage *with* diverse communities and possess the leadership skills to build support amongst their colleagues as well as communities. Burns's (1978) model of transformational leadership has been most commonly used to capture the requirements of senior police leaders but Vinzant and Crothers (1994) argue that this model can be stretched further and applied to the role of a police officer undertaking restorative work.

As the previous section noted, Schein's (1996) work on organisational culture points to the importance of recruiting police officers who have the critical thinking skills to challenge managers and traditional modes of thinking as outlined in the literature on police culture. This perspective paved the way for the more recent work by Wood *et al.* (2008) on the role of street-level officers as active social agents with strong social capital who influence and determine the environment they work in. The concern that emerges here relates to the cultural capture and adaptation of enhanced discretion by the punitive and authoritarian values that are embedded in some parts of police organisations and communities (Clamp and Paterson 2011). There is a large body of academic literature that focuses on challenges presented by police culture but, equally as important, if not more, are the conceptualisations of, and expectations from, communities for policing agencies to actively engage in the mitigation of conflict and the restoration of a hegemonic social order (Fukuyama 2012).

Problems such as enhancing community engagement in conflict resolution and repairing social harm are so complicated and convoluted that they fit the definition of a 'wicked' problem utilised by complexity theory (Grint 2010). A wicked problem is inherently complex, cannot be removed from its social context and cannot be subjected to simple forms of measurement. Wicked problems tend to require a response that embraces the collective rather than just an edict from above and an acceptance that constructing a solution to the problem is an often inelegant process that takes a long time (Grint 2010). Shared leadership emerges as a key factor in addressing wicked problems (Flynn and Herrington 2015) which means the process of change must harness drivers that emerge from the bottom-up. Built into this change process is recognition that there is a Janus face, or dark side, to the development of restorative policing, as there are with other wicked issues. Hence, restorative-policing proponents must acknowledge that police officers and communities may misuse their enhanced discretion and active citizenship. Given these circumstances, one of the most difficult challenges for police managers and supervisors is to provide their officers with sufficient trust and space to take risks from the 'bottom up' (Skogan 2008).

Following on from this, the emphasis upon innovation and creativity needs to be backed up with freedom from organisational restraint. Police organisations are directed by processes related to data collection, analysis and reporting, all of which inform strategic and tactical direction. Yet, these systems could be adapted to incorporate the coordination of both police and community intelligence and resources to understand where best to use diversionary measures. This requires senior leaders to separate this work from more centralised planning and performance management, which limit the discretion and empowerment of front line officers. Community collaboration and shared leadership is central to the generation of trust that will support the development of sustainable restorative policing. First, this approach challenges the inbuilt inequities between police officer and community. Second, in areas where there are longstanding difficulties in police-community relations this offers the opportunity for rebuilding community relations from the bottom-up through personalised relationships between people in the community who develop and maintain an active investment in community justice and policing.

From implementation to investigation and beyond

This chapter has argued that there is a distinction that can be made between top-down and bottom-up approaches to public policy development and implementation and how they might coalesce with a social justice-oriented vision of policing. A social justice vision includes a commitment to a process of democratisation and empowerment; the satisfaction of human physical, social and economic needs; and respect for human rights (including principles of fairness, equity and non-discrimination). Restorative justice has traditionally been conceived as a 'bottom-up' process which when engaging the police requires both street-level police support coupled with strong political leadership and political and organisational climates that are supportive of change. Within this context, it becomes a strategic imperative for police organisations to both facilitate change from the top-down and to cultivate change with communities from the bottom-up.

The examples drawn upon in this chapter demonstrate that restorative policing can help drive forward a more democratic and participatory approach from police organisations to the value of frontline officers and the creativity and intimate knowledge that can be drawn from this area. The extent to which empowerment activities are successful, however, depends on the availability of good horizontal and vertical communication practices (Hann and Mortimer 1994). This requires transformational leadership from senior police officers who use their positions to reflect on the way police organisations meet their mission and purpose (Burns 1978) in combination with street-level policing changes agents. We are cognisant of the challenges this approach presents but, in a climate of economic instability and diminishing resources across Anglo-American societies, governments and police organisations are increasingly thinking in a more radical manner.

Restorative policing has been subject to significant experimentation across international jurisdictions, but much of this work has slipped out of sight due to the inherently local nature of the work and the absence of capacity for sustained empirical evaluation. Sustained development requires the generation of clear empirical and theoretically informed foundations to support the transformative potential of restorative policing for individuals, communities and criminal justice. This process requires engagement with both the 'restorativeness' of new initiatives but, as this chapter has illustrated, also often unexplored interpretations of 'policeness' (Hills 2014). The final chapter will articulate what this research agenda could look like.

8 Reframing the research agenda for restorative policing

Introduction

Restorative policing is a complex and heated area of study. This is not unusual for restorative justice applications, particularly in areas like domestic violence and sexual assault, but the fervour of debate initiated by the introduction of conferencing within the realms of policing has been unmatched by other applications within criminal justice. In part, as the preceding chapters have shown, this was (and still is) due to the perceived risks associated with increasing the unfettered and largely unchecked discretion of police officers in holding a monopoly over dealing with crime. However, we contend that this overlooks the particular nuances of restorative policing and that of operational policing environments. As such, the purpose of this book has been to, first, survey the landscape of restorative policing over a 25-year period during which its use and influence over criminal justice has waxed and waned and, second, to situate this discussion within a criminological discussion about neo-liberal responses to crime control, particularly that located within the policing literature.

Usefully, comparative analyses of restorative policing raise fundamental questions about how societies do justice and this is why the comparative case study approach was adopted. It is by no means a complete review of restorative policing but it is an attempt to address the lay of the land and to offer an exploration of the role of restorative thinking and practice set against a backdrop of turn of the millennium crime control. The aim has been to chart the emergence of restorative policing and to identify trajectories in thinking and doing restorative policing. In our view, the book provides a platform for those new to restorative policing to start with as well as a reference point for those well versed in these debates to challenge and adapt ideas that have been put forward. The approach taken by the authors has sought to draw together a broad range of restorative policing literature that is often only drawn upon in a partial manner.

As such, it has not been the aim here to generate new knowledge, but to critique the field as it stands and to explore appropriate ways of studying this topic. Because of this, the book now concludes with the identification of the topics we think are of the most urgent need of research if restorative policing is to situate itself within the everyday parlance of restorative justice and policing scholars and practitioners. The chapter first reviews the key empirical and theoretical conclusions from the book before exploring some of the core themes that have emerged. These themes are then situated within the context of other contemporary academic debates to inform the proposed research agenda which takes up most of the final part of this chapter.

Connecting restorative justice and policing

Much of this book has referred to the complexity that emerges when you connect restorative justice and policing. This complex array of influences upon restorative policing can be viewed as local and global as well as inextricably linked to variables such as legal context, organisational structure, ideological predisposition and politics. Yet, there has often been only superficial debate about how the concepts of 'restorative justice' and 'policing' sit alongside each other and how they may be connected or disconnected in theoretical and conceptual terms within the restorative policing literature. The concept of justice, in particular, has been problematic for policing agencies and scholars as it requires a shift in thinking away from the traditional emphasis upon crime prevention, public protection, order maintenance and law enforcement and presents difficulties in connecting 'restorative justice' and 'policing' in meaningful ways. Similarly, discussions about 'policing' within the context of restorative justice have been dominated by concerns about police culture, which have led to an oversimplification of the challenges faced when splicing the concepts of 'restorative justice' and 'policing' in operational practice.

As this book has acknowledged, an appreciation of the symbolic importance of the 'police use of force' paradigm is of particular importance in neoliberal settings and a failure to recognise this can lead to unrealistic expectations from those in the field of restorative justice about how police officers will interpret restorative initiatives and a continued frustration with unintended outcomes such as net-widening and creeping punitiveness. In this section we therefore provide a brief overview of the key empirical and theoretical findings that have emerged out of our attempts, inspired initially by Bazemore and Griffiths (2003), but subsequently by many others to, problematise, conceptualise and somehow connect restorative justice and policing.

The role of the police in building and supporting community linkages

A clear argument has been put forward by the authors for a strong police role in restorative policing. Police officers are ideally positioned to undertake this work as they are already assigned to work in particular territories in which they develop a detailed understanding of a range of dynamic social problems. Furthermore, the evidence from the case studies in Chapter 3 clearly indicates the active role played by police officers at different points in the police hierarchy as drivers of change. This reconceptualised position provides police officers with an opportunity to facilitate change within communities and to influence behaviour for broader purposes such as improved public health and the protection of vulnerable people (Wood *et al.* 2013). In this context, police officers can be understood as holding responsibility for guidance through procedure whilst also delivering a guardianship role.

We view restorative policing simultaneously as a criminal and non-criminal method of intervention that seeks to promote beneficial forms of *social capital*. This requires an extension and enhancement of the concept of community policing to incorporate strategic models of community partnership that are designed to actively and systematically identify local organisations and other community supports that build professional-community coalitions and generate the confidence and ownership in the community to develop effective partnership approaches. The key distinction here is the removal of the police officer from their traditional sovereign position as the owner of the conflict with its cultural links to the 'police use of force' paradigm. This shift has profound implications for the recruitment, training and leadership development of those involved in policing who will require considerably greater community engagement and awareness in taking a leading role in generating partnerships that transcend traditional inter-agency arrangements to draw on the full panoply of community assets.

Problem solving thus occurs in the community with active participation of community members and is not externally imposed by professionals who have a limited stake in the community. This model generates ownership, engagement and a form of legitimacy and sustainability that cannot be achieved by professionally imposed solutions. This approach is consistent with the model outlined in the informal social control ties of Sampson and Laub (2003) in which it is suggested that higher levels of engagement by social networks imposes control through positive support and engagement in the change process. Moreover, this approach draws on Bazemore (2000a), Mastrofski *et al.* (2002) and Manning's (2010) critical comments that the academic field of policing is weaker due to an absence of engagement with the work on collective efficacy which promotes a social network approach to policing that resonates with the multi-lateralised shifts to nodal networks of policing identified by Shearing and colleagues (Bayley and Shearing 2001; Shearing and Johnston 2003). It should be noted at this point, however, that these connections are only being introduced in this book and thus require further theoretical and empirical testing to assess their rigour in community contexts.

Policy implementation and organisational development

The learning that emerged out of the review in Chapter 1 on police reforms in the areas of community policing, problem-oriented and restorative policing identified difficulties in translating abstract and reflective policing ideas into tangible programmes and tactical action (Bazemore 2000a; Bazemore and Griffiths 2003; Skogan 2008) as well as an absence of work on the science of implementation that could inform developments in these areas. The authors have consistently stressed in this book that there are mechanisms, which can help facilitate organisational development (leadership, training and education, changes to organisational structures, empowering the frontline) but, historically, these changes have followed long after programme implementation. Studies of restorative policing have therefore demonstrated similar challenges in the area of organisational development in the form of difficulties in digesting core restorative values and a subsequent dilution of restorative principles in practice.

A comparative analysis of case studies has helped us to identify a range of characteristics that can support the successful implementation of restorative policing and which encourage programme developers to consider: local and organisational context and pressures, the extent of change that the implementation of restorative programmes require, and whether individuals have the relevant skills and capacities to drive forward new projects. The history of community-based conferencing, community-based mediation and consultation projects has been littered with evidence of low levels of community participation and especially poor engagement with those communities that experience the worst crime problems. This indicates that a simple policy implantation approach is unlikely to work. Yet, little consideration has been given to implementation science and a theory of change for the inversion of the police role required to embed restorative policing in a systematic manner (Bazemore 2000a).

Help in relation to this can be found from other disciplines, which have separated empirical study at the macro-, meso- and micro-levels to ascertain where research findings can inform public policy. At the macro-level, restorative policing has developed in an uneven and inconsistent manner both within and across territorial jurisdictions and an understanding of this can be drawn from analysis of changes in the shape and forms of global crime control. At the meso-level, it is clear that restorative policing is most suited to common law jurisdictions and democratic modes of policing where front-line officers are encouraged to use their discretion in a flexible manner – although there remain concerns that an absence of structured discretion could lead to more authoritarian policing. At the micro-level, the influence of community and organisational culture is a key indicator in predicting how restorative policing will be shaped at the local level. Many studies of restorative policing have focused their lens of analysis here, particularly upon the police but there remains little understanding of how other new, and hybrid, policing nodes function.

Micro-level community capacity

The major finding at the micro-level has been the value of social and community capital approaches in informing and understanding how restorative policing works. This theoretical connection emerged out of a rediscovery of the work of Moore and Forsythe (1995) and Bazemore (2000), which identified connections between restorative policing, neighbourhood social capital and community capacity. Restorative policing has been most successful in relatively homogenous social contexts where there is an identifiable voice emanating out of a community rather than the cacophony of divergent voices that emerge out of more complex, often urban, con-texts with competing demands. This does not mean that restorative policing cannot be used in complex urban settings, rather, that there are risks to doing so and more careful implementation planning is required. This positivist critique of community-oriented policing policy has emerged out of a structural emphasis upon community deficits, which underestimates the potential of new initiatives to tap into local agency and weak ties to develop new social resources that increase social inter-action between otherwise disconnected sub-groups (Granovetter 1973; Paterson and Best 2016).

This approach suggests it is possible to transform both physical and social space into a supportive environment in which police officers feel more empow-ered to address neighbourhood problems and become actively engaged in com-munity coalitions that provide access to the support, expertise, time and commitment to address these problems. This approach to restorative policing builds on notions of asset based community development and the principles of both community and problem-oriented policing to develop a scientific and sys-tematic approach to effective community engagement and conflict resolution. There are two important points that emerge here. First, the need to engage with a more interdisciplinary approach to restorative policing, in particular the health field which has made much more use of the concepts of social capital and col-lective efficacy and developed ways of measuring success. Second, there is still much that can be learned, in both empirical and theoretical terms, from com-munity and problem-oriented policing experiments to inform future develop-ments in policy and practice. Much of our insight has been drawn from work that is around 20 years old and which has been largely forgotten in contemporary studies of restorative policing.

Changing configurations of policing

Much of the restorative policing literature has remained disconnected from the theoretical literature on changes in the configuration of policing which have long hypothesised that changes in neoliberal governance are likely to produce new modes of policing which indirectly lead to changes in the public police role. The preference of the authors for the term 'restorative policing' recognises the central role played by the police in restorative practices that focuses on diversion and informal social control in conjunction with new modes of policing that emerge out of communities. The new hybrid mode of policing that emerges out of this process should capture the value of restorative approaches in helping to build community capital that leads to lower rates of offending (Sampson *et al.* 1997; Sampson and Laub 2003) but as the chapters have noted, there is no guarantee that this is the trajectory that will be followed.

The postmodern emphasis on community values, engagement and interaction remains a challenge for police institutions founded on modernity's conception of an all-powerful state that provides security and order across society yet restora-tive policing presents two potentially powerful responses to these postmodern changes. First, the integration of restorative principles, as well as restorative programmes, into day-to-day policing provides a framework for police officers at all levels of the organisation to make sense of restorative policing and to see what this interpretation produces. Second, if one takes Manning's normative standpoint that policing should, at worst, do no more harm when managing day-to-day issues of public order then restorative policing can be benchmarked against its potential to produce more just outcomes for societies. At the very least, these changes require policing agents to look at their roles in very different ways and it may mean that police organisations have to reassess who they recruit.

We still know little about how this trajectory will unfold. Policing scholars have demonstrated little interest in restorative policing as a coordinated field of study although there has been intensification in the study of non-state modes of policing in the twenty-first century. Policing, as a concept and emergent academic discipline, is only loosely grounded in theory and more commonly draws on other academic disciplines such as sociology, political science, law and philosophy for insight and reflection. As a consequence of this atheoretical position, reflections on the purpose of policing tend to focus on functions (what the police do) and roles (who should do it and how) which, in turn, draw upon cultural assumptions about how policing should be done. Because of this, although the theoretical complexities of restorative policing have largely been ignored, there has been significant growth in studies of the social justice functions of the police role. This includes analyses of the policing of vulnerability, mental ill-health, domestic violence and addictions. Following on from this, Wood *et al.* (2013) have called for recognition of the public health aspects of the police role and others, for example Neyroud and Beckley (2001), have referred to the next generation of police officers as being a mixture of crime-fighters, social engineers and enablers. It is not the purpose of this chapter to explore this terminology here but just to note that these conversations about the future of policing are emerging out of police organisations. There is, however, we would argue, value in further exploring and interrogating these concepts and assessing what impact they could have on our thinking about restorative policing.

This book furthers the research agenda suggested by Bayley and Shearing (2001) to investigate these broader contextual changes and has used a comparative case study approach that illustrates how shifts in configurations of governance at the global level impact upon the micro-level practices of a range of individuals and agencies who do policing. The book has placed an emphasis upon changes to the police role, the theoretical lenses of macro-level governance and micro-level social capital, and the need for more sophisticated forms of organisational development to adapt to new modes of policing. All of these ideas have been explored in other studies of restorative justice and policing and they remain subject to critique, which leads the following section to pause and reflect upon potential challenges and limitations to the ideas we have presented.

Reflections on empirical and theoretical findings

Raising questions about changes in the role and function of state police organisations always has the potential to initiate a, generally conservative, backlash that reflects upon contemporary challenges to security and the need to toughen rather than soften the police role. It is not the aim in this book to neglect the state security function of police organisations in neoliberal societies but to note, as others have (Brodeur 2010), that policing low level crime in communities is a different and distinct function that can draw on different people and organisations who require different skill sets. This is widely recognised within police organisations, but it is rarely spoken about publicly due to the political challenge of acknowledging the limits of the sovereign state (Garland 1996). It is also our perspective that we are not advocating for an ideological shift that sits outside the current sociopolitical thinking about potential trajectories in policing. The basis for the emergence of police organisations in democratic societies has always been trust in impersonal authority and the symbolic and cultural capital this provides the police to undertake their role. It follows that where this trust exists police can act as contributors to, and facilitators of, collective efficacy but where this trust does not exist there is a challenge to the implementation of restorative policing.

For many restorative proponents, restorative interventions are not only seen as a means through which to deal more effectively with the causes and consequences of offending behaviour, but also as a mechanism through which to facilitate community cohesion. The authors do not disagree with this position, but argue that this benevolent endeavour should be contextualised with the prevailing winds of punitive and offender-oriented mentalities that prevail across the neoliberal democracies. To paraphrase Bittner (1970), policing in Anglo-American societies continues to be defined in both police organisations and the collective public conscience as the *state-sanctioned capacity to use force*. Because of this, state police tend to be defined by their legal authority to use violence and the more commonplace policing functions such as the maintenance of social order and keeping the peace are neglected. This presents challenges for restorative policing in relation to support for diversion to restorative programmes and the adaptation of restorative initiatives to fit in with more traditional conceptions of the purpose of police work. Many of the challenges faced by restorative initiatives during the first wave of programmes during the 1990s emerged due to an underestimation of the impact of this change for all those involved in these processes. Yet, 25 years later it is now apparent that there are countless examples of community-based practices that can inform the future direction of restorative policing.

A research agenda

The final section of the book outlines a research agenda for restorative policing that harnesses the same structure put forward by Bayley and Shearing (2001) when they promoted the necessity of research into the new structure of policing. The four sections are *foundational design* which focuses on descriptive gaps in knowledge, *social impact* which addresses areas such as the ways in which restorative policing has addressed changes in policing technologies and mentalities, *policy development* and the potential ways forward for restorative policing, before closing with *causation* and the theoretical insights required to take this field forward.

Foundational description

As Bazemore (2000a: 234) has noted, ultimately, nothing short of a complete national inventory is needed to determine the range of variation in conferencing models from community to community. The systematic review of the restorative policing literature led to the clearest empirical finding being the absence of information from particular jurisdictions. Most glaringly, the picture from the United States has generated recognition of much work within police organisations that could be situated under the umbrella term 'restorative policing' but with useful data so scarce, it has been impossible to come to clear descriptive conclusions about what the scale and scope of restorative policing looks like at the time of writing. This is largely due to the size of the United States with its 18,000, mainly small, police forces but it is certainly not beyond the abilities of researchers to audit activity in a bid to start making sense of how restorative justice has or has not established itself across the country. A similar case could be made for Europe where there are pockets of restorative policing but little understanding of the extent or types of use. In contrast, England and Wales, with its much smaller population and landmass, has audited restorative practice across the country (Institute for Crime Policy Research 2016).

Social impact

The preceding chapters have detailed significant changes to police practice as a result of engagement with restorative policing but these studies have remained locally focused with many of the findings representing hypotheses that have not yet been further tested elsewhere. While we know a lot about police culture, we still do not know the extent of the impact that restorative policing has upon how police organisations function – that is, the impact upon arrest rates, court processes and officer behaviour. There are a number of implications from the comparative case study analysis that can be tested. These include: the impact of restorative policing upon community confidence, any potential impact upon changing individual and collective policing mentalities, and the indirect impact upon the state police role and function as well as new nodes of governance. New policing mentalities will emerge out of these hybrid nodes as the influence of other statutory and voluntary sector agencies takes hold. However, there remains an absence of understanding of new policing mentalities emerging out of new configurations of policing (Shearing 2016).

Second, an important dynamic in the successful implementation of restorative policing has been the micro-level bonds and structures that tie people and groups together as well as the macro-level social ecology that either helps or hinders social organisation (Sampson and Groves 1989). Restorative policing seeks to mobilise action at the micro-level, which helps to strengthen community linkages and build citizen-institution partnerships, which perform, where appropriate, both activist and mentorship roles in communities. The process is built from the micro-level upwards for communities and consolidated at the meso and macro-levels, but its impact upon communities needs to be monitored and evaluated. The challenge is ascertaining the extent to which communities have the capacity, or community collective efficacy to engage in such processes and to use them to help them to strengthen relationships between at-risk individuals and groups within the wider community. Shearing (2016: 88) has already promoted design principles for the analysis of such nodal networks which he describes as concentrating power nodally and then using it to steer governance; recognising and using all of your power resources; and focusing on nodes where one can be creative and assertive. These principles can arguably be mapped onto communities where restorative policing functions.

Policy development

A clear understanding of the process of policy implementation is central to the delivery of effective restorative policing. Recent studies have demonstrated a clear understanding of the nuances of restorative policing at a senior level but, simultaneously, more varied appreciation and understanding in the middle ranks (see, for example, Stockdale 2015). It is at these middle rank levels that further research is required to ascertain how restorative policing can be most effectively delivered. It is at this point that cultural influences mould and shape the type of restorative policing that emerges. This process potentially facilitates the misinterpretation of the role of restorative programmes in dealing with the harm caused by offending and incorporates additional aims that were not constituent parts of its underlying philosophy. The way to avoid this is to focus on the selection of appropriate officers who embrace restorative principles and have the relevant skill sets to influence both their colleagues and communities so that enhanced discretion does not become exclusionary policing. Chapter 7 has presented a number of ideas concerning how restorative policing can be taken forward in this way, but they require further research.

Causation

There is evidence from police cultural studies that indicates a cultural disposition towards crime control within police organisations, which is replicated in policy discussions, research by government agencies and large swathes of academic work yet there is little discussion of the ways in which policing compounds existing inequalities or the impact upon over-policed populations' conceptions of democracy and social justice. Following on from this, there has been a presumption in some areas of the literature that bringing police officers into contact with restorative approaches can result in a change of behaviour and, at the collective level, this means that restorative policing can be a key facilitator of change. There is huge complexity to this question and it remains untested. Conversely, scholars such as Shearing and Manning have argued that policing remains in a state of perpetual flux and contest and thus its functions, behaviours and activities change much more than other scholars have recognised. Herewith, there is a gap in our understanding of causation. Further research is required to identify clear links between the intention and impact of restorative policing that are both theoretically and empirically informed. It is also essential to review other existing policing practices to assess whether the aims of restorative policing are being met by other, potentially invisible, 'restorative-like' activities.

Some final thoughts

Much of the outlined research agenda is asking for a fundamental shift in how we think about restorative policing. As the earlier chapters noted, there are very different perspectives, in ideological terms, concerning how restorative policing should be developed. Criminological and policing studies have tended to focus on traditional criminal justice institutions and have oft neglected those who sit in other agencies. At the same time, those undertaking or researching social justice roles have sometimes been reluctant to engage with the coercive arm of the state. As Bayley and Shearing (2001) have noted, these obstacles constitute challenges to developing a sustained research agenda for modes of security and policing which sit (at least partly) outside of the traditional remit of criminal justice. This is due to the dominance of institutionally oriented thinking which addresses questions of efficiency and effectiveness and leads to disciplinary modes of thinking that emphasise the good or bad functioning of criminal justice ahead of a more nuanced appreciation of changes in the configuration of crime control and the new hybrid modes of responding to justice that this produces. Our aim has been to adopt both a comparative and interdisciplinary approach to avoid this tendency to drift into administrative analysis and to shine a light on the opportunities that emerge out of identifying similarities across jurisdictions.

There remains a question about the extent to which existing analyses, which continue to conceptually separate restorative justice and policing can make sense of the hybrid mode of policing that is restorative policing. Without this intellectual leap, scholars, policy makers and practitioners will continue to compartmentalise elements of the challenges they face in ways that are inappropriate and which create distinctions in places where they may not lie. There is much evidence already available to support a case for understanding restorative policing as a new mode of governance or policing, but the implications of this conclusion are not yet clear. It is certainly the case that restorative policing offers a potentially transformative vision of the future of policing but it is not yet clear whether it is a realistic, credible or sustainable one.

References

Abramson, A.M. (2003) 'Sustainable relationships and competing values: Restorative justice initiatives and the police – a case study'. *Police Practice and Research: An International Journal*, 4(4): 391–398.

ACPO. (2011) *Restorative Justice Guidance and Minimum Standards*, Association of Chief Police Officers. [Online]. Available from: www.restorativejustice.org.uk/sites/default/files/resources/files/ACPO%20restorative%20justice%20guidance%20and%20minimum%20standards.pdf

Acton, E. (2015) 'Restorative justice: A postcode lottery?' *Safer Communities*, 14(3): 120–125.

Aertsen, I. (2009) 'Restorative police practices in Belgium: A research into mediation processes and their organisation', in L. Moor, T. Peters, P. Ponsaers, J. Shapland and B. van Stokkom (eds) *Restorative Policing*. Netherlands: Maklu-Publishers.

Aertsen, I., Vanfraechem, I. and Crawford, A. (2010) *Restorative Justice and Crime Prevention: Presenting a Theoretical Explanation, an Empirical Analysis and the Policy Perspective*. Final Report of the European Prroject 'Restorative Justice and Crime Prevention'. Italy: Department of Juvenile Justice. [Online]. Available from: www.giustiziaminorile.it/rsi/pubblicazioni/Restorative_Justice_and%20Crime_Prevention_Final%20report_2010.pdf

Alarid, L. and Montemayor, C. (2012) 'Implementing restorative justice in police departments', *Police Practice and Research: An International Journal*, 13(5): 450–463.

Alder, C. and Wundersitz, J. (1994) *Family Conferencing and Juvenile Justice: The Way Forward or Misplaced Optimism?* Canberra: Australian Institute of Criminology.

Alderson, J. (1979) *Policing Freedom*. Plymouth: McDonald and Evans.

Ashworth, A. (2001) 'Is restorative justice the way forward for criminal justice?' *Current Legal Problems*, 54, 347–376.

Banton, M. (1964) *The Policeman in the Community*. London: Tavistock.

Barton, C. (2003) *Restorative Justice: The Empowerment Model*. Annandale, NSW: Hawkins Press.

Batton, C. (2011) 'Durham police and restorative justice', paper presented at the Restorative Justice: Building Consensus in Theory and Practice conference, Nottingham Law School, England, 7–8 April 2011.

Bauman, Z. (2001) *Community: Seeking Safety in an Insecure World*. Cambridge: Polity Press.

Bayley, D. (2003) 'Security and justice for all', in H. Strang and J. Braithwaite (eds) *Restorative Justice and Civil Society*. Cambridge: Cambridge University Press.

Bayley, D. and Shearing, C. (1996) 'The future of policing'. *Law and Society Review*, 30: 585–606.

Bayley, D. and Shearing, C. (2001) *The New Structure of Policing: Description, Conceptualization and Research Agenda*, Washington, DC: National Institute of Justice. [Online]. Available from: www.ncjrs.gov/pdffiles1/nij/187083.pdf

Bazemore, G. (2000a) *Community Justice and a Vision of Collective Efficacy: The Case of Restorative Conferencing*. Washington, DC: National Institute of Justice. [Online]. Available from: www.ncjrs.gov/criminal_justice2000/vol_3/03f.pdf

Bazemore, G. (2000b) 'Community justice and a vision of collective efficacy: The case of restorative conferencing', in J. Horney (ed.) *Policies, Processes, and Decisions of the Criminal Justice System*. Washington, DC: National Institute of Justice.

Bazemore, G. (2001) 'Young people, trouble, and crime: Restorative justice as a normative theory of informal social control and social support', *Youth & Society*, 33(2): 199–226.

Bazemore, G. and Griffiths, C. (2003) 'Police reform, restorative justice, and restorative policing', *Police, Practice and Research*, 4(4): 335–346.

Bazemore, G. and McLeod, C. (2011) 'Restorative justice and the future of diversion and informal social control', in E. Weitekamp and H. Kerner (eds) *Restorative Justice: Theoretical Foundations*. London: Routledge.

Bazemore, G., Nissen, L. and Dooley, M. (2000) 'Mobilising Social Support and Building Relationships: Broadening Correctional and Rehabilitative Agendas', *Corrections Management Quarterly*, 4(4): 10–21.

Bazemore, G. and Schiff, M. (2001) 'Understanding restorative community justice: What and why now?', in G. Bazemore and M. Schiff (eds) *Restorative Community Justice: Repairing Harm and Transforming Communities*. Cincinnati: Anderson.

Bazemore, G. and Schiff, M. (2002) *Understanding restorative justice conferencing: A case study in informal decision making in the response to youth crime (Draft Report)*, National Institute of Justice, US Department of Justice.

Bazemore, G. and Schiff, M. (2005) *Juvenile Justice Reform and Restorative Justice: Building Theory and Policy*. Cullompton: Willan Publishing.

Bazemore, G. and Schiff, M. (2015) *Restorative Community Justice: Repairing Harm and Transforming Communities*. Oxon/New York: Routledge.

Bazemore, G. and Stinchcomb, J. (2004) 'A civic engagement model of re-entry: Involving community through service and restorative justice', *Federal Probation*, 68(2): 14–24.

Bazemore, G. and Umbreit, M. (1994) *Balanced and Restorative Justice*. Washington, DC: Office for Juvenile Justice and Delinquency Prevention.

Bazemore, G. and Umbreit, M. (2001) 'A comparison of four restorative conferencing models', *Juvenile Justice Bulletin*. Washington, DC: Office of Justice Programmes, US Department of Justice.

Bazemore, G. and Walgrave, L. (1999) 'Restorative justice: In search of fundamentals', in G. Bazemore and L. Walgrave (eds) *Restorative Juvenile Justice: Repairing the Harm of Youth Crime*. Monsey, NY: Criminal Justice Press.

Beck, U. (1992) *Risk Society*. London: Sage.

Bentham, J. (1791/2009) *Panopticon*. Whitefish, MT: Kessinger.

Berkeley, G. (1969) *The Democratic Policeman*. Boston: Beacon Press.

Biggs, J. (1999) *Teaching for Quality Learning at University*. Buckingham: Society for Research into Higher Education and Open University Press.

Bigo, D. (2000) 'When two becomes one: Internal and external securitisations in Europe', in M. Kelstrup and M. Williams (eds) *International Relations Theory and the Politics of European Integration: Power Security and Community*. London: Routledge.

Bittner, E. (1970) *The Functions of the Police in Modern Society*. Washington DC: National Institute of Justice.

Blagg, H. (1997) 'A just measure of shame? Aboriginal youth and conferencing in Australia', *British Journal of Criminology*, 37(4): 481–501.

Bottomley, K. and Coleman, C. (1981) *Understanding Crime Rates*. Aldershot: Ashgate.

Bottoms, A. (1977) 'Reflections on the renaissance of dangerousness', *Howard Journal of Criminal Justice*, 16(2): 70–96.

Bottoms, A. (1995) 'The philosophy and politics of punishment and sentencing', in C. Clarkson and R. Morgan (eds) *The Politics of Sentencing Reform*. Oxford: Clarendon Press.

Bourdieu, P. (1980) *The Logic of Practice*. Stanford, CA: Stanford University Press.

Bourdieu, P. (1985) 'The forms of capital', in J. Richardson (ed.) *Handbook of Theory and Research for the Sociology of Education*. New York: Greenwood.

Bouwman, J. and Purdy, G. (1997) 'Sparwood Youth Assistance Program'. Paper presented at the National Conference: Dawn or Dusk in Sentencing, Montreal, Canada, 24–26 April.

Boyes-Watson, C. (2005) 'Community is not a place but a relationship: Lessons for organisational development', *Public Organisation Review: A Global Journal*, 5(4): 359–374.

Bradford, B. and Jackson, J. (2010) 'Cooperating with the police: Social control and the reproduction of police legitimacy', Paper presented at the annual meeting of the ASC Annual Meeting, San Francisco Marriott, San Francisco, California, 17 November.

Bradford, B. and Jackson, J. (2011) *Legitimacy and the Social Field of Policing*. [Online]. Available from: http://ssrn.com/abstract=1914458

Bradley, K. (2009). 'The Bradley Report: Lord Bradley's Review of People with Mental Health Problems or Learning Disabilities in the Criminal Justice System'. London: Department of Health.

Bradley, T., Tauri, J. and Walters, R. (2006) 'Demythologising youth justice in Aotearoa/ New Zealand', in J. Muncie and B. Goldson (eds) *Contemporary Youth Justice*. London: Sage.

Braithwaite, J. (1989) *Crime, Shame and Reintegration*. Cambridge: Cambridge University Press.

Braithwaite, J. (1993) 'Juvenile offending: New theory and practice', in L. Atkinson and S. Gerull (eds) *National Conference on Juvenile Justice Conference Proceedings No. 22*, Canberra: Australian Institute of Criminology.

Braithwaite, J. (1994) 'Thinking harder about democratising social control', in C. Alder and J. Wundersitz (eds) *Family Conferencing and Juvenile Justice: The Way Forward or Misplaced Optimism?* Canberra: Australian Institute of Criminology.

Braithwaite, J. (1997) Restorative justice: Assessing an immodest theory and a pessimistic theory. [Online]. Available from: www.aic.gov.au/rjustice/braithwaite.html

Braithwaite, J. (1998) 'Restorative justice', in M. Tonry (ed.) *The Handbook of Crime and Punishment*. Oxford: Oxford University Press.

Braithwaite, J. (1999) 'Restorative justice: Assessing optimistic and pessimistic accounts', *Crime and Justice*, 25(5): 1–127.

Braithwaite, J. (2000) 'Democracy, community and problem solving', in G. Burford and J. Hudson (eds) *Family Group Conferencing: New Directions in Community-Centred Child and Family Practice*. New York: Aldine de Gruyther.

Braithwaite, J. (2002) *Restorative Justice and Responsive Regulation.* Oxford: Oxford University Press.

Braithwaite, J. (2003) 'Principles of restorative justice', in A. von Hirsch, J. Roberts, A. Bottoms, K. Roach and M. Schiff (eds) *Restorative Justice and Criminal Justice: Competing or Reconcilable Paradigms?* Oxford: Hart.

Braithwaite, J. (2004) 'Restorative justice and de-professionalization', *The Good Society*, 13(1): 28–31.

Braithwaite, J. and Parker, C. (1999) 'Restorative justice is republican justice', in G. Bazemore and L. Walgrave (eds) *Restorative Juvenile Justice: Repairing the Harm of Youth Crime*. Monsey, NY: Willow Tree Press.

Brannigan, A. (2007) 'Restorative justice in post-genocidal Rwanda: From community to citizenship as a basis for social justice', in A. Brannigan and G. Pavlich (eds) *Governance and Regulation in Social Life: Essays in Honour of W.G. Carson*. Oxon: Routledge.

Brodeur, J.P. (1983) 'High policing and low policing: Remarks about the policing of political activities'. *Social Problems*, 30(5): 507–520.

Brodeur, J. (2010) *The Policing Web*. London: Routledge.

Brogden, M. (1999) 'Community Policing as Cherry Pie', in R. Mawby (Ed.) *Policing Across the World: Issues for the Twentieth Century*. London: Routledge.

Brogden, M. and Nijhar, P. (2005) *Community Policing: National and International Models and Approaches*. Cullompton: Willan Publishing.

Brown, M. and Polk, K. (1996) 'Taking fear of crime seriously: The Tasmanian approach to community crime prevention', *Crime and Delinquency*, 42(3): 398–420.

Bullock, K. and Tilley, N. (2009) 'Evidenced-based policy and crime reduction'. *Policing: A Journal of Policy and Practice*, 3(4): 381–387. Oxford: Oxford Journals.

Burns, J. (1978) *Leadership*. New York: Harper and Row.

Campbell, C., Devlin, R., O'Mahony, D., Doak, J., Jackson, J., Corrigan, T. and McEvoy, K. (2005) *Evaluation of the Northern Ireland Youth Conference Service*. Belfast: Northern Ireland Office.

Campeau, H. (2015) ' "Police Culture" at work: Making sense of police oversight'. *British Journal of Criminology*, 55(4): 669–687.

Canadian Report on the Future of Policing (2014) *Policing Canada in the Twenty-first Century: New policing for new challenges*. Ottawa, ON: Council of Canadian Academies.

Cantor, G. (1976) 'An end to punishment', *The Shingle (Philadelphia Bar Association)*, 39(4): 99–114.

Carpenter, J., Gassner, L. and Thomson, N. (2016) 'Enhancing the participation of police as collaborative leaders in responding to complex social and public health issues in Australia', *Policing: A Journal of Policy and Practice*, 10(1): 17–25.

Carrington, P. (1998) *Factors Affecting Police Diversion of Young Offenders: A Statistical Analysis*, Ottawa: Solicitor General of Canada.

Carroll, M. (1994) 'Implementational issues: Considering the options for Victoria', in C. Alder and J. Wundersitz (eds) *Family Conferencing and Juvenile Justice: The Way Forward or Misplaced Optimism?* Canberra: Australian Institute of Criminology.

Cavadino, M. and Dignan, J. (2006) *The Penal System: An Introduction*, London: Sage Publications.

Chambliss, W. (2011) *Police and Law Enforcement*. Thousand Oaks, CA: Sage.

Chan, J. (1996) 'Changing police culture', *British Journal of Criminology*, 36(1): 109–134.

Chan, J. (1997) *Changing Police Culture: Policing in a Multicultural Society*. Cambridge: Cambridge University Press.

Chatterjee, J. (1999) *A report on the evaluation of RCMP restorative justice initiative: Community justice forum as seen by participants*. Ottawa: Research and Evaluation Branch, Community, Contract and Aboriginal Policing Services.

Chatterjee, J. (2000) 'RCMP's restorative justice initiative', *Forum on Corrections Research*, 12(1): 35–37.

Chatterjee, J. and Elliott, L. (2003) 'Restorative policing in Canada: The Royal Canadian Mounted Police, Community Justice Forums, and the Youth Criminal Justice Act', *Police Practice and Research: An International Journal*, 4(4): 347–359.

Cheliotis, L. (2006) 'How 'iron' is the iron cage of the new penology?' *Punishment and Society*, 8(3): 313–340.

Choi, J. and Gilbert, M. (2010) 'Joe everyday, people off the street: A qualitative study on mediators' roles/skills in victim offender mediation', *Contemporary Justice Review*, 13(2): 207–227.

Christie, N. (1977) 'Conflicts as property', *British Journal of Criminology*, 17(1): 1–15.

Christie, N. (1982) *Limits to Pain*. Oxford: Martin Robertson.

Christie, N. (1993) *Crime Control as Industry*. New York: Routledge.

Christie, N. (2004) *A Suitable Amount of Crime*. London: Routledge.

Claassen, R. (1996) *Restorative Justice Principles: Primary Focus on People, Not Procedures*. California: Center for Peacemaking and Conflict Studies.

Clairmont, D. and Kim, E. (2013) 'Getting past gatekeepers: The reception of restorative justice in the Nova Scotia criminal justice system', *The Dalhousie Law Journal*, 36(2): 359–391.

Clamp, K. (2008) 'Assessing alternative forms of localised justice in post-conflict societies – youth justice in Northern Ireland and South Africa', in D. Frenkel and C. Gerner-Beuerle (eds) *Selected Essays on Current Legal Issues*. Athens: ATINER.

Clamp, K. (2010) 'The receptiveness of countries in transition to restorative justice: A comparative analysis of the role of restorative justice in transitional processes and criminal justice reform', unpublished thesis, University of Leeds.

Clamp, K. (2014a) *Restorative Justice in Transition*. London/New York: Routledge.

Clamp, K. (2014b) 'A "local" response to community problems?: A critique community justice panels', *British Journal of Community Justice*, 12(2): 21–34.

Clamp, K. (2016a) 'Clearing the conceptual haze: Restorative justice concepts in transitional settings', *Restorative Justice in Transitional Settings*. London/New York: Routledge.

Clamp, K. (2016b) 'Restorative justice as a contested response to conflict and the challenge of the transitional context: An introduction', *Restorative Justice in Transitional Settings*. London/New York: Routledge.

Clamp, K. (2016c) 'Towards a Transformative Vision of Restorative Justice as a Response to Mass Victimisation: Some Concluding Thoughts', *Restorative Justice in Transitional Settings*, London/New York: Routledge.

Clamp, K. and Paterson, C. (2011) 'Rebalancing criminal justice: Potentials and pitfalls for community neighbourhood panels', *British Journal of Community Justice*, 9(2): 21–35.

Clamp, K. and Paterson, C. (2013) 'An exploration of the role of leadership in restorative policing in England and Wales', in A. Normore and N. Erbe (eds) *Collective Efficacy: Interdisciplinary Perspectives on International Leadership*. Bingley: Emerald.

Clark, M. (2005) 'The importance of a new philosophy to the post-modern policing environment'. *Policing: An International Journal of Police Strategies and Management*, 28(4): 642–653.

Clear, T. (2007) *Imprisoning Communities: How Mass Incarceration Makes Disadvantaged Neighbourhoods Worse*. New York: Oxford University Press.

Coates, R. and Gehm, J. (1989) 'An empirical assessment', in M. Wright and B. Galaway (eds) *Mediation and Criminal Justice*. London: Sage.

Coates, R., Umbreit, M. and Vos, B. (2006) 'Responding to hate crimes through restorative justice dialogue', *Contemporary Justice Review: Issues in Criminal, Social, and Restorative Justice*, 9(1): 7–21.

Cohen, S. (1985) *Visions of Social Control*. Cambridge: Polity Press.

Coleman, J. (1988a) 'Social capital in the creation of human capital', *American Journal of Sociology*, 94: 95–121.

Coleman, J. (1988b) 'The creation and destruction of social capital: Implications for the law', *Notre Dame Journal of Law, Ethics and Public Policy*, 3: 37–404.

Colquhoun, P. (1796/2010) *A Treatise on the Police of the Metropolis*. 4th edition. London: British Library.

Cooper, C. (1997) 'Patrol police officer conflict resolution processes', *Journal of Criminal Justice*, 25(2): 87–101.

Cordner, G. (1997) 'Community policing: Elements and effects', in R. Dunham and A. Alpert (eds) *Critical Issues in Policing: Contemporary Readings*. Illinois: Waveland Press.

Cornwell, D., Blad, J. and Wright, M. (2013) Civilising Criminal Justice: An International Restorative Agenda for Penal Reform, Hampshire: Waterside Press.

Council of Canadian Academies (2014) *Policing Canada in the Twenty-First Century: New Policing for New Challenges*. [Online] Available from: http://www.scienceadvice.ca/uploads/eng/assessments%20and%20publications%20and%20news%20releases/policing/policing_fullreporten.pdf

Cox, D. (2011) 'Educating police for uncertain times: The Australian experience and the case for a normative approach'. *Journal of Policing, Intelligence and Counter-Terrorism*, 6(1): 3–22.

Crawford, A. (2005) *Plural Policing: The Mixed Economy of Visible Patrols in England and Wales*. Bristol: Policy Press.

Crawford, A. (2008) 'Refiguring the community and professional in policing and criminal justice: Some questions of legitimacy', in J. Shapland (ed.) *Justice, Community and Civil Society: A Contested Terrain*. Cullompton: Willan Publishing.

Crawford, A. (2015) 'Temporality in restorative justice: On time, timing and time-consciousness', *Theoretical Criminology*, 19(4): 470–490.

Crawford, A. and Clear, T. (2001) 'Community justice: Transforming communities through restorative justice?', in G. Bazemore, and M. Schiff (eds), *Restorative Community Justice: Repairing Harm and Transforming Communities*. Cincinnati: Anderson Publications.

Crawford, A. and Evans, K. (2012) 'Crime prevention and community safety', in R. Morgan, M. Maguire and R. Reiner (eds) *The Oxford Handbook of Criminology*. Oxford: Oxford University Press.

Crawford, A. and Newburn, T. (2003) *Youth Offending and Restorative Justice: Implementing Reform in Youth Justice*. Cullompton: Willan Publishing.

Crocker, D. (2013) 'The effects of regulated discretion on police referrals to restorative justice', *The Dalhousie Law Journal*, 36(2): 393–418.

Cullen, F., Wright, J. and Chamlin, M. (1999) 'Social support and social reform: A progressive crime control agenda', *Crime & Delinquency*, 45(2): 188–207.

Cunneen, C. (1997) 'Community conferencing and the fiction of indigenous control', *Australian & New Zealand Journal of Criminology*, 30(3): 292–311.

Cunneen, C. (2002) 'Restorative justice and the politics of decolonization', in E. Weitekamp and H. Kerner (eds) *Restorative Justice: Theoretical Foundations*, Cullompton: Willan Publishing.

Cunneen, C. (2008) 'Exploring the relationship between reparations, the gross violation of human rights, and restorative justice', in D. Sullivan and L. Tifft (eds) *Handbook of Restorative Justice: A Global Perspective*. London and New York: Routledge.

Cunneen, C. (2010) 'The limitations of restorative justice', in C. Cunneen and C. Hoyle (eds) *Debating Restorative Justice*. Oxford: Hart Publishing.

Cunneen, C. (2016) 'When does transitional justice begin and end? Colonised peoples, liberal democracies and restorative justice', in K. Clamp (ed.) *Restorative Justice in Transitional Settings*. London/New York: Routledge.

Cunneen, C., Brown, D., Schwartz, M., Stubbs, J. and Young, C. (2016) *Justice Reinvestment: Winding Back Imprisonment*. Basingstoke: Palgrave Macmillan.

Cutress, L. (2015) 'The use of *Restorative Justice* by the police in England and Wales', unpublished PhD thesis, University of Sheffield.

D'haese, W. and Grunderbeeck, S. (2009) www.maklu-online.eu/en/tijdschrift/cahiers-politiestudies/jaargang-2009/11-restorative-policing/restorative-policing-police-mediation-during-polic/. Restorative Policing: Police Mediation during Police Investigation: A procedure and a project to achieve Excellent Police Care', in L. Moor, T. Peters, P. Ponsaers, J. Shapland and B. van Stokkom (Ed.) Restorative Policing, Netherlands: Maklu-Publishers.

Daly, K. (2000) 'Restorative Justice in Diverse and Unequal Societies', *Law in Context*, 17(1): 167–90.

Daly, K. (2001) 'Conferencing in Australia and New Zealand: Variations, research findings and prospects', in A. Morris and G. Maxwell (eds) *Restoring Justice for Juveniles: Conferencing, Mediation and Circles*. Oxford: Hart Publishing.

Daly, K. (2002) 'Restorative justice – The real story', *Punishment and Society*, 4(1): 55–79.

Daly, K. (2003) 'Making Variation a Virtue: Evaluating the Potential and Limits of Restorative Justice', in E. Weitekamp and H. Kerner (eds) *Restorative justice in context: International practice and direction*. Cullompton: Willan Publishing.

Dandurand, Y. and Griffiths, C. (2006) *Handbook on Restorative Justice Programmes*. United Nations Office on Drugs and Crime: New York.

Darcy, D. (2005) 'Policing the socially disadvantaged, the value of rekindling community policing in Woolloomooloo – A Police Commander's perspective', *Current Issues in Criminal Justice*, 17(1): 144–153.

Davey, L. (2007) Restorative Practices in Workplaces, Paper presented at the 10th International Institute for Restorative Practices World Conference, 'Improving Citizenship & Restoring Community', Budapest, Hungary.

Davis, M. (1990) *City of Quartz*. New York: Verso.

De Jong, C. (2004) 'Gender differences in officer attitude and behavior: Providing comfort to citizens', *Women and Criminal Justice*, 15(3): 1–32.

De Jong, C., Mastrofski, S. and Parks, R. (2001) 'Patrol officers and problem-solving: An application of expectancy theory', *Justice Quarterly*, 18(1): 1–62.

Dean, M. (2010) A response to the question 'What is neoliberalism?' Paper presented to 'Contesting Neoliberalism and its Future', Australian Academy of the Social Sciences Workshop, University of Sydney, 2–4 December. Available at: http://sydney.edu.au/arts/political_economy/downloads/Mitchell_Dean.pdf.

Dignan, J. (2002) 'Restorative justice and the law: The case for an integrated, systemic approach', in L. Walgrave (eds) *Restorative Justice and the Law*. Collumpton: Willan Publishing.

Dignan, J. (2003) 'Towards a systemic model of restorative justice: Reflections on the concept, its context, and the need for clear constraints', in A. Von Hirsch, J. Roberts,

A. Bottoms, K. Roach and M. Schiff (eds) *Restorative Justice and Criminal Justice: Competing or Reconcilable Paradigms*. Oxford: Hart Publishing.

Dignan, J. (2005) *Understanding Victim and Restorative Justice*. Maidenhead: Open University Press.

Dinnen, S. (1997) 'Restorative justice in Papua New Guinea', *International Journal of Sociology of Law*, 25(3): 245–262.

Dixon, D. (1997) *Law in Policing: Legal Regulation and Police Practices*. Oxford: Clarendon.

Doob, A. and Cesaroni, C. (2004) *Responding to Youth Crime in Canada*. Toronto: University of Toronto Press.

Doob, A. and Chan, J. (1982) 'Factors affecting police decisions to take juveniles to court', *Canadian Journal of Criminology*, 24(1): 25–37.

Duekmedjian, J. (2008) 'The rise and fall of RCMP community justice forums: Restorative justice and public safety interoperability in Canada', *Canadian Journal of Criminology and Criminal Justice*, 50(2): 117–151.

Duff, P. (1986) *Trials and Punishments*. Cambridge: Cambridge University Press.

Dugan, M. (1996) 'A nested theory of conflict', *A Leadership Journal: Women in Leadership – Sharing the Vision*, 1(1): 9–20.

Durkheim, E. (1893) *The Division of Labour in Society*. Glencoe: Free Press.

Durkheim, E. (1912/2008) *The Elementary Forms of Religious Life*. Oxford: Oxford University Press.

Durkheim, E. (1925/1961) *Moral Education: A Study in the Theory and Application of the Sociology of Education*. New York: The Free Press.

Dyck, D. (2008) 'Reaching toward a structurally responsive training and practice of restorative justice', in D. Sullivan and L. Tifft (eds) *Handbook of Restorative Justice: A Global Perspective*. London: Routledge.

Eck, J. and Spelman, W. (1987) *Problem-solving: Problem-Oriented Policing in Newport News*. Washington, DC: Police Executive Research Forum.

Emsley, C. (1991) *The English Police: A Political and Social History*. London: Harvester Wheatsheaf.

Engel, R.S. and Worden, R.E. (2003) Police officer attitudes, behaviour and supervisory influences: An analysis of problem-solving. *Criminology*, 41(1): 131–166.

Erez, E. and Ibarra, P. (2007) 'Making your home a shelter: Electronic monitoring and victim re-entry in domestic violence cases', *The British Journal of Criminology*, 47(1): 100–120.

Erez, E. and Rogers, L. (2001) 'Victim impact statements and sentencing outcomes and processes: The perspectives of legal professional', in B. Williams and H. Chong (eds) *Victims and Victimisation: A Reader*. Maidenhead: Open University Press.

Ericson, R. (1982) *Reproducing Order: A Study of Police Patrol Work*. Toronto: Toronto University Press.

Ericson, R. and Haggerty, K. (1997) *Policing the Risk Society*. Oxford: Oxford University Press.

Eriksson, A. (2009) *Justice in Transition: Community Restorative Justice in Northern Ireland*. Cullompton, Devon: Willan Publishing.

Eterno, J. and Silverman, E. (2012) *The Crime Numbers Game*. New York: CRC Press.

Faulkner, D. (2003) 'Taking citizenship seriously: Social capital and criminal justice in a changing world', *Criminal Justice*, 3(3): 287–315.

Feeley, M. and Simon, J. (1992) 'The new penology: Notes on the emerging strategy of corrections and its implications', *Criminology*, 30(4): 449–474.

Findlay, M. (2000) 'Decolonising restoration and justice in transitional cultures', in H. Strang and J. Bathwater (eds) *Restorative Justice: Philosophy to Practice*. Aldershot: Dartmouth Publishing Company Limited.

Fleming, J. and O'Reilly, J. (2007) 'The small-scale initiative: The rhetoric and reality of community policing in Australia'. *Policing: A Journal of Policy and Practice*, 1(2): 1–17.

Fletcher, L. and Weinstein, H. (2002) 'Violence and social repair: Rethinking the contribution of justice to reconciliation', *Human Rights Quarterly*, 24: 573–639.

Flew, T. (2014) 'Six theories of neoliberalism', *Thesis Eleven*, 122(1): 49–71.

Flynn, E. and Herrington, V. (2015) *Towards a Profession of Police Leadership. New Persepctives in Policing*. Boston: Harvard Kennedy School/ National Institute of Justice.

Foster, J. and Jones, C. (2010) 'Nice to do and essential: Improving neighbourhood policing in an English police force', *Policing: A Journal of Policy and Practice*, 4(4): 395–402.

Foucault, M. (1991) 'Governmentality', in G. Burchell, C. Gordon and P. Miller (eds) *The Foucault Effect: Studies in Governmentality*. London: Harvester Wheatsheaf, pp. 87–104.

Foucault, M. (2008) *The Birth of Biopolitics: Lectures at the Collège de France 1978–1979*, ed. Sennelart M, trans. Burchell, G. Basingstoke: Palgrave.

Friedmann, R. (1992) *Community Policing: Comparative Perspectives and Prospects*. New York: St. Martin's Press.

Froestad, J. and Shearing, C. (2007) 'Conflict resolution in South Africa: A case study. A South African Innovation: The Zwelethemba Model', in G. Johnstone and D. Van Ness (eds) *The Handbook of Restorative Justice*. Cullompton, Devon: Willan Publishing.

Froestad, J. and Shearing, C. (2013) *Security Governance, Policing, and Local Capacity*. Boca Raton, FL: CRC Press.

Fry, M. (1951) *Arms of the Law*. London: Gollancz.

Fukuyama, F. (2012) *The Origins of Political Order: From Pre-human Times to the French Revolution*. London: Profile Books.

Galaway, B. and Hudson, J. (2007) 'Introduction', in B. Galaway and J. Hudson (eds) *Restorative Justice: International Perspective*. Monsey, NY: Criminal Justice Press.

Gardner, J. (1990) *Victims and Criminal Justice*. South Australia: Office of Crime Statistics, South Australia Attorney General's Department.

Garland, D. (1996) 'The limits of the sovereign state', *British Journal of Criminology*, 36(4): 445–471.

Garland, D. (2001) *The Culture of Control: Crime and Social Order in Contemporary Society*. Oxford: Oxford University Press.

Geddis, D. (1993) 'A critical analysis of the family group conference', *Family Law Bulletin*. 3: 141–144.

Gehm, J. (1998) 'Victim-offender mediation programs: An exploration of practice and theoretical frameworks', *Western Criminology Review*, 1(1): 1–28.

Giddens, A. (1990) *The Consequences of Modernity*. Cambridge: Polity Press.

Gilbert, R. (2012) 'Place-based initiatives and indigenous justice', *Indigenous Justice Clearinghouse Research Brief 13*, Sydney: Indigenous Justice Clearinghouse.

Gill, D. (2006) 'Toward a radical paradigm of restorative justice', in D. Sullivan and L. Tifft (eds) *Handbook of Restorative Justice: A Global Perspective*. London: Routledge.

Goldstein, H. (1977) *Policing a Free Society*. Cambridge, MA: Ballinger.

Goldstein, H. (1979) 'Improving policing: A problem-oriented approach', *Crime & Delinquency*, 25(2): 236–258.

Goldstein, H. (1990) *Problem-oriented Policing*. New York, NY: McGraw-Hill.

Goldstein, H. (1997) 'LEN Interview: Herman Goldstein, the father of problem-oriented policing', *Law Enforcement News*, 23(461): 8–11.

Goldstein, H. (2010) 'On further developing problem-oriented policing: The most critical need, the major impediments, and a further proposal', in J. Knutsson (ed.) *Problem-Oriented Policing: From Innovation to Mainstream. Crime Prevention Studies Vol. 15*. London: Lyne Rienner.

Gottfredson, M. and Hirschi, T. (1990) *A General Theory of Crime*. Stanford: Stanford University Press.

Gould, L. (1999) 'The impact of working in two worlds and its effect on Navajo police officers', *Journal of Legal Pluralism*, 44: 53–71.

Granovetter, M. (1973) 'The strength of weak ties', *American Journal of Sociology*, 78(6): 1360–1380.

Grimshaw, R. and Jefferson, T. (1987) *Interpreting Policework*. London: Allen and Unwin.

Grint, K. (2010) 'The cuckoo clock syndrome: Addicted to command, allergic to leadership', *European Management Journal*, 28: 306–313.

Guzik, K. (2008) 'The agencies of abuse: Intimate abusers' experience of presumptive arrest and prosecution', *Law Society Review*, 42, 111–144.

Haberfeld, M.R. and Cerrah, I. (2008) *Comparative Policing: The Struggle for Democratization*. London: Sage.

Hall, S., Roberts, B., Clarke, J., Jefferson, T. and Critcher, C. (1978) *Policing the Crisis: Mugging, the State and Law and Order*. London: Palgrave Macmillan.

Hann, J. and Mortimer, B. (1994) 'Strategic planning and performance evaluation for operational policing', in D. Biles and S. McKillop (eds) *Criminal Justice Planning and Coordination*. Conference Proceedings no. 24, Canberra: Australian Institute of Criminology.

Harris, K. (2008) 'Transformative justice: The transformation of restorative justice', in D. Sullivan and L. Tifft (eds) *Handbook of Restorative Justice: A Global Perspective*, London and New York: Routledge.

Harris, N. (2006) 'Reintegrative shaming, shame and criminal justice', *Journal of Social Issues*, 62(2): 327–346.

Henry, S. and Milovanovic, D. (1994) 'The constitution of constitutive criminology: A postmodern approach to criminological theory', in D. Nelken (ed.) *The Futures of Criminology*, London: Sage.

Henry, S. and Milovanovic, D. (1996) *Constitutive Criminology: Beyond Postmodernism*. London: Sage.

Herbert, N. (2011) *Restorative Justice, Policing and the Big Society*. Available at: www.homeoffice.gov.uk/media-centre/speeches/Herbert-Restorative-Justice

Herrington, V. and Colvin, C. (2016) 'Police leadership for complex times', *Policing: A Journal of Policy and Practice*, Forthcoming.

Heslop, R. (2011) 'Reproducing police culture in a British university', *Police Practice and Research*, 12(4): 298–312.

Hills, A. (2014) 'What is policeness? On being police in Somalia', *The British Journal of Criminology*, 54(5): 765–783.

Hines, D. (2000) *The Woodbury Police Department Restorative Justice Program Recidivism Study*. Woodbury, MN: Inter-faith Ministries.

Hines, G. and Bazemore, D. (2003) 'Restorative policing, conferencing and community', *Police Practice and Research: An International Journal*, 4(4): 411–427.

Hipple, N. and McGarrell, E. (2008) 'Comparing police- and civilian-run family group conferences', *Policing: An International Journal of Police Strategies & Management*, 31(4): 553–577.

Hirschi, T. (1969) *Causes of Delinquency*. Berkeley, CA: University of California Press.

Hobsbawm, E. (1995) *Age of Extremes: The Short Twentieth Century, 1914–1991*. London: Abacus.

Holland, B. (2007) 'View from within: The realities of promoting race and diversity inside the police service', in M. Rowe (ed.), *Policing Beyond Macpherson: Issues in Policing, Race and Society*. Cullompton: Willan Publishing.

Home Office. (2010) *Policing in the 21st Century: Reconnecting Police and the People*. London: HMSO.

Home Office. (2011) *A New Approach to Fighting Crime*. London: Home Office.

House of Commons Home Affairs Committee. (2011) *New Landscape of Policing*. London: HMSO.

Howard, B. and Purches, L. (1992) 'A discussion of the Police Family Group Conferences and the Follow-up Program (Stage 2) in the Wagga Wagga juvenile cautioning process', *Rural Society*, 2(2): 20–23.

Hoyle, C. (2002) 'Securing *restorative justice* for the "non-participating" victim', in C. Hoyle and R. Young (eds) *New Visions of Crime Victims*. Oxford, UK: Hart Publishing.

Hoyle, C. (2007) 'Policing and restorative justice', in G. Johnstone and D. Van Ness (eds) *Handbook of Restorative Justice*. Cullompton: Willan Publishing.

Hoyle, C. and Rosenblatt, F. (2016) 'Looking back to the future: Threats to the success of restorative justice in the United Kingdom', *Victims & Offenders*, 11(1): 30–49.

Hoyle, C. and Young, R. (2003) 'Restorative justice, victims and the police', in T. Newburn (ed.) *Handbook of Policing*. Cullompton: Willan Publishing.

Hoyle, C., Young, R. and Hill, R. (2002) *Proceed with Caution: An Evaluation of the Thames Valley Police Initiative in Restorative Cautioning*. York: Joseph Rowntree Foundation.

Huang, H., Braithwaite, V. Tsutomi, H. Hosoi, Y. and Braithwaite, J. (2012) 'Social capital, rehabilitation, tradition: Support for restorative justice in Japan and Australia', *Asian Criminology*, 7(4): 295–308.

Hudson, B. (2003) *Justice in the Risk of Society*. London: Sage Publications.

Hughes, G. (1998) *Understanding Crime Prevention*. Maidenhead: Open University Press.

Hunter, A. (1985) 'Private, parochial and public social orders: The problem of crime and incivility in urban communities', in G. Suttles and M. Zald (eds) *The Challenge of Social Control: Citizenship and Institution Building in Modern Society*. Norwood, NJ: Aldex Publishing.

Ianni, E. and Ianni, F. (1983) 'Street cops and management cops: The two cultures of policing'. In M. Punch (ed.) *Control in the Police Organisation*. Cambridge, MA: MIT Press.

Jackson, J., Bradford, B., Hough, M., Myhill, A., Quinton, P. and Tyler, T. (2012) 'Why do people comply with the law? Legitimacy and the influence of legal institutions', *British Journal of Criminology*, 52(6): 1051–1071.

Jackson, S., Cleverly, S., Poland, B., Burman, D., Edwards, R. and Robertson, A. (2013) 'Working with Toronto neighbourhoods towards developing indicators of community capacity', *Health Promotion International*, 18(4): 339–350.

Jaschke, H. and Neidhart, K. (2007) 'A modern police science as an integrated academic discipline', *Policing and Society*, 17(4), 303–320.

Jefferson, T. and Grimshaw, R. (1984) *Interpreting Police Work: Policy and Practice in Forms of Beat Policing*. London: Harper Collins.

Johnson, N. (2010) *Separate and Unequal*. London: Fabian Society.

Johnstone, G. (2008) 'The agendas of the restorative justice movement', in H. Millar (ed.) *Restorative Justice: From Theory to Practice*. Bingley, UK: Emerald Group.

Johnstone, G. and Van Ness, D. (2007) 'The meaning of restorative justice', in G. Johnstone and D. Van Ness (eds) *Handbook of Restorative Justice*. Collumpton, UK: Willan Publishing.

Johnston, L. and Shearing, C. (2003) *Governing Security*. London: Routledge.

Jones, T. and Newburn, T. (2002) 'The transformation of policing? Understanding current trends in policing systems', *British Journal of Criminology*, 42(1): 129–146.

Jones, T. and Newburn, T. (2006) *Plural Policing: A Comparative Perspective*. London: Routledge.

Kappeler, V., Sapp, A., Carter, D. (1992) 'Police officer higher education, citizen complaints and departmental rule violations', *American Journal of Police*, 11: 37–54.

Karp, D. and Walther, L. (2001) 'Community reparative boards in Vermont', in G. Bazemore and M. Schiff (eds) *Restorative Community Justice: Repairing Harm and Transforming Communities*. Cincinnati, OH: Anderson.

Katz, J. (1988) *The Seduction of Crime*. Basic Books: New York.

Katz, J. and Bonham, G. (2006) 'Restorative justice in Canada and the United States: A comparative analysis', *Journal of the Institute of Justice and International Studies*, 6: 187–196.

Kkrameddine, Y., De Marco, D., Hassel, R. and Silverstone, P. (2013) 'A novel trading program for police forces that improves relations with people with mental health problems and is cost effective', *Frontiers in Psychiatry*, 4(9): 1–10.

Kurki, L. (1999) 'Incorporating restorative and community justice into American sentencing and corrections', *Sentencing and Corrections Issues for the 21st Century*. Washington, DC: U.S. Department of Justice.

Kurki, L. (2003) Evaluating restorative justice practices', in A. von Hirsch, J. Roberts, A. Bottoms, K. Roach and M. Schiff (eds) *Restorative Justice and Criminal Justice: Competing or Reconcilable Paradigms?* Oxford: Hart Publishing.

La Mare, N. (1722) *Traite de Police*. Paris: Michel Brunet.

Landry, J. (2011) *Learning Styles of Law Enforcement Officers: Does Police Work Affect how Officers Learn?* Unpublished PhD thesis, Capella University, Minneapolis.

Lee, M. (1995) 'Pre-court diversion and youth justice', in L. Noaks, M. Maguire and M. Levi (eds) *Contemporary Issues in Criminology*. Cardiff: University of Wales Press.

Leigh, A., Read, T. and Tilley, N. (1996) *Brit POP II: Problem-Oriented Policing*. Police Research Group. Crime Detection and Prevention Series Paper 93, London: Home Office.

Leishman, R., Cope, S. and Starie, P. (1996) 'Reinventing and restructuring: towards a new policing order', in F. Leishman, B. Loveday and S. Savage (eds.) *Core Issues in Policing*. London: Longman.

Lentz, S. and Chaires, R. (2007) 'The invention of Peel's principles: A study of policing 'textbook' history', *Journal of Criminal Justice*, 35(1): 69–79.

Levrant, S., Cullen, F., Fulton, B. and Wozniak, J. (1999) 'Reconsidering restorative justice: The corruption of benevolence revisited?', *Crime & Delinquency*, 45(1): 3–27.

Liang, H. (1992) *The Rise of Modern Police and the European State System from Meternich to the Second World War*. Cambridge: Cambridge University Press.

Lipsky, M. (1980) *Street-Level Bureaucracy: The Dilemmas of Individuals in Public Services*. MA: MIT Press.

Llewellyn, J. (2007) 'Truth commissions and restorative justice', in G. Johnstone and D. Van Ness (eds) *Handbook of Restorative Justice*. Cullompton, Devon: Willan Publishing.

Loader, I. (2006) 'Policing, recognition and belonging', *Annals of the American Academy of Political Social Science*, 605(1): 202–221.

Loader, I. and Mulcahy, A. (2003) *Policing and the Condition of England: Memory, Politics and Culture*. Oxford: Oxford University Press.

Loader, I. and Walker, N. (2007) *Civilising Security*. Cambridge: Cambridge University Press.

Lofty, M. (2002) 'Restorative Policing', paper presented at the Third International Conference on Conferencing, Circles and other Restorative Practices. August 8–10, Minneapolis, Minnesota.

Loury, G. (1977) 'A dynamic theory of racial income differences', in P. Wallace and A. La Mond (eds) *Women, Minorities and Employment Discrimination*. Lexington, MA: Heath.

Lyon, D. (2003) *Surveillance after September 11*, Cambridge: Polity.

McAra, L. and McVie, S. (2007) 'Youth justice: The impact of system contact on patterns of desistance from offending', *European Journal of Criminology*, 4(3): 315–345.

McCold, P. (1996) 'Restorative justice and the role of community', in B. Galaway and J. Hudson (eds) *Restorative Justice: International Perspectives*. Monsey, NY: Criminal Justice Press.

McCold, P. (1998) *Police-facilitated restorative conferencing: What the data show*. Paper presented to the Second Annual International Conference on Restorative Justice for Juveniles, Florida Atlantic University, and the International Network for Research on Restorative Justice for Juveniles, Fort Lauderdale, FL, 7–9 November. Available at: fp.enter.net/restorativepractices/policeconferencing.pdf

McCold, P. (2000) 'Toward a holistic vision of restorative juvenile justice: A reply to the maximalist model', *Contemporary Justice Review*, 3(4): 357–372.

McCold, P. (2003) 'An experiment in police-based restorative justice: The Bethlehem (PA) Project, *Police Practice and Research: An International Journal*, 4(4): 379–390.

McCold, P. and Stahr, J. (1996) *Bethlehem Police Family Group Conferencing Project*. Paper presented at the American Society of Criminology Annual Meeting, Chicago, November 20–23.

McCold, P. and Wachtel, B. (1996) *Police officer orientation and resistance to implementation of community policing*. Paper presented to the American Society of Criminology, Chicago, 20–23 November.

McCold, P. and Wachtel, B. (1998a) *Restorative Policing Experiment: The Bethlehem Pennsylvania Police Family Group Conferencing Project*. Pipersville, PA: Community Service Foundation.

McCold, P. and Wachtel, B. (1998b) 'Community is not a place: A new look at community justice initiatives', *Contemporary Justice Review*, 1(1): 71–85.

McCold, P. and Wachtel, T. (2001) 'Restorative justice in everyday life', in J. Braithwaite and H. Strang (eds) *Restorative Justice and Civil Society*. Cambridge: Cambridge University Press.

McCold, P. and Wachtel, B. (2003) *In Pursuit of Paradigm: A Theory Of Restorative Justice*. Paper presented at the XIII World Congress of Criminology, Rio de Janeiro, Brazil. www.realjustice.org/library/paradigm.html.

McCold, P. and Wachtel, B. (2012) *Restorative Policing Experiment: The Bethlehem Pennsylvania Police Family Group Conferencing Project*. Eugene, OR: Wipf and Stock Publishers.

McCulloch, H. (1996) *Shop Theft: Improving the Police Response*. Crime Detection and Prevention Series Paper 76, London: Home Office Police Research Group.

McDonald, J. and Moore, D. (2001) 'Community conferencing as a special case of conflict transformation', in H. Strang and J. Braithwaite (eds) *Restorative Justice and Civil Society*. Cambridge: Cambridge University Press.

McDonald, J., Moore, D., O'Connell, T. and Thorsborne, M. (1995) *REAL JUSTICE Training Manual: Coordinating Family Group Conferences*. Pipersville, PA: Piper's Press.

McGarrell, E. (2001) *Restorative Justice Conferences as an Early Response to Young Offenders*. Washington, DC: US Department of Justice, Office of Juvenile Justice and Delinquency Prevention.

McGarrell, E. and Hipple, N. (2008) 'Family group conferencing and re-offending among first-time juvenile offenders: The Indianapolis Experiment', *Justice Quarterly*, 24(2): 221–246.

McGarrell, E., Olivares, K. Crawford, K. and Hipple, N. (2000) *Returning Justice to the Community: The Indianapolis Juvenile Restorative Justice Experiment*. Indianapolis: Hudson Institute.

McLaughlin, E. and Johansen, A. (2002) 'A force for change? The prospects for applying restorative justice to citizen complaints against the police in England and Wales, *British Journal of Criminology*, 42(3): 635–653.

MacPherson, W. (1999) *The Stephen Lawrence Inquiry*, London: HMSO.

Maguire, M. and Pointing, J. (1988) *Victims of Crime: A New Deal?*, Milton Keynes: Open University Press.

Manning, P. (1984) 'Community policing', *American Journal of Police*, 3(2): 205–227.

Manning, P. (1993) 'Toward a theory of police organization: Polarities and change'. Paper presented at the 'International Conference on Social Change in Policing', 3–5 August, Taipei.

Manning, P. (2002) 'Introduction', *Policing: An International Journal of Police Strategies & Management*, 25(1): 9–13.

Manning, P. (2010) *Democratic Policing in a Changing World*. Boulder, CO: Paradigm Publishers.

Mantle, G., Fox, D. and Dhami, M. (2005) 'Restorative justice and three individual theories of crime', *Internet Journal of Criminology*, 1–36.

March, J. (1991) 'Exploration and exploitation in organisational learning', *Organisational Science*, 2(1): 71–87.

Marenin, O. (1982) 'Parking tickets and class repression: the concept of policing in critical theories of criminal justice', *Contemporary Crises*, 6(3): 241–266.

Marenin, O. (2004) 'Police training for democracy', *Police Practice and Research: An International Journal*, 5(2), 107–123.

Marinos, V. and Innocente, N. (2008) 'Factors influencing police attitudes towards extrajudicial measures under the youth criminal justice act', *The Canadian Journal of Criminology and Criminal Justice*, 50(4): 469–489.

Marshall, T. (1990) 'Results of research from British experiments in restorative justice', in B. Galaway and J. Hudson (eds) *Criminal Justice, Restitution and Reconciliation*. Monsey, NY: Criminal Justice Press.

Marshall, T. (1999) *Restorative Justice: An Overview*. London: Home Office.

Marx, G. (1988) *Undercover: Police Surveillance in America*. Berkeley, CA: University of California Press.

Mason, B. (1992) 'Reparation and mediation programmes: The perspective of the victim of crime', *Criminal Law Journal*, 16(6): 402–414.

Mastrofski, S., Reisig, M. and McCluskey, J. (2002) 'Police disrespect toward the public: An encounter-based analysis', *Criminology*, 40(3): 519–552.

Mastrofski, S. and Ritti, R. (2000) 'Making sense of community policing: A theory-based analysis', *Police Practice and Research*, 1(2): 183–210.

Mastrofski, S., Willis, J. and Snipes, J. (2002) 'Styles of patrol in a community policing context', in M. Morash and K. Ford (eds) *The Move to Community Policing: Making Change Happen*. Thousand Oaks, CA: Sage.

Maxwell. G. (1999) 'Researching Re-Offending', in A. Morries and G. Maxwell (eds) *Youth Justice in Focus: Proceedings of an Australiasion Conference held 27-30 October 1998 held at the Michael Fowler Centre*, Wellington. Wellington: Institute of Criminology, Victoria University of Wellington.

Maxwell, G., Kingi, V. Robertson, J. and Morris, A. (2004) *Achieving Effective Outcomes in Youth Justice: Final Report to the Ministry of Social Development*. Wellington: Ministry of Social Development.

Maxwell, G. and Morris, A. (1993a) *Family Participation, Cultural Diversity and Victim Involvement in Youth Justice: A New Zealand Experiment*, Wellington, New Zealand: Victoria University.

Maxwell, G. and Morris, A. (1993b) *Family, Victims and Culture: Youth Justice in New Zealand*. Wellington, New Zealand: Social Policy Agency and Institute of Criminology, Victoria University of Wellington.

Maxwell, G. and Morris, A. (1994a) 'The New Zealand model of family group conferences', in C. Alder and J. Wundersitz (eds) *Family Conferencing and Juvenile Justice: The Way Forward or Misplaced Optimism?* Canberra: Australian Institute of Criminology.

Maxwell, G. and Morris, A. (1994b) 'Rethinking youth justice: For better or worse', *Occasional Papers in Criminology New Series: No. 3*, Wellington, New Zealand: Victoria University of Wellington, Institute of Criminology.

Maxwell, G. and Morris, A. (1996) 'Research on family group conferences with young offenders', in J. Hudson, A. Morris, G. Maxwell and B. Galaway (eds) *Family Group Conferences: Perspectives on Policy and Practice*. Annandale, New South Wales: Federation Press.

Maxwell, G. and Morris, A. (2000) 'Restorative justice and re-offending', in H. Strang and J. Braithwaite (eds) *Restorative Justice: From Philosophy to Practice*. Aldershot, England: Ashgate/Dartmouth.

Meadows, L., Albertson, K. Ellingworth, D. and Senior, P. (2012) *Evaluation of the South Yorkshire Restorative Justice Programme*. Sheffield: Hallam Centre for Community Justice.

Meadows, L., Clamp, K., Culshaw, A., Cadet, N., Wilkinson, K. and Davidson, J. (2010) *Evaluation of Sheffield City Council's Community Justice Panels Project*. Hallam Centre for Community Justice. Unpublished Report. [Online]. Available from: www.cjp.org.uk/publications/ngo/hccj-evalutation-of-sheffield-citycouncilscommunity-justice-panels-project

Merry, S. (1979) 'Going to court: Strategies of dispute management in an American urban neighbourhood', *Law and Society Review*, 13(4): 891–925.

Messmer, H. and Otto, H. (1992) 'Restorative justice: Steps on the way towards a good idea', in H. Messmer and H. Otto (eds) *Restorative Justice on Trial*. Dordrecht: Kluwer Academic Publications.

Meyer, J., Paul, R. and Grant, D. (2009) 'Peacekeepers turned peacemakers: Police as mediators', *Contemporary Justice Review*, 12(3): 331–344.

Miers, D., Maguire, M., Goldie, S., Sharpe, K., Hale, C., Netten, A., Uglow, S., Doolin, K., Hallam, A., Enterkin, J. and Newburn, N. (2001) *An Exploratory Evaluation of Restorative Justice Schemes*. London: HMSO.

Mika, H. (1989) *Cooling the Mark Out? Mediating Disputes in a Structural Context*, paper presented at the North American Conference on Peace-making and Conflict Resolution, Montreal, Quebec, 27 February–5 March.

Miller, L., Hess, K. and Orthmann, C. (2013) *Community Policing: Partnerships for Problem Solving*. Independence, KY: Cengage Learning

Miller, S. (1999) *Gender and Community Policing: Walking the Talk*. Boston, MA: Northeastern University Press.

Minor, K. and Morrison, J. (1996) 'A theoretical study and critique of restorative justice', in B. Galaway and J. Hudson (eds) *Restorative Justice: International Perspectives*. Monsey, NY: Criminal Justice Press.

Mirsky, L. (2003) *Family Group Conferencing Worldwide*, Bethlehem, PA: International Institute for Restorative Justice.

Moor, L., Peters, T., Ponsaers, P., Shapland, J. and van Stokkom, B. (2009) 'Restorative practices within community oriented policing, or meeting the needs of the officer on the beat', in L. Moor, T. Peters, P. Ponsaers, J. Shapland and B. van Stokkom (eds) *Restorative Policing*. Antwerp: Maklu.

Moore, D. (1991) 'Police responses to community policing', in S. McKillop and J. Vernon (eds) *Police and the Community, Conference Proceedings No. 5*. Canberra: Australian Institute of Criminology.

Moore, D. (1992) 'Criminal justice and conservative government in New South Wales (1988–1992): The significance of police reform', *Police Studies*, 15(2): 41–54.

Moore, D. (1993a) 'Facing the consequences', in L. Atkinson and S. Gerull (eds) *National Conference on Juvenile Justice Conference Proceedings*. Canberra: Australian Institute of Criminology.

Moore, D. (1993b) 'Shame, forgiveness and juvenile justice', *Criminal Justice Ethics*, 12(1): 3–25.

Moore, D. (1994) 'Evaluating family group conferences', in D. Biles and S. McKillop (eds) *Criminal Justice Planning and Coordination*. Canberra: Australian Institute of Criminology.

Moore, D. (1995) *A New Approach to Juvenile Justice: An Evaluation of Family Conferencing in Wagga Wagga, A Report to the Criminology Research Council*. Wagga Wagga, Australia: Center for Rural Social Research, Charles Sturt University–Riverina.

Moore, D. (2004) 'Managing social conflict – The evolution of a practical theory', *Journal of Sociology and Social Welfare*, 31(1): 71–91.

Moore, D. and Forsythe, L. (1995) *A New Approach to Juvenile Justice: An Evaluation of Family Conferencing in Wagga Wagga: A Report to the Criminology Research Council*. Wagga Wagga, AUS: Centre for Rural Social Research, Charles Stuart University-Riverina.

Moore, D. and McDonald, J. (1995) 'Achieving the "good community": A local police initiative and its wider ramifications', in K. Hazlehurst (ed.) *Perceptions of Justice*. Aldershot: Avebury.

Moore, D. and McDonald, J. (2001) 'Community conferencing as a special case of conflict transformation', in H. Strang and J. Braithwaite (eds) *Restorative Justice and Civil Society*. Cambridge: Cambridge University Press.

Moore, D. and O'Connell, T. (1994) 'Family conferencing in Wagga Wagga: A communitarian model of justice', in C. Alder and J. Wundersitz (eds) *Family Conferencing and Juvenile Justice: The Way Forward or Misplaced Optimism?* Canberra: Australian Institute of Criminology.

Morris, A. (1999) 'Creative Conferencing: Revisiting Principles, Practice and Potential', in A. Morris and G. Maxwell (eds) *Youth Justice in Focus: Proceedings of an Australiasion Conference held 27–30 October 1998 held at the Michael Fowler Centre, Wellington.* Wellington: Institute of Criminology, Victoria University of Wellington.

Morris, A. (2002) 'Critiquing the Critics. A Brief Response to Critics of Restorative Justice', *British Journal of Criminology*, 42(3): 596–615.

Morris, A. and Maxwell, G. (1998) 'Restorative justice in New Zealand: Family group conferences as a case study', *Western Criminology Review*, 1(1): 1–17.

Morris, A. and Maxwell, G. (2000) 'The practice of family group conferences in New Zealand: Assessing the place, potential and pitfalls of restorative justice', in A. Crawford and J. Goodey (eds) *Integrating a Victim Perspective within Criminal Justice.* Aldershot: Ashgate.

Morrison, B. (2001) 'The school system: Developing its capacity in the regulation of civil society', in H. Strang and J. Braithwaite (eds) *Restorative Justice and Civil Society.* Cambridge: Cambridge University Press.

Munro, R. (2006) 'Nanaimo restorative justice program', in J. Wwang (ed.) *An Overview of Community Corrections in China and Canada.* Vancouver, BC: International Centre for Criminal Law Reform and Criminal Justice Policy (ICCLR).

Murphy, K., Tyler, T. and Curtis, A. (2009) 'Nurturing regulatory compliance: Is procedural justice effective when people question the legitimacy of the law?', *Regulation and Governance*, 3: 1–26.

Neocleous, M. (2006) 'Theoretical foundations of the new police science', in M. Dubber and M. Valverde (eds) *The New Police Science.* Stanford: Stanford University Press.

Neyroud, P. (2013) *Review of Police Leadership and Training.* London: Home Office.

Neyroud, P. and Beckley, R. (2001) *Policing, Ethics and Human Rights.* Cullompton: Willan Publishing.

Nicholl, C. (1999) *Community Policing, Community Justice, and Restorative Justice.* Washington DC: U.S. Department of Justice, Office of Community Oriented Policing Services.

Nonini, D. (2008) 'Is China becoming neoliberal?' *Critique of Anthropology*, 28(2): 145–176.

O'Connell, T. (1992) 'Wagga juvenile cautioning process: The general applicability of family group conferences for juvenile offenders and their victims', *Rural Society*, 2(2): 16–19.

O'Connell, T. (1993) 'Wagga Wagga juvenile cautioning program: It may be the way to go!', in L. Atkinson and S. Gerull (eds) *National Conference on Juvenile Justice Conference Proceedings.* Canberra: Australian Institute of Criminology.

O'Connell, T. (1996a) 'Safety in the community: Make it happen'. Unpublished paper presented to the Restorative Justice Group, Human Resources & Development, Belfast, Northern Ireland, May.

O'Connell, T. (1996b) 'Community accountability conferences'. Paper presented at ACPO Summer Conference in Manchester, England, 2–4 July.

O'Connell, T. (1998) 'From Wagga Wagga to Minnesota'. Paper presented at the First International Conference on Conferencing, Minneapolis, *MN*, USA. Available from: www.iirp.edu/article_detail.php?article_id=NDg5

O'Connell, T. (2008) 'Restorative justice pioneer honored: His graduation address at Australian Catholic University', *IIRP Restorative Practices Eforum*, 1–4.

O'Mahony, D. and Campbell, C. (2006) 'Mainstreaming restorative justice for young offenders through conferencing: The experience of Northern Ireland', in J. Junger-tas and S. Decker (eds) *International Handbook of Youth*. Amsterdam: Springer Academic Press.

O'Mahony, D. and Doak, J. (2004) 'Restorative justice – is more better? The experience of police-led restorative cautioning pilots in Northern Ireland', *Howard Journal of Criminal Justice*, 43(3): 484–505.

O'Mahony, D., Chapman, T. and Doak. J. (2002) *Restorative cautioning: a study of police based restorative cautioning pilots in Northern Ireland*, Belfast: Northern Ireland Office.

O'Mahony, D. and Doak, J. (2009) 'Restorative justice and police-led cautioning practice: Tensions in theory and practice', in L. Moor, T. Peters, P. Ponsaers, J. Shapland and B. van Stokkom (eds) *Restorative Policing*. Netherlands: Maklu-Publishers.

Paterson, C. (2011) 'Adding value? A review of the international literature on the role of higher education in police training and education', *Police Practice and Research: An International Journal*, 12(4): 286–297.

Paterson, C. (2016) 'Higher education, police training and police reform', in P. Kratcoski and M. Edelbacher (eds) *Collaborative Policing: Police, Academics, Professionals, and Communities Working Together for Education, Training and Program Implementation*. Boca Raton, FL: CRC Press.

Paterson, C. and Best, D. (2016) 'Policing vulnerability through building community connections', *Policing: A Journal of Policy and Practice*. Advance access.

Paterson, C. and Clamp, K. (2012) 'Exploring recent developments in restorative policing in England and Wales', *Criminology & Criminal Justice*, 12(5): 593–611.

Paterson, C. and Clamp, K. (2014) 'Innovating responses to risk: Exploring the potential of a victim-focused policing strategy', *Policing: A Journal of Policy and Pratice*, 8(1): 51–58.

Paterson, C. and MacVean, A. (2007). 'Defining deviant lifestyles: Understanding anti-social behaviour and problem drug use through critical methodologies', in E. Hogard, R. Elllis and J. Varren (eds), *Community Safety: Innovation and Evaluation*. Chester: Chester University Press.

Paterson, C. and Pollock, E. (2010) *Policing and Criminology*. Exeter: Learning Matters.

Paterson, C. and Pollock, E. (2012) 'Developments in police education in England and Wales', in M. Cowburn, M. Duggan, A. Robinson and P. Senior (Eds.) *Values in Criminology and Community Justice*. Bristol: Polity Press.

Patten Report. (1999) *A New Beginning, Policing in Northern Ireland: The Report of the Independent Commission on Policing for Northern Ireland*. Belfast: HMSO.

Pavlich, G. (1996a) *Justice Fragmented*. London: Routledge.

Pavlich, G. (1996b) 'The power of community mediation: Government and formation of self-identity', *Law and Society Review*, 30(4): 707–733.

Pavlich, G. (2001) 'The force of community', in H. Strang and J. Brathwaite (eds) *Restorative Justice and Civil Society*. Cambridge: Cambridge University Press.

Pavlich, G. (2005) *Governing Paradoxes of Restorative Justice*. London: Glasshouse Press.

Peace, R. (2006) 'Probationer training for neighbourhood policing in England and Wales'. *Policing: An International Journal of Police Strategies and Management*, 29(2): 335–346.

Peak, K. and Glensor, R. (1996) *Community Policing and Problem Solving: Strategies and Practices*. Engelwood Cliffs, NJ: Prentice Hall.

Pearson-Goff, M. and Herrington, V. (2013) 'Police leadership: A systematic review of the literature', *Policing: A Journal of Policy and Practice*, 8(1): 14–26.

Polk, K. (1994) 'Family conferencing: Theoretical and evaluative concerns', in C. Alder and J. Wundersitz (eds) *Family Conferencing and Juvenile Justice: The Way Forward or Misplaced Optimism?* Canberra: Australian Institute of Criminology.

Pollard, C. (2001) 'If your only tool is a hammer, all your problems will look like nails', in H. Strang and J. Braithwaite (eds) *Restorative Justice and Civil Society*. Cambridge: Cambridge University Press.

Pollitt, C. (1986) 'Beyond the managerial model: The case for broadening performance assessment in government and the public services', *Financial Accountability and Management*, 2(3): 155–170.

Ponsaers, P. (2001) 'Reading about community (oriented) policing and police model', *Policing: An International Journal of Police Strategies & Management*, 18(2): 470–496.

Portes, A. (1998) 'Social capital: Its origins and applications in modern sociology', *Annual Review of Sociology*, 24(1): 1–24.

Pratt, J. (1996) 'Colonization, power and silence: A history of indigenous justice in New Zealand society', in B. Galaway and J. Hudson (eds) *Restorative Justice: International Perspectives*. Monsey: Criminal Justice Press.

Putnam, R. (1993) 'The prosperous community: Social capital and public life', *American Prospect*, 13: 35–42.

Putnam, R. (2000) *Bowling Alone: The Collapse and Revival of American Community*. New York: Simon & Schuster.

Putt, J. (2010) *Community Policing in Australia*, Canberra: Australian Institute of Criminology. Available from: www.aic.gov.au/media_library/publications/rpp/111/rpp.111.pdf

Rawls, J. (1971/1999) *A Theory of Justice*. Oxford: Oxford University Press.

Reiner, R. (2010) *The Politics of the Police*. Oxford: Oxford University Press.

Reiss, A. (1992) 'Police organisation in the 20th century', in M. Tonry and N. Morris (eds) *Modern Policing*. Chicago, IL: University of Chicago Press.

Reith, C. (1948) *A Short History of the British Police*. Oxford: Oxford University Press.

Richards, K. (2004) *Exploring the History of the Restorative Justice Movement*. Paper presented at the '5th International Conference on Conferencing and Circles', International Institute for Restorative Practices, Vancouver, Canada, 5–7 August.

Richards, K. (2010) 'Police-referred restorative justice for juveniles in Australia', *Trends & issues in crime and criminal justice* no. 398, Canberra: Australian Institute of Criminology.

Ritchie, J. and O'Connell, T. (2001) 'Restorative justice and the need for restorative environments in bureaucracies and corporations', in H. Strang and J. Braithwaite (eds) *Restorative Justice and Civil Society*. Cambridge: Cambridge University Press.

Rix, A., Joshua, F., Maguire, M. and Morton, S. (2009) *Improving Public Confidence in the Police: A Review of the Evidence*. [Online] Available from: www.gov.uk/government/uploads/system/uploads/attachment_data/file/115848/horr50-report.pdf

Rix, A., Skidmore, K., Self, R., Holt, T. and Raybould S. (2011) *Youth Restorative Disposal Process Evaluation*. London: Youth Justice Board for England and Wales.

Roach, K. (2005) 'Enhancing criminal justice reform, including restorative justice', paper presented at the 11th United Nations Congress on 'Crime Prevention and Criminal Justice Synergies and Responses: Strategic Alliances in Crime Prevention and Criminal Justice', Bangkok, Thailand April 18–25. [Online]. Available from: www.icclr.law.ubc.ca/Publications/Reports/11_un/KENT%20ROACH%20Speaking%20Notes.pdf

Roberts, A. and Masters, G. (1999) *Group Conferencing: Restorative Justice in Practice*, Minneapolis, MN: University of Minnesota, Centre for RJ and Mediation, School of Social Work.

Robinson, A. (2003) 'The impact of police social capital on officer performance of community policing', *Policing: An International Journal of Police Strategies & Management*, 26(4): 656–689.

Roche, D. (2001) 'The evolving definition of restorative justice', *Contemporary Justice Review*, 4(3–4): 341–353.

Roche, D. (2003) *Accountability in Restorative Justice*. Oxford: Oxford University Press.

Rose, D. and Clear, T. (1998) 'Incarceration, social capital, and crime: Implications for social disorganization theory', *Criminology*, 36(3), 441–478.

Rosenbaum, D. (1998) 'The changing role of the police: Assessing the current transition to community policing', in J. Brodeur (ed.) *How to Recognize Good Policing*. Thousand Oaks, CA: Sage Publications.

Rossner, M. (2008) 'Healing victims and offenders and reducing crime: A critical assessment of restorative justice practice and theory', *Sociology Compass*, 2(6): 1734–1749.

Royal Commission into Aboriginal Deaths in Custody. (1991) *Royal Commission into Aboriginal Deaths in Custody National Report: Overview and Recommendations (Commissioner Elliott Johnson)*, Australian Government Publishing Service, Canberra.

Sabatier, P. (1986) 'Top-down and bottom-up approaches to implementation research: A critical analysis and suggested synthesis', *Journal of Public Policy*, 6(1): 21–48.

Sampson, R. (1987) 'Communities and crime', in M. Gottfredson and T. Hirschi (eds) *Positive Criminology*. Beverly Hills, California: Sage.

Sampson, R. (1988) 'Local friendship ties and community attachment in mass society: A multilevel systemic model', *American Sociological Review*, 53: 766–779.

Sampson, R. and Graif, C. (2009) 'Neighborhood social capital as differential social organization: Resident and leadership dimensions', *American Behavioural Scientist*, 52(11): 1579–1605.

Sampson, R. and Groves, W. (1989) 'Community structure and crime: Testing social disorganization theory', *American Journal of Sociology*, 94: 774–802.

Sampson, R. and Laub, J. (1993) *Crime in the making: pathways and turning points through life*, Cambridge, MA: Harvard University Press.

Sampson, R. and Laub, J. (2003). 'Life-course desisters? Trajectories of crime among delinquent boys followed to age 70', *Criminology*, 41(3): 555–592.

Sampson, R., Raudenbush, S. and Earls, F. (1997) 'Neighbourhoods and violent crime: A multi-level study of collective efficacy', *Science*, 227(5328): 918–924.

Sandor, D. (1994) 'The thickening blue wedge in juvenile justice', C. Alder and J. Wundersitz (eds) *Family Conferencing and Juvenile Justice: The Way Forward or Misplaced Optimism?* Canberra: Australian Institute of Criminology.

Scarman, J. (1982) *The Brixton Disorders, 10–12 April 1981*. London: HMSO.

Schafft, K. and Brown, D. (2003) 'Social capital, social networks, and social power', *Social Epistemology: A Journal of Knowledge, Culture and Policy*, 17(4): 329–342.

Schein, E. (1985) *Organisational Culture and Leadership*. San Francisco, CA: John Wiley.

Schein, E. (1996) 'Culture: The missing concept in organization studies'. *Administrative Science Quarterly*. 41(2): 229–240.

Schwartz, S., Hennessey, M. and Levitas, L. (2003) 'Restorative justice and the transformation of jails: An urban sheriff's case study in reducing violence'. *Police Practice and Research: AN International Journal*, 4(4): 399–410.

Settles, T. (2009) 'Restorative reentry: A strategy to improve reentry outcomes by enhancing social capital', *Victims and Offenders*, 4(4): 285–302.

Shapland, J. (2003) 'Restorative justice and criminal justice: Just responses to crime?', in A. von Hirsch, J. Roberts, A. Bottoms, K. Roach and M. Schiff (eds) *Restorative Justice and Criminal Justice: Competing or Reconcilable Paradigms*. Oxford: Hart Publishing.

Shapland, J. (2009) 'Restorative justice conferencing in the context of community policing', in L. Moor, T. Peters, P. Ponsaers, J. Shapland and B. van Stokkom (eds) *Restorative Policing*. Netherlands: Maklu-Publishers.

Shapland, J., Atkinson, A., Atkinson, H., Chapman, B., Colledge, E., Dignan, J., Howes, M., Johnstone, J., Robinson, G. and Sorsby, A. (2006) *Restorative Justice in Practice: The Second Report from the Evaluation of Three Schemes*. Sheffield: The University of Sheffield.

Shapland, J., Atkinson, A., Atkinson, H., Chapman, B., Dignan, J., Howes, M., Johnstone, J., Robinson, G. and Sorsby, A. (2007) *Restorative Justice: The Views of Victims and Offenders, Ministry of Justice Research Series 3/07*. London: Ministry of Justice.

Shapland, J., Robinson, G. and Sorsby, A. (2011) *Restorative Justice in Practice: Evaluating What Works for Victims and Offenders*. London: Routledge.

Shearing, C. (2001) 'Transforming community: A South African experiment', in H. Strang and J. Braithwaite (eds) *Restorative Justice and Civil Society*. Cambridge: Cambridge University Press.

Shearing, C. (2005) 'Nodal security', *Police Quarterly*, 8(1): 57–63.

Shearing, C. (2016) 'Reflections on the nature of policing and its development', *Police Practice and Research*, 17(1): 84–91.

Shearing, C. and Johnston, L. (2003) *Governing Security: Explorations in Policing and Justice*. London: Routledge.

Shearing, C. and Stenning, P. (1987) 'Say "Cheese!": The Disney order that is not so Mickey Mouse', in C. Shearing and P. Stenning (eds) *Private Policing*. California: Sage.

Sherman, L. (1993) 'Defiance, deterrence and irrelevance: A theory of the criminal sanction', *Journal of Research in Crime and Delinquency*, 30(4): 445–473.

Sherman, L. and Barnes, G. (1997) 'Restorative justice and offenders' respect for the law, reintegrative shaming experiment', working paper #3, Canberra: Law Programme, Research School of Social Sciences, Australian National University.

Sherman, L. and Strang, H. (1997) *The Right Kind of Shame for Crime Prevention*, RISE Working Paper No. 1. Canberra: Australian National University, Research School of Social Sciences. Online. Available from: www. aic.gov.au/rjustice/rise/index.html

Sherman, L. and Strang, H. (2007) *Restorative Justice: The Evidence*. London: The Smith Institute.

Sherman, L., Gottfredson, D., MacKenzie, D., Eck, J., Reuter, P. and Bushway, S. (1997) *Preventing Crime: What Works, What Doesn't, What's Promising, Report to the U.S. Congress*. Washington, D.C.: U.S. Dept. of Justice.

Sherman, L., Strang, H., Barnes, G., Braithwaite, J. and Inkpen, N. and The, M. (1998) *Experiments in Restorative Policing: A Progress Report to the National Police Research Unit on the Canberra Reintegrative Shaming Experiments (RISE)*. Canberra: Australian Federal Police and Australian National University.

Sherman, L., Strang, H. and Woods, D. (2000) *Recidivisim Patterns in the Canberra Reintegrative Shaming Experiments (RISE)*, Canberra: Centre for Restorative Justice, Australian National University.

Sherman, L., Strang, H. and Woods, D. (2003) 'Captains of restorative justice: Experience, legitimacy and recidivism by type of offence', in E. Weitekamp and H. Kerner (eds) *Restorative Justice in Context: International Practice and Directions*. Cullompton: Willan Publishing.

Sherman, L., Strang, H., Woods, D. and Barnes, G. (2004) 'Restorative justice effects on repeat offending after violent and property crimes: Differential effects on two random-ised trials', Paper presented at the American Society of Criminology, Nashville.

Shewan, G. (2010) *A Business Case for Restorative Justice*, Available from: www.restor-ativejustice.org.uk/resource/the_business_case_for_restorative_justice_and_policing/.

Shewan, G. (2011) 'Restorative justice and policing in Manchester', paper presented at the Restorative Justice: Building Consensus in Theory and Practice conference, Not-tingham Law School, England, 7–8 April 2011.

Silvestri, M. (2007) 'Doing police leadership: Enter the new smart macho', *Policing and Society*, 17(1): 38–58.

Simon, J. (2006) *Governing Through Crime*. Oxford: Oxford University Press.

Skinns, L. (2008) 'A prominent participant: The role of the state in police partnerships', *Policing and Society*, 18(3): 311–321.

Sklansky, D. (2005) Police and democracy. *Public Law and Legal Theory Research Paper Series No. 05-11*. Los Angeles, CA: University of California.

Sklansky, D. and Marks, M. (2008) 'The role of the rank and file in police reform', *Polic-ing and Society*, 18(1): 1–6.

Skogan, W. (1998) 'Community policing in Chicago', in G. Alpert and A. Piquero (eds) *Community Policing: Contemporary Readings*, Prospect Heights, IL: Waveland.

Skogan, W. (1999) *On the Beat: Police and Community Problem Solving*. Boulder, CO: Westview.

Skogan, W. (2008) 'Why reforms fail', *Policing and Society*, 18(1): 23–34.

Skogan, W. and Hartnett, S. (1997) *Community Policing, Chicago Style*. New York: Free Press.

Skogan, W., Hartnett, S., DuBois, J., Comey, J., Laiser, M. and Lovig, J. (1999) *On the Beat: Police and Community Problem Solving*. Boulder: Westview Press.

Skolnick, J. (1966) *Justice Without Trial: Law Enforcement in a Democratic Society*. New York: Wiley and Sons.

Skolnick, J. and Bayley, D. (1988) *Community Policing: Issues and Practices around the World*. Washington, DC: National Institute of Justice.

Spelman, W. and Eck, J. (1987) *Problem-oriented Policing*. Washington, DC: Depart-ment of Justice, National Institute of Justice.

Spruce, G. (2010) *Restorative Justice Pilot in Greater Manchester Police: Final Evalu-ation Report*. Manchester: Greater Manchester Police.

Standing Committee on Justice and Legal Affairs. (1997) *Renewing Youth Justice: Thir-teenth Report of the Standing Committee on Justice and Legal Affairs*. Ottawa: Cana-dian Communication Group – Publishing, Public Works and Government Services Canada.

Stenson, K. (1998) 'Beyond histories of the present', *Economy and Society*, 27(4): 33–352.

Stenson, K. (2001) 'The new politics of crime control', in K. Stenson and R. Sullivan (eds) *Crime, Risk and Justice*. Cullompton: Willan Publishing.

Stenson, K. (2005) 'Sovereignty, biopolitics and the local government of crime in Britain', *Theoretical Criminology*, 9(3): 265–287.

Steven's Report. (2013) *Policing for a Better Britain*. Essex: Anton.

Stockdale, K. (2015) 'Police understandings of restorative justice – The impact of rank and role', *Restorative Justice: An International Journal*, 3(2): 212–232.

Storch, R. (1975) 'The plague of the blue locusts: Police reform and popular resistance in Northern England', *International Review of Social History*, 20(1): 61–90.

Stout, B. (2006) 'Is diversion the appropriate emphasis for South African child justice?', *Youth Justice*, 6(2): 129–142.

Strang, H. (1999) 'Recent Research on Conferencing: The Canberra Experiments', Sherman, L., Strang, H. Barnes, G. Braithwaite, J. and Inkpen, N. (1998) *Experiments in restorative policing: A progress report to the National Police Research Unit on the Canberra Reintegrative Shaming Experiments (RISE)*, Canberra: Australian Federal Police and Australian National University.

Strang, H. (2000) 'The future of restorative justice', D. Chappell and P. Wilson (eds) *The Australian Criminal Justice System: 2000 and Beyond*. Sydney: Butterworths.

Strang, H. (2002) *Repair or Revenge: Victims and Restorative Justice*. Oxford: Clarendon Press.

Strang, H., Barnes, G.. Braithwaite, J. and Sherman, L. (1999) *Experiments in Restorative Policing: A Progress Report on the Canberra Reintegrative Shaming Experiments (RISE)*, Canberra: Australian National University.

Strang, H., and Braithwaite, J. (1998) 'Pros and cons of police-led conferencing', in B. Sobey (ed.), *Diversionary Conferencing Advisory Committee Discussion Paper*. Canberra ACT: Australian Federal Police Diversionary Conferencing Team.

Stuart, B. (1997) *Building Community Partnerships: Community Peacemaking Circles*. Ottawa: Minister of Public Works and Government Services.

Stubbs, J. (1997) 'Shame, defiance and violence against women', in S. Cook and J. Bessant (eds) *Women's Encounters with Violence: Australian Experiences*. London: Sage.

Sullivan D. and Tifft, L. (2001) *Restorative Justice: Healing the Foundations of Our Everyday Lives*. Monsey: NY Willow Tree Press.

Sullivan, D. and Tifft, L. (2006) 'Transformative justice and structural change', in D. Sullivan and L. Tifft (eds) *Handbook of Restorative Justice*. London: Routledge.

Sunshine, J. and Tyler, T. (2003) 'The role of procedural justice and legitimacy in shaping public support for policing', *Law and Society Review*, 37(3): 555–589.

Sutcliffe, S. (2003) *Children of the New Age: A History of Spiritual Practices*. London: Routledge.

Sykes, G. and Matza, D. (1957) 'Techniques of neutralisation: A theory of delinquency', *American Sociological Review*, 22(6): 664–670.

Tavuchis, N. (1991) *Mea Culpa: A Sociology of Apology and Reconciliation*. Stanford, CA: Stanford University Press.

Taylor, C. (2012) *Policing Just Outcomes*. Perth: Edith Cowan University.

Taylor, J. (2008) *An Evaluation of the Impact of Restorative Justice in Cheshire*, Cheshire, UK: Cheshire Constabulary.

Thaler, R. and Sunstein, C. (2008) *Nudge: Improving Decisions About Wealth, Health and Happiness*. New Haven: Yale University Press.

The Times (1829) 'New police instructions', *The Times*, 25 September 1829.

Tilley, N. and Burrows, J. (2005) *An Overview of Atrition Patterns in the Investigative Process. RDS Online Report 45/05*, London: Home Office.

Trojanowicz, R. (1994) *Community Policing: A Survey of Police Departments in the United States.* Washington, DC: Federal Bureau of Investigation.

Trojanowicz, R. and Bucqueroux, B. (1998) *Community Policing: How to Get Started*. London: Routledge.

Trojanowicz, R., Kappeler, V. and Gaines, L. (2002) *Community Policing: A Contemporary Perspective*. London: Routledge.

Turner, S. (2002) *Young People's Experiences of the Young Offenders Act*. Sydney, New South Wales: Law and Justice Foundation of New South Wales.

Tyler, T. (1990) *Why People Obey the Law: Procedural Justice, Legitimacy, and Compliance*. New Haven, CT: Yale University Press.

Tyler, T. (1997) 'Citizen discontent with legal procedures', *American Journal of Comparative Law*, 45: 869–902.

Tyler, T. (2003) 'Procedural justice, legitimacy, and the effective rule of law', in M. Tonry (ed.) *Crime and Justice: A Review of Research*. Chicago: University of Chicago Press.

Tyler, T. (2006a) 'Legitimacy and legitimation', *Annual Review of Psychology*, 57: 375–400.

Tyler, T. (2006b) 'Restorative justice and procedural justice: dealing with rule breaking', *Journal of Social Issues*, 62(2): 307–326.

Tyler, T. (2011) *Why People Cooperate*. Princeton: Princeton University Press.

Umbreit, M. (1988) 'Mediation of victim-offender conflict', *Journal of Dispute Resolution*, 31: 85–105.

Umbreit, M. (1994) *Victim Meets Offender: The Impact of Restorative Justice in Mediation*. Monsey, NY: Criminal Justice Press.

Umbreit, M. (1995) *Mediation of Criminal Conflict: An Assessment of Programs in Four Canadian Provinces*. Minnesota Center for Restorative Justice & Mediation, School of Social Work, University of Minnesota.

Umbreit, M. (1996a) 'Restorative justice through mediation: The impact of programs in four Canadian Provinces', in B. Galaway and J. Hudson (eds) *Restorative Justice: International Perspectives*. Monsey, NY: Criminal Justice Press, 373–386.

Umbreit, M. (1996b) 'A humanistic mediation model: Moving to a higher plane', *VOMA Quarterly*, 7(3): Fall/Winter. [Online]. Available from: www.voma.org/docs/vomaq 96.html

Umbreit, M. (1996c) 'Beyond fast food mediation: implementation issues in restorative justice'. Paper presented at the American Society of Criminology Conference, Annual Meeting, Chicago, November 20–23.

Umbreit, M. (1999) 'Avoiding the marginalization and "McDonaldization" of victim–offender mediation', in G. Bazemore and L. Walgrave (eds) *Restorative Juvenile Justice: Repairing the Harm of Youth Crime*. New York: Criminal Justice Press.

Umbreit, M. (2001) 'Humanistic mediation: A transformative journey of peacemaking', in M. Umbreit (ed.) *The Handbook of Victim Offender Mediation: An Essential Guide to Practice and Research*. San Francisco: Jossey-Bass.

Umbreit, M. and Coates, R. (1993) 'Cross-site analysis of victim-offender mediation in four states', *Crime and Delinquency*, 39(4): 565–585.

Umbreit, M. and Farcello, C. (1997) *Woodbury Police Department's Restorative Justice Community Conference Program: An Initial Assessment of Client Satisfaction*. Minnesota: Centre for Restorative Justice & Mediation, University of Minnesota.

Umbreit, M. and Zehr, H. (1996a) 'Family group conferences: A challenge to victim-offender mediation?, *VOMA Quarterly*, 7(1): 4–8.

Umbreit, M. and Zehr, H. (1996b) 'Restorative family group conferences: Differing models and guidelines for practice', *Federal Probation*, 60(3): 24–29.

Van Dijk, J. (2001) 'Attitudes of victims and repeat victims toward the police: Results of the International Crime Victims Survey', in G. Farrell and K. Pease (eds) *Repeat Victimization. Crime Prevention Studies*. Monsey, NY: Criminal Justice Press.

Van Ness, D. (1990) 'Restorative justice', in B. Galaway and J. Hudson (eds) *Criminal Justice Restitution and Reconciliation*. Monsey, NY: Criminal Justice.

Van Ness, D. and Strong, K. (2002) *Restoring Justice: An Introduction to Restorative Justice*. Cincinnati, OH: Anderson.

van Stokkom, B. and Moor, L. (2009) 'Passing the buck: Restorative policing in the Netherlands', in L. Moor, T. Peters, P. Ponsaers, J. Shapland and B. van Stokkom (eds) *Restorative Policing*. Netherlands: Maklu-Publishers.

Vanfraechem, I. (2009) 'Restorative policing: In pursuit of principles', in L. Moor, T. Peters, P. Ponsaers, J. Shapland and B. van Stokkom (eds) *Restorative Policing*. Netherlands: Maklu-Publishers.

Vinzant, J. and Crothers, L. (1994) 'Street-level leadership: The role of patrol officers in community policing', *Criminal Justice Review Autumn*, 19(2): 189–211.

Volpe, M. (1989) 'The police role', in M. Wright and B. Galaway (eds) *Mediation and Criminal Justice: Victims, Offenders and Communities*. Newbury Park, CA: Sage.

Vynckier, G. (2009) 'A comparative view on the role of police in different restorative practices in Flanders', in L. Moor, T. Peters, P. Ponsaers, J. Shapland and B. van Stokkom (eds) *Restorative Policing*. Netherlands: Maklu-Publishers.

Wachtel, T. (2013) 'Defining restorative justice'. Paper presented at the 2013 IIRP Graduate School, Bethlehem, Pennsylvania: International Institute for Restorative Practices. [Online]. Available from: www.iirp.edu/pdf/Defining-Restorative.pdf

Wachtel, T. and McCold, P. (2001) 'Restorative justice in everyday life', in H. Strang and J. Braithwaite (eds) *Restorative Justice and Civil Society*. Cambridge: Cambridge University Press.

Waddington, P.A.J. (1998) *Policing Citizens: Police, Power and the State*. London: Routledge.

Walker, S., Archbold, C. and Herbst, L. (2002) *Mediating Citizen Complaints against Police Officers: A Guide for Police and Community Leaders*. Washington, DC: US Department of Justice, Office of Community Oriented Policing Services.

Walklate, S. (2005) 'Victimhood as a source of oppression', *Social Justice*, 32(1): 88–99.

Warner, K. (1994) 'Family group conferences and the rights of the offender', C. Alder and J. Wundersitz (eds) *Family Conferencing and Juvenile Justice: The Way Forward or Misplaced Optimism?* Canberra: Australian Institute of Criminology.

Weisburd, D., Telep, C., Hinkle, J. and Eck, J. (2008) *The Effects of Problem-Oriented Policing on Crime and Disorder*. Campbell Systematic Reviews, Oslo: The Campbell Collaboration.

Weitekamp, E. (1989) *Restitution: A New Paradigm of Criminal Justice or a New Way to Widen the System of Social Control?* Ann Arbor, MI: University Microfilms.

Weitekamp, E., Kerner, H. and Meier, U. (2003) 'Community and problem-oriented policing in the context of restorative justice', in E. Weitekamp and H. Kerner (eds) *Restorative Justice in Context: International Practice and Directions*. Collumpton: Willan.

White, R. (1994) 'Shame and reintegration strategies: individuals, state power and social interests', C. Alder and J. Wundersitz (eds) *Family Conferencing and Juvenile Justice: The Way Forward or Misplaced Optimism?* Canberra: Australian Institute of Criminology.

Wilcox, A. and Young, R. (2007) 'How green was Thames Valley? Policing the appearance of the effectiveness of restorative justice cautions', *Policing and Society*, 17(2): 141–163.

Williams, A. (2014) *Policing and Security in the Post 2001 Era: Model Development and the transferability of western models to the Arab Islamic states*. Unpublished PhD thesis. University of Cumbria.

Willis, J., Mastrofski, S. and Kochel, T. (2010) 'The co-implementation of Compstat and community policing', *Journal of Criminal Justice*, 38, 969–980.

Wilson, J.Q. and Kelling, G.L. (1982) 'The police and neighbourhood safety: broken windows', *Atlantic Monthly*, 249(3): 29–38.

Winkel, F. and Vrij, A. (1993) 'Rape reporting to the police: Exploring the social psychological impact of a persuasive campaign on cognitions, attitudes, normative expectations and reporting intentions', *International Review of Victimology*, 2(4): 277–294.

Wisler, D. and Ihekwoaba, D.O. (2009) *Community Policing: International Patterns and Comparative Perspectives*. CRC Press: Boca Raton, Florida.

Wisler, D. and Onwudiwe, I. (2007) *Community Policing: A Comparative View*. Geneva: IPES/DCAF.

Wood, J. and Shearing, C. (2007) *Imagining Security*. Cullompton, Devon: Willan Publishing.

Wood, J., Fleming, J. and Marks, M. (2008) 'Building the capacity of police change agents: the nexus policing project', *Policing and Society*, 18(1): 72–87.

Wood, J., Taylor, C., Groff, E. and Ratcliffe, J. (2013). 'Aligning policing and public health promotion: Insights from the world of foot patrol', *Police Practice and Research*, 16(3): 211 223.

Wood, J. and Shearing, C. (2007) *Imagining Security*, Cullompton, Devon: Willan Publishing.

Wright, M. (1991) *Justice for Victims and Offenders: A Restorative Response to Crime*. Milton Keynes: Open University Press.

Wrong, D. (1979) *Power: Its Forms, Bases and Uses*. Chicago: Chicago University Press.

Wycoff, M. and Skogan, W. (1994) *Community Policing in Madison: Quality from the Inside Out; An Evaluation of Implementation and Impact; A Final Summary Report Presented to the National Institute of Justice*. Rockville, MD: U.S. Department of Justice.

Young, J. (1988) 'Radical criminology in Britain; The emergence of a competing paradigm. *British Journal of Criminology*. 28(2): 159–183.

Young, J. and Matthews, J. (2003) *The New Politics of Crime and Punishment*. Cullompton: Willan Publishing.

Young, R. (2001) 'Just cops doing "shameful" business? Police-led restorative justice and the lessons of research', in A. Morris and G. Maxwell (eds) *Restorative Justice for Juveniles Conferencing, Mediation and Circles*. Oxford: Hart Publishing.

Young, R. (2002) 'Testing the limits of restorative justice: the case of corporate victims', in C. Hoyle and R. Young (eds) *New Visions of Crime Victims*. Portland, OR: Hart Publishing.

Young, R. (2003) 'Just cops doing "shameful" business? Police-led restorative justice and the lessons of research', in A. Morris and G. Maxwell (eds) *Restorative Justice for Juveniles Conferencing, Mediation and Circles*. Oxford: Hart Publishing.

Young, R. and Gould, B. (2003) 'Restorative police cautioning in Aylesbury – From degrading to reintegrative shaming ceremonies', in E. McLaughlin, R. Fergusson, G. Hughes and L. Westmarland (eds) *Restorative Justice: Critical Issues*. Thousand Oaks, CA: Sage Publications.

Young, R. and Hoyle, C. (2003) 'New improved police-led restorative justice?', in A. von Hirsch, J. Roberts, A. Bottoms, and M. Schiff (eds) *Restorative Justice and Criminal Justice Competing or Reconcilable Paradigms*. Oxford: Hart Publishing.

Zedner, L. (1994) 'Victims', in M. Maguire, R. Morgan and R. Reiner (eds) *The Oxford Handbook of Criminology*. Oxford: Oxford University Press.

Zehr, H. (1990) *Changing Lenses*. Scottdale, PA: Herald Press.

Zehr, H. (2002) *The Little Book of Restorative Justice*. Intercourse, PA: Good Books.

Zureik, E. and Salter, M. (eds.) *Global Surveillance and Policing: Borders, Security and Identity*. Cullompton: Willan.

Index

Page numbers in *italics* denote tables, those in **bold** denote figures.